# SPECIAL AGENT, VIETNAM

## Related Titles from Potomac Books

*Counterspy: Memoirs of a Counterintelligence Officer in World War II and the Cold War*
by Richard Cutler

*Prodigal Soldiers: How the Generation of Officers Born of Vietnam Revolutionized the American Style of War*
by James Kitfield

*Silent Warfare: Understanding the World of Intelligence, 3rd Ed.*
by Abram N. Shulsky and Gary N. Schmitt

*Soldiering: Observations from Korea, Vietnam, and Safe Places*
by Henry Gole

*Spymaster: My Life in the CIA*
by Ted Shackley with Richard A. Finney

*The U.S. Navy in the Vietnam War: An Illustrated History*
by Edward J. Marolda

# SPECIAL AGENT, VIETNAM

**A NAVAL INTELLIGENCE MEMOIR**

DOUGLASS H. HUBBARD JR.

Potomac Books, Inc.
Washington, D.C.

ISBN-10:  1-57488-970-2
ISBN-13:  978-1-574-88970-3

Printed in the United States of America

Potomac Books, Inc.
22841 Quicksilver Drive
Dulles, Virginia 20166

# CONTENTS

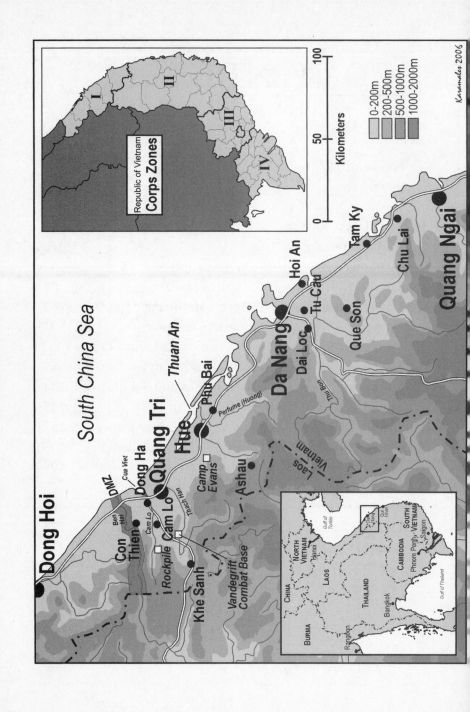

South China Sea

Dong Hoi

DMZ

Con Thien

Khe Sanh

Rockpile

Vandegrift Combat Base

Cam Lo

Cam Lo

Dong Ha

Quang Tri

Ben Hai

Cua Viet

Thach Han

Camp Evans

Ashau

Hue

Phu Bai

Thuan An

Perfume (Huong)

Laos / Vietnam

Da Nang

Hoi An

Dai Loc

Tu Cau

Thu Bon

Que Son

Tam Ky

Chu Lai

Quang Ngai

Republic of Vietnam
Corps Zones

I  II  III  IV

Kilometers

0        50        100

0-200m
200-500m
500-1000m
1000-2000m

Karremder 2006

CHINA

NORTH VIETNAM
Hanoi

Gulf of Tonkin

Da Nang

LAOS

BURMA

THAILAND
Bangkok

CAMBODIA
Phnom Penh

SOUTH VIETNAM
Saigon

Rangoon

Gulf of Thailand

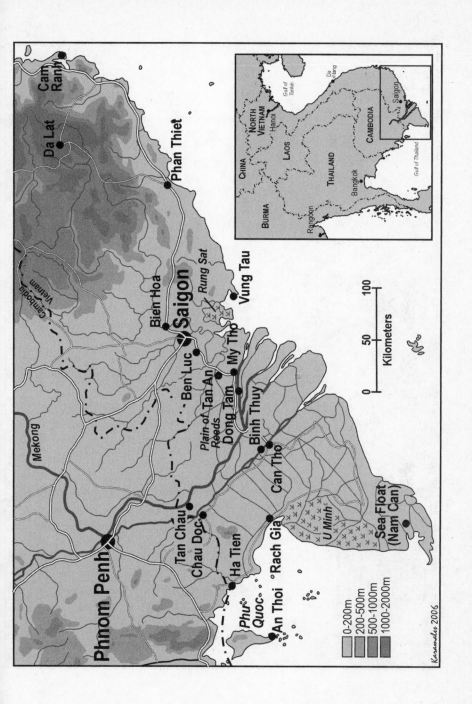

Kerenseler 2006

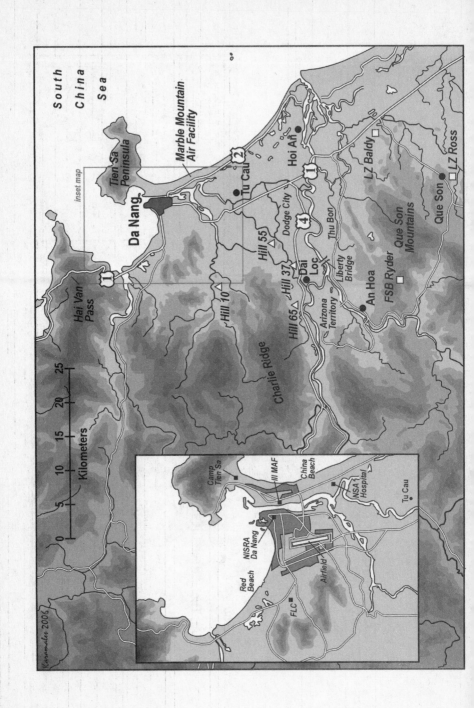

# FOREWORD

**More than a quarter century has passed,** and even for those of us who served in Vietnam, the war has sunk into the recesses of our memories. For some it is because recollections of combat are simply too unpleasant; for others it is because of painful memories of the dreadful internal divisions the war generated between the peoples of the United States. Still others regard as shameful our abandoning an ally whom we had persuaded to make common cause with us.

After decades of books and movies focused on what was wrong with our efforts in Vietnam, the past several years have seen several good books that simply examine how dedicated Americans answered the call of their country and served with honor and pride—and some remarkable successes. This is one of those books. A well-written story, *Special Agent, Vietnam* comes to life with a collection of previously unpublished material and photographs illustrative of those difficult days. It is an important contribution to the history of the conflict written by a man who served three consecutive Vietnam tours as a special agent.

Here is the story of a highly dedicated and thoroughly professional group of men who served as officers, enlisted, and civilian special agents of the Office of Naval Intelligence in Vietnam—and of some of the equally dedicated Vietnamese with whom they operated. The civilian special agent contingent never numbered more than two dozen; yet they provided counterintelligence and investigative support to the entire force of U.S. Navy and Marine Corps deployed to Vietnam. Despite their rather uncertain status as civilians, special agents wore uniforms, carried rifles—and worked and lived in the field with sailors and marines, sharing the same dangers and discomforts. I was privileged to be associated with them and found them to be the most dedicated, professional, and capable people I had the privilege of serving with in my thirty-five years of naval service.

Virtually nothing has been written about the Office of Naval Intelligence in Vietnam. This is in part because it was a very small part of a very large war and partially because it has only recently become acceptable to write about things pertaining to intelligence. This is an important story not only because it captures interesting and significant history, but what is more, because it tells a tale of a unit that served with dedication, honor, and dignity and whose members—myself included—look back with great pride on the part we played.

Thomas A. Brooks
Rear Admiral, U.S. Navy (Ret.)
Fairfax Station, Virginia
Former Director of Naval Intelligence

# PREFACE

**The story of the Naval Intelligence special agents** who volunteered for service in the Republic of Vietnam during our nation's most prolonged and controversial war has been waiting to be told for more than three decades. This is a chronicle of events that began in 1962 and continued through to the ignoble fall of Saigon thirteen years later; in many ways, the tales of these men are also a reflection of the political and military events of the Vietnam conflict.

At the peak of American involvement in Vietnam, with more than 550,000 military personnel assigned, the special agent task force was also at its zenith, with only about twenty professionals available to provide support to all U.S. Navy and Marine Corps elements in the republic. The chosen few accomplished much with very little.

Agent volunteers transferred from duty stations around the world, but most moved from the relative safety of a Stateside posting to the most remote, dangerous site the service could provide. Wives and families were left behind for a minimum of one year. Most agents found upon their arrival that they were expected to conduct complex and demanding investigations of a nature they could only have imagined in the United States—and in many instances the expectation was that they would do so alone and without supervision in dangerous circumstances. More often than not, resources that an agent might take for granted elsewhere, like transportation, were difficult to arrange in Vietnam and dangerous when they were available. The challenges tempered these men, and the younger ones matured very quickly.

Vietnam service changed and affected every man who did the twelve-month tour of duty, and it has certainly drawn alumni together into the tightest imaginable group—as close as brothers can be in many instances. These ties endured the passing years, despite the passage of decades between meetings or even communication. But as the years advanced, agents retired from Naval Intelligence. More alarmingly, they began to die before their stories had been told, and with each death, something of the story of Naval Intelligence was lost. I was both the youngest special agent to deploy to the Republic of Vietnam and the longest serving—from March 1969 to March

1972. Thus it fell to me, more than four decades after the first agent deployment, to tell as much of that story as possible.

This work is a compendium of the recollections of the men who served in Vietnam. My intention had always been to underpin our aging memories through a process of reviewing and researching the original reports that were dispatched for case review at the Naval Investigative Service (NIS) headquarters in Washington, D.C.; that, unfortunately, proved impossible. Lawyers at NCIS (the new name for NIS) twice refused my requests for assistance under Freedom of Information Act provisions, and less formal requests to headquarters personnel were no more successful. The Navy refused to confirm or deny the existence of all the documents and photographs that we had written and submitted, even though the contents of one important report had previously been published in a U.S. government history.

*Special Agent, Vietnam* would not have been possible without modern communication and the patient encouragement of my former colleagues and their families. With the exception of a single group reunion in 2000 and various interviews on the fly, it was researched and composed remotely and written in a variety of disparate locales, including Australia and Africa. The support of agents was a powerful stimulus for me to write of the dedicated, brave brethren who were Naval Counterintelligence Support Activity, Saigon, and, later, Naval Investigative Service Office, Vietnam. Their names are interspersed through the chapters that follow.

Being the author of these stories has been an intensely personal experience. I had the advantage of familiarity with the people, venues, sights, sounds, and smells referred to as my predecessors told of the earlier days in Vietnam. I have done my best to capture the experiences and thoughts of my colleagues in ways that communicate the experience and history of each man, including those not individually interviewed or named. It was simply not possible to interview everyone who served, nor was it possible to name them all.

Many parts of the story that occurred during the period 1969 to 1972 have been written in the first person. I sought to portray fairly what those involved saw and felt, as well as my own experiences, many of which are today nearly as intense as they were more than thirty years ago.

Special thanks go to R.Adm. T. A. Brooks, USN (Ret.), who never lost faith in the importance of this work, and to my parents, Doug and Fran Hubbard—both authors in their own right—whose support for the project was unfailing. Judith Anderson Sager, who shared the Vietnam experience with me from afar, returned to help with final editing steps, encouragement, and support. Her critical eye and unerring sense of story context were catalytic in the last days of preparation, when years of work finally coalesced into a complete manuscript.

Vietnam marked every person who served there. For me it was a milestone of such significance that scarcely a day has passed since 1972 when the events and impressions of those days are not somehow considered. For the men I served with, certainly as many profited from the incredible intensity of the year's tour as those who received scars tipped the scale the other direction. We all continue to decide in our own way, all these years later, what the experience meant to each of us.

# 1

# EARLY DAYS, 1962 TO 1964

**Saigon slumbered on a Sunday morning** in the spring of 1964. The so-called Paris of the Orient was quiet after the preceding night's weekend revelry. Broad boulevards stood still, rows of tamarind trees reflecting morning dew as the tropical sun began its rise over the tiled roofs of villas, business establishments, and squatter camps that characterized the capitol of the Republic of Vietnam (RVN)—known throughout the Western world simply as South Vietnam.

Split from the communist North by a border called the demilitarized zone (DMZ), South Vietnam's fragile pro-Western regime led by President Ngo Dinh Diem was struggling against both a communist insurgency and shrinking support from the citizenry. The United States, under President John F. Kennedy, while denying that U.S. forces were actually engaged in military operations in the republic, had moved much closer to initiating such operations. By the end of 1962 there were more than three thousand advisers present, including Special Forces, Air Force personnel, and both Army and Marine Corps helicopter units. Fourteen Americans had been killed in operations supporting South Vietnamese forces, and in February the first of hundreds of U.S. helicopters was shot down while ferrying Vietnamese troops into battle.

Nevertheless, life in Saigon for expatriates and the wealthy remained pleasant during 1962 and 1963. The expected amenities were present, the security situation was manageable, and the residue of France's former colonial lifestyle was largely intact. The U.S. military advisory staff had their families with them, often billeted in splendid former-French villas with tall walls and manicured gardens. Behind the growing tension of an expanding counterinsurgency war in South Vietnam, life generally remained quite civilized.

Virtually from the outset, the U.S. Navy provided all of the logistical support for the U.S. military effort in Vietnam. Every ration, round of ammunition, and aircraft part required passed through the Navy's logistical support system. Responding to the need for the protection of the forces' assets and personnel, the Office of Naval Intelligence (ONI) directed that agents

1

be assigned to Saigon to provide counterintelligence and investigative support for Navy commands. Special Agent Robert Kain was assigned as the first full-time special agent in the Republic of Vietnam.

Awakened from a deep sleep at dawn that May Sunday morning by banging on his door, Bob Kain, staggered to his bachelor officers' quarters (BOQ) room door and hurriedly opened it. Standing in the doorway was a young Army military policeman who had been dispatched from the Saigon Provost Marshals Office to Kain's room at the Five Oceans BOQ in Cholon.

"Mr. Kain," he said, "There's a carrier been sunk down at the docks."

Stunned, Kain replied, "You've got to be shitting me." Then, recovering his senses, he thanked the soldier and said he would be at the scene as soon as possible. He returned to his adjoining bedroom, quickly dressed, and walked downstairs to where his jeep was parked.

That morning, May 2, 1964, there was little traffic on the normally crowded thoroughfares of Saigon. Kain made good time driving down the boulevards to central Saigon and the dock area where ships were berthed on the Saigon River. Approaching the river, he could see the looming superstructure of USNS *Card*, a carrier converted for use as an aircraft transport.

Kain was no stranger to Vietnam. In the days after France's final ignoble defeat at Dien Bien Phu in 1954, then-Lieutenant Kain, aboard the U.S. Navy landing ship tank *Hampden County* (LST803), participated in the evacuation of Catholic Vietnamese refugees from the northern seaport of Haiphong to Saigon. The evacuation allowed many thousands of Vietnamese to escape control of communist Viet Minh under the leadership of Ho Chi Minh, then rapidly taking control of the North as the French pulled out. As many as three thousand refugees were packed into the bowels of the vessel, designed to transport tanks and land them through opening bow doors.

After leaving the Navy, Kain was an insurance adjustor for a while. Then in 1958 he joined the Office of Naval Intelligence as an agent and was assigned to the Los Angeles field office. Volunteering in 1961 for duty with the Office of Naval Intelligence at Subic Bay, Philippines, put him in line for periodic working trips to Vietnam as the U.S. presence grew there. A permanent ONI was set up in Saigon in late 1962, and Kain became its first senior agent.

That Sunday morning Special Agent Kain arrived at the gates of the Port of Saigon to an air of urgency and tension. Identifying himself to a jumpy sentry, he was passed through and drove his jeep toward the towering superstructure of the carrier berthed at dockside. Kain's experience at sea told him *Card* had been badly wounded. The vessel was settling in the water, and he could hear a clatter of hammers and air compressors from within the bowels of the ship. Crewmembers and shore-based damage control personnel rushed to a multitude of tasks, all designed to save the damaged vessel. Kain boarded, explained his presence to the master, and went below to see the damage firsthand. There he found damage-control parties fabricating temporary patches and reinforcements over a gaping hole. They had placed beams, scaffolding, and patching materials over and around the hole, but water continued to flood the interior of the ship. Pumps hummed in the bilges as sailors began to stabilize the ship's buoyancy.

The rather obvious evidence, both inside and on the ship's exterior, suggested that a number of explosive charges had been placed against the exterior of the hull in tandem below the waterline. These were simultaneously detonated to cause maximum damage—tearing a twenty-five-foot rift in the metal plates of the hull. The damage showed all the indications of an especially audacious attack by Viet Cong (VC) swimmer-sappers.

Some time later, Kain was joined by agent Mord Tucker, who set about photographing the engine room while workers struggled to stop further flooding.

When interviewed by Kain, crewmembers were unable to provide useful information about the events before the explosion, which had come as a complete surprise. Kain focused his attention on the area of the dockside, from where he believed the explosive charge had been fired. Vietnamese Navy (VNN) divers conducted a careful search around and under the hull and then began examining the dock itself. A large storm-water sewer was found to open into the river at this point, and closer scrutiny of the drain gave indications that the attackers might have entered the sewer labyrinth under Saigon, later leaving the scene the same way.

Kain's secret report carefully documented all evidence available at the time, but it could not say with certainty who actually carried out the daring attack. The enemy had clearly been concerned about the arrival of more allied helicopters and their potential effect on the ongoing fight in the field against communist Viet Cong forces.

During this period in the Vietnam conflict, VC increasingly used explosives in urban terrorism. The enemy began specifically targeting Americans and places frequented by them. ONI agents responded to a number of blasts at bars frequented by service personnel.

Kain recalls, "One particularly clever means of getting bombs close to their targets was to pack the hollow tubing of a bicycle frame with plastic explosive, then place it against an outer wall or window where the explosion would have maximum effect."

With their countrymen being killed and injured on the streets, Americans were quickly learning the necessity of vigilance in Saigon.

Agents assigned to U.S. Naval Counterintelligence Support Unit, Saigon, had little leisure time. After his arrival in late 1963, Kain shouldered a majority of the investigative workload, assisted by officer in charge Lt. Bud Siler, USN, and enlisted agents Jake Jacobson, Mord Tucker, and William G. "Sam" Houston. The office in Cholon was shared with the U.S. Army Provost Marshal, the only U.S. law enforcement agency then in Vietnam.

Kain soon tired of the menu at the nearby BOQ and began exploring the many restaurants of Saigon. For recreation, handball courts were available both at Tan Son Nhut Air Base and at the Cercle Sportif Saigonnais for interludes from the daily routine. Kain's regular partner in these days was Marine Capt. Don Koelper. Koelper and Kain had met in the aftermath of the Korean War, shortly after *Hampden County*'s final evacuation voyage from North Vietnam to Saigon. Kain's ship had been ordered to Korean waters to return elements of the battle-weary First Marine Division to Hawaii; one of the officers who clambered aboard the LST at a small port on the east coast of Korea that day had been 1st Lt. Don Koelper, USMC. Koelper and Kain were roommates and became fast friends in the exceptionally long voyage that followed: one of the LSTs in the squadron was disabled and had to be taken under tow. The voyage from Korea to Hawaii, at speeds seldom exceeding three knots, took thirty-seven days.

Don Koelper had been assigned as an adviser to the Vietnamese Marine Corps; this meant most of his time was spent away from Saigon in the field. During Koelper's periods of leisure in Saigon, the two friends always tried to get together. One Sunday night in February 1964 following a handball game, they agreed to meet at the Capital Kinh Do Theater, a recreational facility operated by the Navy for military personnel in the area, to see *The Diary of Anne Frank*. That afternoon, Kain received an official call out, which forced him to cancel his plans. Later that evening he was told by Army military police (MPs) that Viet Cong had bombed the movie theater and that there had been a fatality.

Kain went directly to the theater blast scene to join in the investigation. There he learned that the enemy had shot a military policeman outside the theater and then rushed into the lobby to plant the bomb. A Marine officer, seeing the bomb planted just after purchasing his ticket, had rushed down the aisle calling for people to take cover. That officer was Don Koelper; he was the only fatality in the bombing.

Later, at the dispensary, doctors told Kain that the blast had removed most of the rear of his friend's skull. But his selfless action had undoubtedly saved many others that day.

The Vietnamese language uses tonal inflection to give meaning to different words. Thus, a word might have many different meanings, depending on how it is spoken. This makes Vietnamese a difficult language for most Westerners to master. Interpreters, therefore, were particularly important for agents needing to interact with Vietnamese who spoke no English.

Bob Kain, like virtually every agent who followed him, was transferred to Vietnam without the benefit of any language training. Upon his arrival, the ONI office was relying on the U.S. embassy translator pool for its communication requirements. Among this pool, one translator quickly stood out as superior; his name was Lo Han Thang. Kain requested authority from headquarters in Sangley Point to hire Thang and it was granted. Thus, the longest-serving individual in ONI's Vietnam era was hired.

Interestingly, a young Lo Han Thang had been evacuated with his family from Hai Phong in North Vietnam to Saigon aboard a U.S. Navy LST, the very same rescue mission that first introduced Kain to Vietnam in 1954. Thang cannot recall the name of the vessel that carried him and his family to the South, but both Kain and Thang have speculated that it may have been Kain's LST, *Hampden County*. Thang remained an integral, important part of the office until its final closure and assisted Naval Intelligence until Saigon fell in 1975.

Bob Kain learned early in his tour that Saigon could be an unpredictable and dangerous place. Though South Vietnam had initially enjoyed relative peace, enemy North Vietnamese activities, Viet Cong insurgents, and internal political strife all contributed to unrest and violence as communists turned up the heat in their attempts to undermine the South. Despite numerous attempts to destabilize and remove him, South Vietnam's Catholic president, Ngo Dinh Diem, remained a titular leader—as he had since Vietnam's last king, Emperor Bao Dai, appointed him prime minister in 1954.

Perhaps as many as 80 percent of the people of South Vietnam were Buddhist. Ten percent were Catholic. Groups of Catholics, some lead by their priests, migrated from the North, assisted by the U.S. Navy and U.S. government refugee resettlement programs. They formed a loyal, devoutly anticommunist political base for President Diem. The president wasted little time appointing Catholics to key positions of leadership. Indeed, Diem considered Catholics the only Vietnamese he could trust in his bid to stay in power.

During the Eisenhower presidency, Diem was well received in the United States when he toured as a visiting chief of state. U.S. leadership threw their support behind him and his vocally anticommunist government. But eventually cracks appeared in the foundations of his Catholic-led regime. Vietnamese students demanded long-delayed democratic reforms. Even more vocal was the leadership of the republic's Buddhist majority. In the old imperial city, Hue, the Catholic deputy province chief ordered troops to fire on Buddhists celebrating a religious holiday in May 1963. Controversial monk Thich Tri Quang, himself born in North Vietnam and previously jailed on suspicion of supporting the communist Viet Minh in their war against France, began speaking out against Diem. Advising U.S. officials that he considered them responsible for Diem's abuses, the cleric insisted they urge the president to reform or resign. Then-U.S. ambassador to South Vietnam Henry Nolting personally pressed Diem to moderate his position but was rebuffed.

The man behind the scenes in the Diem regime was the president's brother, Ngo Dinh Nhu. Nhu, a shady character well known for his machinations with the secret police, pulled the strings that kept his devout, single brother in power. Madam Ngo Dinh Nhu, self-appointed, flamboyant first lady of South Vietnam, had the ear of certain members of the press contingent. Sensing her own power base, Madam Nhu attacked Buddhist leaders by alleging they were being manipulated by Americans against Diem. The first lady achieved global notoriety in June 1963 after Buddhist monks, demanding "peace and charity" to all religions, began burning themselves to death on public street corners. Characterizing the self-immolations as barbecues, she offered to supply matches to other similarly inclined Buddhist clerics.

American leadership became increasingly uncomfortable with Diem's leadership. The Vietnamese president had rejected all pleas to moderate policies and find real internal peace. Perhaps sensing an opportunity, a group of Vietnamese general officers began plotting Diem's overthrow. They were careful to let key players in the U.S. embassy know their intentions. President John F. Kennedy was given a White House briefing as events unfolded; he urged there be no direct U.S. involvement in any potential change of government.

On November 1, 1963, dissident troops laid siege to the presidential palace in central Saigon. Although Kain was privy to rumors about possible coup plans among Vietnamese general officers, he was surprised when a telephone call from a news source found him in his room at the Five Oceans BOQ. The newsman said simply that some sort of military action was occurring in central Saigon.

Kain hurried to find the office's radio-equipped jeep and, by carefully navigating through back streets to avoid potential roadblocks and troop movement, found his way to the downtown headquarters building of Military Assistance Command, Vietnam (MACV), where Agent Sam Houston already was. By now there was considerable gunfire in the area only a short distance from the presidential palace, some of it near MACV. Parking immediately in front of the headquarters building, Kain began transmitting his observations of the fighting. He was the sole link Navy headquarters in Cholon had at their disposal, and thus he was integral to Navy command decisions designed to protect personnel and assets.

South Vietnamese Air Force (VNAF) aircraft roared overhead to put air strikes into the palace grounds a mere two blocks away from Kain's position. Firing, some indiscriminate, ranged up and down the boulevard ahead. Kain continued the radio transmissions for about forty-five minutes, until a South Vietnamese soldier manning a .50-caliber machine gun at the traffic circle ahead swung the weapon around and trained it directly on Kain's jeep. Temporarily abandoning the vehicle, the special agent entered the MACV headquarters building until the firing subsided somewhat, then returned to his vehicle and began a patrol of the downtown area, radioing his observations.

Diem and Nhu, unable to rally support to expel dissident army and air force elements, later escaped the presidential palace via a secret tunnel. Taking refuge at St. Francis Xavier Church in Cholon the next day, the two brothers negotiated by telephone with coup leaders, who assured them their lives would be spared. Diem finally agreed to surrender. He and his brother were then picked up by rebel troops in an armored personnel carrier. Instead of being taken to staff headquarters, both were shot, apparently on the orders of South Vietnamese Gen. Duong Van Minh.

President Kennedy was shocked at news of the bloody end of the Diem dynasty, but in Saigon the generals were quickly recognized as the new, legitimate power. Embassy officials hoped General Minh would prosecute the war more effectively, without the rancor that had characterized Diem's rule. They were to be disappointed.

Bob Kain and his fellow agents began hearing rumors of Diem's death only a few hours after the coup broke out. The next morning the grim details of the two brothers' demise began to surface, together with a rash of rumors as to who was responsible. President Kennedy was dead days later, also at the hand of an assassin.

# 2
## SAIGON, 1964 TO 1967

**Something about a three-year tour of duty** in the Philippines did not appeal to Special Agent Maynard Anderson. After completing the Agent Basic Course the year previously, Anderson was advised by ONI headquarters in 1964 that he could expect a transfer from Chicago either to Sangley Point or Subic Bay. Concerned at the prospect, he wrote to headquarters and then discussed his options with Special Agent Sherman Bliss. Saigon was, Bliss said, an alternative to the Philippines.

Anderson had heard tales of the Pearl of the Orient, as Saigon had long been known during the halcyon days of French rule. A certain mystique was associated with it; besides, the location augured well for professional travel to other points of interest in Southeast Asia and there seemed a good likelihood of action there. Anderson volunteered. He was to be senior agent, Saigon—not senior resident agent. At that time, the post was not important enough to rate an SRA.

Anderson's trip to Vietnam began on July 14, 1964. Like the many who would follow him, he overnighted in San Francisco at the Treasure Island BOQ, leaving nearby Travis Air Force Base aboard a World Airways midnight flight—a chartered Boeing 707 loaded with service personnel and dependents bound for destinations across the Pacific. After Hawaii, they made a fuel stop at Anderson Air Force Base, Guam, in time for breakfast with Supervising Agent Jim Ritchie before the onward journey continued.

A briefing period had been planned at the headquarters element under which the Saigon office functioned: U.S. Naval Counterintelligence Support Activity, Philippines. Supervising Agent Harry Doyle met Anderson at Clark Air Force Base, driving him to Sangley Point in the teeth of an impending typhoon. At Sangley Point, Anderson learned a little about what to expect at his new assignment in Saigon, and he was to be met and briefed by the existing senior agent, Robert M. Kain. Ultimately, he would relieve Kain.

After an overnight delay caused by mechanical problems on the aircraft, the World Airways charter flight from Clark Air Force Base finally got away,

Saigon-bound, on August 2. Also aboard were Lt. Gen. Creighton Abrams, USA, and his family bound for Abram's new assignment as Gen. William Westmoreland's deputy at Military Assistance Command, Vietnam. Over Saigon at last, a spiral landing approach, designed to reduce the likelihood of damage by ground fire, gave passengers their first look at the city that would be home for most of them in the year ahead.

Soon after landing, Anderson was introduced to staff at ONI: two enlisted agents (the last so-assigned to Vietnam), YNC Mord Tucker and YN1 Sam Houston. The office was situated behind a high wall within the Cholon compound, then home to the U.S. Navy–operated Headquarters Support Activity, Saigon, under the command of Capt. Archie Kuntze, USN (a colorful character who later fell from grace, charged with impropriety). With the Naval Intelligence Detachment assigned as an element of his command, Captain Kuntze was a strong supporter who had supplied agents with transport and office space that would not have been forthcoming from Naval Intelligence resources.

Quartered at the Brink BOQ in central Saigon near the famous Continental and Caravelle Hotels, Anderson shared space with Air Force Capt. Michael Stevens, aide to Brig. Gen. Robert Rowland, chief of the Air Force Advisory Group. General Rowland later provided useful information about the activities and intentions of the Vietnamese Air Force during periods of political upheaval in South Vietnam.

Maynard Anderson set about learning his way around the power circles of Saigon. Special Agent Bob Kain, a skilled criminal investigator, would remain in the office for some months to come, so Maynard saw that the intervening time would be best used in finding out as much as possible about what factors and people made things happen in Saigon—and what effect those forces had on the well-being of the U.S. forces he was sent to protect.

He got off to a good, if unexpected start: afflicted with a parasitic disease that baffled U.S. doctors and was only successfully diagnosed by a Vietnamese doctor, Anderson was hospitalized in Saigon where he met Mrs. William Westmoreland. Kitsie Westmoreland, a long-serving Gray Lady, called regularly at his quarantined private room. It was an auspicious acquaintance that paid dividends later.

Finally out of hospital and back at his Cholon desk, he could begin the task of establishing relations with agencies—local and U.S.—in earnest. Central to the mission was protection of U.S. assets and personnel. Information of the right sort could go a long way toward fulfilling this tenet, and a combined effort by the agencies represented in Saigon seemed most likely to succeed.

In 1964 the conflict in Vietnam was not at the stage of a full-blown war, but many activities, real and potential, affected U.S. personnel: political unrest, theft and corruption, and potential terrorism. The Army Counterintelligence Corps (CIC) had a mandate similar to that of the Naval Intelligence detachment, as did the U.S. Air Force Office of Special Investigations (OSI). Anderson found agents of the CIC with whom he had associated in Chicago, among them Special Agent Jim Bryant. With Embassy Security Officer Tom Gaffney, CIC, OSI, and ONI formed the Saigon Security Committee to ensure that information developed by one agency could quickly be shared with all with a minimum of bureaucracy. The Central Intelligence Agency (CIA) station chief was also represented.

Though ONI retained its responsibility for investigation of serious criminal matters, the counterintelligence mission became almost primary as unrest and terrorism became more prevalent. The Saigon atmosphere began changing from one of colonial comfort—with all the attendant social life—to one of a culture touched by unexpected violence. The people of Saigon were a long way from the soldiers struggling for their lives in nearby rice paddies and fields, but they were often reminded of reality by surreal-seeming evening views of firefights in the distance and air strikes visible from building rooftops. As time went on, these sights were punctuated by the occasional boom of a terrorist bomb detonated somewhere in the city.

Naval Counterintelligence Support Unit, Saigon, joined with other allied agencies to ferret out information to provide indicators and warning of activities that might imperil their people and their interests. The focus was on VC activities and intentions, North Vietnamese initiatives and activities, and possible enemy infiltrators and potential enemy agents in their midst. Reports that may have seemed innocuous to analysts upstream in Hawaii and Washington had real meaning in the Saigon counterintelligence community, where speed had to be balanced against surety of fact. This was especially so when, for instance, a potential bomb attack was mooted. Navy agents distributed information directly to their affected commands and members of the Saigon Security Committee.

Navy agents developed information sources in many, quite different environments. Mord Tucker and Sam Houston lived in the community with their families. Both were conduits for information—sometimes gossip—that when combined with other information could produce valuable intelligence. At the time, Buddhist clerics were creating angst with acts of self-immolation in protest over fundamental political issues, including endemic corruption in South Vietnam's high-profile leadership. The Buddhist protests and the news that surrounded them were the topic of much discussion in the global press and among the Vietnamese. Tucker and Houston both employed domestic staff who visited the market and gossiped with their friends every day. These sources provided accurate information predicting coup attempts on two occasions during 1964–65. Office employees, the translator, and the driver could also report their feelings and predictions. When they stayed away from work, it was always taken as a worrisome indicator of unknown events perhaps to come.

In September 1964 Maynard Anderson was asked by General Westmoreland to attend a meeting at which he asked Navy agents to investigate allegations that U.S. military supplies were finding their way from Vietnam to Singapore's black market. The information indicated that the trade was of a significant volume: for example, helicopters had reportedly been a part of the inventory stolen. Anderson subsequently flew to Singapore for meetings with the American consulate, the U.S. naval liaison office, and the Singapore CIA station chief. He asked each for assistance in developing information about theft and the Singapore black market. Although the investigation did not produce results sufficient for criminal prosecution, intelligence was developed that helped plug some holes in the leaky Vietnam supply train.

Counterterrorism initiatives were brought very much to home when on Christmas Eve 1964, the Brinks BOQ was bombed. A car bomb exploded in the building's underground garage in the early evening. Maynard Anderson was in his room at the time, seated at a desk, writing a letter. His first recollection was of a muffled explosion, which hurled him to the floor and caused the frame and glass of the window above the desk to implode and strike the wall behind him. The room was showered with glass and the frame fell on him. Dazed, Anderson finally wrenched a jammed door open after he came to his senses; he recalls hearing other muffled blasts. He believed the building was under sustained artillery attack.

In the kitchen, he found his Vietnamese maid bleeding profusely from the myriad of glass shards that had struck her body as she stood in front of a window, curious at the activity occurring outside on the street. He assisted her to the stairs, where medical staff met them and took charge. He returned to his room to dress. After a vain search for his ONI credentials, Anderson started down the stairs to the first floor, where damage was much more severe. There he found large blocks of imploded concrete blocking progress in the hall, now choked with smoke and dust. A Navy employee had been killed in his room on this floor. Finally at ground level, Anderson found Special Agent Bob Kain already on the scene. Kain had responded to messages on his vehicle radio and then raced to the scene, guided by a growing pillar of smoke on the Saigon horizon. He remembers seeing Anderson standing outside as he arrived and being utterly amazed that so many had survived the blast: the central portion of the building over the blast had collapsed into the underground garage. Both agents began assisting in the removal of cars from the burning underground parking area; exploding gas tanks in the area had prompted Anderson's impression of an enemy follow-up attack after the initial blast. Anderson was taken for treatment of cuts received in the blast; Bob Kain later located Anderson's all-valuable credentials after a careful search of the damaged room: they were on top of an armoire.

Bob Kain spent the next several days sifting through the rubble of the blast scene, assisted by Army investigators. The investigation substantiated the theory that a car containing explosives had been driven into the parking area. Collusion of Vietnamese National Police guarding the underground area was suspected but never proven. There was considerable speculation that specific individuals were the targets of this bomb attack.

Bob Hope and his entourage, in Vietnam to entertain troops during the holiday season, were billeted across the street from the Brinks BOQ at the Caravelle Hotel. Bob Kain recalls, "I remember Bob Hope made a special trip to the dispensary to visit and comfort the injured from the attack. Those people really appreciated that." Hope's opening line at the Christmas show was less welcome, "A funny thing happened on the way to the show; a hotel flew by."

The agent force was boosted in January 1965 with the arrival of Special Agent Paul Carr. The product of an Indiana farming community, Carr had served as an Army artilleryman during the Korean War, returning to his native Indiana to attend Indiana University on the GI Bill, graduating with a degree in business management with police administration as a minor. Encouraged by a retired FBI agent professor, Carr submitted an application to join Naval Intelligence and was appointed in October 1963. Carr caught the notice of his trainers during Agent Basic School at headquarters in Washington, D.C., the following year and was asked if he would consider a one-year tour in Vietnam, followed by a second year in the Philippines. Then working almost constantly on prolonged road trips out of the Denver office, bachelor Paul Carr was attracted both by a new challenge and the increased pay and allowances the post offered. He accepted.

Maynard Anderson wrote to Carr from Saigon, passing on useful information as to what he might expect at his new duty station and offering advice that he bring his own sidearm, as issue handguns were scarce in Saigon. Carr, then on leave in Indiana, went out and bought a Smith and Wesson Chief's Special, which he carried through two tours in Vietnam and which serves him to this day.

With orders instructing him to report to headquarters in the Philippines, Carr stepped off the charter flight at Clark Air Force Base after the long flight from California and caught a Navy commuter flight to Sangley Point, on the other side of the bay from Manila. Here he received more briefings as to what he might expect in Vietnam. Paul Carr was not that impressed with the Philippines. This indoctrination helped convince him to stay in Vietnam for his two-year commitment.

His January 1965 arrival in Saigon uneventful, Carr settled into a top-floor room at the Hong Kong BOQ in Cholon, perhaps six blocks away from the office. Because the facility had no operating elevator, he was able to obtain a private room that would normally have been reserved for senior field-grade officers. Soon, he learned a nearby ladderway provided access to the rooftop, a perfect place to sit on Saturday night with a cold drink and his portable radio, listening to *The Grand Old Opry* on Armed Forces Radio. In the distance, over the canal, tracers and flares from a skirmish with VC were often added entertainment.

Soon after his arrival in Saigon, Paul Carr found his energies being channeled toward the counterintelligence mission. Special Agent Milt Steffen showed his origins as a Chicago police officer in a preference for criminal investigation. Mord Tucker, then about to complete his time in Vietnam, had carried much of the counterintelligence load. He told Carr he thought he might be good at counterintelligence; Tucker's observation was prescient.

In the weeks before his transfer, Mord Tucker began to introduce Carr to his contacts and informants, the people who had provided information about impending unrest and even of possible enemy targets. One of the first introductions was to the family of civil engineer Frank Hessler. Hessler's Vietnamese wife, Jeanette, was well connected in Vietnamese political circles and sympathetic to the Navy's need for accurate information about the local situation. In the years ahead, Paul Carr helped the Hessler family by doing commissary shopping in Frank's absence. At a time when some of the dissident Buddhist elements had been infiltrated by communist agents, Jeanette Hessler used her extensive contacts to glean useful information about monks intentions and objectives.

Mrs. Hessler also introduced Carr to Lt. Cdr. Nguyen Anh, who held an important staff position at VNN headquarters in Saigon. A northerner who had escaped communist rule, Anh was the personification of the self-discipline characteristic of many North Vietnamese. He had been trained in the United States.

During the period Paul Carr was learning his way in Saigon, ONI received a lead from agents in Japan about illegal firearms entering the country, probably from Vietnam. Authorities were alarmed to discover that semi- and full-automatic military weapons had found their way into the Japanese underworld; they suspected personnel from the CIA's proprietary airline, Air America, were bringing arms into Japan and selling them as a lucrative illegal business venture. Given the case, Carr found his way to a nearby Special Forces compound where he interviewed a noncommissioned officer (NCO) at the armory. The unit, he learned, had been established several years previously, early in the U.S. counterinsurgency assistance program, to arm groups of sympathetic Vietnamese who wanted to fight the Viet Cong. The weapons were mostly of World War II vintage, of both U.S. and European manufacture. Carr saw German Schmeissers, Swedish K submachine guns, and full-automatic M2 Carbines present. No system for documenting weapons issuance had ever been introduced, nor was one planned for the future. Soon he learned that Air America had hired some rough characters who didn't mind dabbling in the gun-running business, but little could be done about any of it. Paul Carr wrote up and submitted his findings and heard nothing more.

Carr's contacts in the community expanded. He was introduced to a Navy lieutenant whose Vietnamese wife's family was well connected in the transport industry. Her father owned a fleet of trucks that regularly transited the major thoroughfares of South Vietnam, particularly the national highway, Route 1. Through this contact, he learned Viet Cong "tax collectors" on remote stretches of the highway routinely stopped truckers, removing some of the truck cargo as a levy to "the cause." Realizing this information had potential value as a means of identifying enemy units, their operating areas and objectives, Carr requested the truck drivers take note of road mile markers when stopped and report details about guerrilla armament and what had been taken. Large quantities of rice, for instance, might indicate an enemy training facility was nearby, while a desire for concrete and reinforcing rod might be a sign that fortifications were being constructed. As the information began to flow, Carr took it to intelligence analysts at MACV J-2; several successful military operations were formulated and launched against VC as a result.

A man from Oklahoma probably owes his life to the effectiveness of Carr's trucker network: realizing opportunities existed in Vietnam for those with construction skills, he had applied for a position as a dozer operator with construction conglomerate Raymond Morrison Knudsen–Brown Root Jones (RMK-BRJ) when his Army enlistment ended. His application was accepted. The man completed out-processing from the U.S. Army in Japan and returned to Saigon, where he learned he had been hired. Told to wait a few days in Saigon for the next flight north to Cam Ranh, he opted, against the advice of many, to ride through "Indian country" on a motorcycle to his new job. He never made it.

Tipped about the missing man by the American embassy, Carr began checking his trucker contacts and the same afternoon received a report that a driver on Route 1 had seen a blond man being led by Vietnamese down a riverbank. One of the Vietnamese men had been pushing a motorcycle. Late that afternoon, this information made it into the hands of J-2, and a sweep of the area by U.S. Army infantry was set up for the following morning. Early the next day, soldiers sweeping riverbanks in the area where Carr had reported the abduction were surprised as a young American literally ran into their line. It was the Oklahoman. He had successfully slipped his bindings and made his escape. Certainly he was very lucky, in more ways than one.

The Viet Cong continued with their Saigon bombing campaign, next selecting the U.S. embassy as a target. Situated near the riverfront, the embassy had been constructed by French colonizers some years previous. A comfortable building, it was not, however, constructed with the realities of guerrilla warfare in mind.

At about 10:45 AM on March 31, 1965, a Renault sedan pulled up and parked on the street immediately in front of the embassy. The car carried about 250 pounds of plastic explosive in its rear seat. Across the street a second attacker had pulled up on a Lambretta scooter. Vietnamese National Police sentries challenged the car driver almost immediately. He responded by jumping out and firing at them, his accomplice on the Lambretta joining him. Police killed the car driver, but the motorcyclist made good his escape. Moments after the fight, the car bomb detonated causing extensive damage to the embassy and a Chinese restaurant opposite. Twenty-two were killed and 190 injured in the blast. Two U.S. citizens were killed together with several Vietnamese embassy employees.

Early that afternoon the Saigon Security Committee, chaired by the embassy security officer, met. Maynard Anderson represented Naval Intelligence. Members rallied to assist the embassy mission and ensure that a joint effort would be made to help them recover and identify those responsible for the bombing. The CIA station chief was represented and a concerted effort made to find knowledgeable sources. Vietnamese Military Security Service (MSS) personnel identified the dead driver as a Viet Cong agent but the identity of his fellow cell members remained a mystery.

Special Agent Paul Carr visited the site of the bombing the next day. He was drawn immediately to a hole in the street, which he estimated to be about half the size of the automobile in which the bomb had exploded. Train tracks, covered years before with pavement, had been exposed by the blast. Above in the damaged embassy were hollow windows—reminders of clerical staff blinded or killed by the bomb. The sounds of police gunfire had drawn them to the window moments before the car bomb detonation.

Says Carr, "It was this bombing which really added impetus to construction of the new United States embassy in Saigon. The building was in service by the time of the Tet Offensive of 1968, when VC sappers overran part of the compound, and it gained global recognition when embassy staff were evacuated when the South fell in 1975."

The Vietnamese were not the only astute readers of the environment. Members of the Australian Army Training Team, Vietnam, were actively deployed in the South Vietnamese Army (ARVN) field units. These Australians, a high proportion of whom were battle-tested infantry senior NCOs, shared foxholes with Vietnamese soldiers in the field. Like good noncommissioned officers in every service, they were well positioned to pick up signs of unrest in the troops. Given that Vietnamese officers were dabbling in politics and plotting coups, this type of information could be very valuable.

Similarly, the British MI5 officer and political officer at the British embassy in Saigon were very generous about sharing important information that came their way. Both remained valuable sources even after they reposted to Hong Kong.

One of the odder legacies of the 1954 Geneva Treaty that divided North and South Vietnam was the International Control Commission (ICC). With a mission to monitor compliance with the treaty, officers assigned to the ICC were in the unique position of being able to travel to both sides of the demilitarized zone and did so. Staffed by Poles, Indians, and Canadians, the ICC was obviously designed with political balance in mind. The three were odd bedfellows: Poland was then a Soviet satellite and openly hostile to the West; India was a mixed bag, supposedly nonaligned but with ties both to the West and the Soviets; while Canada was perceived as a staunch member of the North American bloc, overseen by the United States.

Maynard Anderson was a regular at the Cercle Sportif Saigonnais, which has been described as French colonial splendor epitomized. Situated in the heart of Saigon on perhaps thirty acres of fenced gardens and trees, the clubhouse had tennis courts and a swimming pool known to attract lovely Eurasian women for an afternoon dip. In the days before war became a full-time occupation in Saigon, it served as a gathering place for members of diplomatic legations and their support staff, as well as the families of wealthy French rubber and tea plantation owners. These people, who maintained Saigon homes, needed a social center for wives and children; many such families spent most of their time at the club playing tennis, swimming, and socializing. Successive American ambassadors regularly played tennis; members of the ICC were in attendance, while MACV staff also regularly used the veranda as a quiet meeting place where information could be shared.

Ambassador Henry Cabot Lodge visited the pool at noon to swim and observe the other swimmers. Ambassador Maxwell Taylor played tennis at least twice weekly at 4:00 PM on court one, immediately over a fence from the street; this made him a potential target, but he refused requests to change to another court. Bill Bludworth, a CIA agent, joined Maynard Anderson to play adjacent to Taylor at those times, just in case something happened.

Despite their access to the North, ICC officers were not considered the best sources of information. Anderson occasionally met Canadian representatives for a social drink and found them to be friendly but apprehensive. His interests were more in the realm of information about potential infiltrators or persons who may have been co-opted to work for the North—rather than information about what the ICC team was seeing on their regular trips to the North. The CIA may have taken a more vigorous approach to sourcing this information, but the Navy did not.

French planters from the tea and rubber plantations northwest of Saigon were not considered particularly reliable sources of information either. Though many were socially friendly, they were disinclined to show support for the United States because it was not in their best interests to do so: they were concerned about maintaining the status quo and often did so by paying off resident Viet Cong and groups of marauding robbers.

Navy agents cultivated a number of the U.S. press corps. Maynard Anderson found several to be helpful, providing information of interest: Garrick Utley of NBC News, Malcolm Brown of Associated Press, and renowned combat photographer Horst Faas. The press had access to information that would have been very difficult for others to obtain, particularly about Buddhist unrest and the political situation generally. Much of the impetus for Buddhist unrest originated in the ancient imperial city, Hue. A center of intellectualism and home to a university, Hue was also home to the militant monk Thrich Tri Quang, whose followers included several clerics who immolated themselves on Saigon streets as acts of protest.

Vietnamese agencies, notably the MSS, were developed as information sources. Their contacts in the community were manifold, but the reliability of their information could vary widely. Navy agents had a string of their own information sources in the Saigon community: restaurateurs heard much of what happened on the streets and behind the scenes but were largely considered unreliable. One of Anderson's better sources was a Chinese tailor who also exchanged local currency for U.S. dollars at highly beneficial rates. Having the means of easily exporting his wealth to a no-questions-asked Hong Kong bank provided the man with a strong incentive to keep agents on his side.

The prime motivation of the majority of those who proffered information was not altruism or ideological belief: it was greed. The unit collection program was enhanced in early 1965 when a shipment of post exchange (PX) liquor and cigarettes was hijacked somewhere between the Port of Saigon and the Navy Exchange. Agents launched an investigation and began searching for the missing trailer, as did MPs from the Army Provost Marshal. At about 10:00 PM that night, the trailer was located with about half the contents missing. The remaining merchandise—including Johnnie Walker scotch and Courvoisier brandy—was loaded into a shipping container and returned to the office compound in Cholon for return to the exchange. The exchange officer, however, did not want it back. It was, he said, more costly to bring it back into the inventory than to simply write the lot off to theft. Agents were suddenly in possession of a large quantity of the best "liaison" material available anywhere. Over time it was dispensed in the acquisition of information necessary to the mission.

✧◆✧◆✧

A Naval Counterintelligence Support Unit trying to come to grips with worsening enemy infiltration and increasing numbers of attacks against allied personnel would logically look to the water for the enemy. Saigon had always been dependant on its rivers and tributaries for supply. Now, with growing evidence that North Vietnamese supply vessels loaded with arms and explosives were finding their way into the South, the unit's attention became focused on the river. Vietnamese naval units in February 1965 had captured and sunk a freighter loaded with arms and medicine destined for Viet Cong forces in the Saigon area.

In those early days, there were no squadrons of U.S. Navy fast patrol craft (PCF), although they would soon come. The only resource for counterintelligence agents was Vietnamese Navy junks and patrol boats inherited from the French. Agents would have to improvise to get necessary surveillance photographs of the river and the vessels using it, and a light aircraft seemed a logical choice for such a mission. They knew that the Vietnamese Air Force had L19 light observation aircraft. What the Air Force required was inducement to provide their allies with aircraft time. The solution was quite unexpected. The Vietnamese liked American combat rations. An enterprising Navy chief petty officer had no problem acquiring several cases of C rations—and these rations bought the air time which resulted in sheaves of useful photographs that cast a new light on riverine activities in and around the Port of Saigon.

In April 1965 the U.S. Navy launched Operation Market Time, a huge blockading operation designed to deny communist insurgents resupply by sea. Until this time, the South Vietnamese coastline had been patrolled by a VNN motorized junk force. Experts estimated that as many as one thousand junks a day moved in offshore waters. In response, Operation Market Time put aerial surveillance into the air, assigned a score of destroyers and escorts to radar picket duty, and began supplementing tired Vietnamese junks with divisions of fast patrol boats. At its peak, thousands of U.S. sailors were required to man Operation Market Time.

Particularly in the early stages of the Vietnam conflict, the imaginary line between overt criminal action and enemy activity was often unclear. The abundance that arrived with Americans and their various assistance programs was a tempting target for diversion to enemy insurgents and their supporters. Why run the risks associated with resupply from North Vietnam if products like medical supplies and ammunition could be obtained from the U.S. supply train?

Further clouding the situation was the temptation that the U.S. supply system provided the South Vietnamese allies. This ranged from small-time

pilferage from targets of opportunity to major theft, sometimes at very senior level. It was fairly common knowledge in Saigon that assassinated South
Vietnamese President Ngo Dinh Diem had $1 million cash in a briefcase
when he was killed; that money found its way into the hands of strongman
Gen. Duong Van "Big" Minh. Minh was also alleged to have taken forty
kilos of gold before Diem was shot. In every instance of theft, the question
as to motive had to be addressed: was it personal enrichment or support for
the enemy?

Opportunity for theft increased as the U.S. supply system ballooned to
support growing troop numbers: 180,000 in 1965 grew to 540,000 by 1968.
Maynard Anderson characterizes the American attitude to property this way:
"If it's ours, we put it somewhere and expect it to be there when we return.
The Vietnamese felt that if somebody turned his back on property, he didn't
care about it and it was thus fair game to steal. The American would simply
get another of whatever it was from the infinite supply house." Anderson
believes this attitude ensured that much of the allied store of material found
its way both to Viet Cong sympathizers and to the soldiers themselves along
the trails of Cambodia and Laos.

Senior Agent Maynard Anderson was relieved at the end of his one-year
tour in July 1965—although he remained on the job in Saigon until September—by Special Agent John Nester. Nester inherited a staff of three special
agents and four military support staff.

Though the focus of Naval Intelligence remained largely in and around
Saigon, increasing activity in the I Corps tactical zone—that northernmost
part of South Vietnam that bordered North Vietnam—necessitated that
agents travel to assist commands. Marines had landed in Da Nang and with
them had come naval construction and logistic forces. With fewer than a
half-dozen agents in Vietnam, it was a strain to send people north but it had
to be done. John Nester, Paul Carr, and Milt Steffen were all called to the
northern port of Da Nang at one time or another after the initial 1965
landings. Nester and Steffen provided support to Marine units during the
highly successful Operation Starlight, when amphibious elements landed
near Chu Lai and routed previously secure VC sanctuaries. Lt. Roger Stauback,
USN, who later became a legendary football player, provided the two agents
with field uniforms.

Steffen and Carr were later dispatched together after reports were received that a Navy LST had been sabotaged in Da Nang Harbor. Getting to
Da Nang was no easy matter, and when they arrived they discovered an all-
Japanese contract crew was manning the ship. Even the master had no command of English. But reports of sabotage were accurate: the LST was beached,

three decks on the stern penetrated. Both agents assumed from the outset that enemy sappers with waterborne demolition charges had attacked the vessel, but they began a thorough investigation assisted by an Air Force master sergeant from Da Nang Air Base, fluent in Japanese. The crewmembers were flighty, obviously frightened, and not keen to wait for the agents to complete inquiries, but they had little choice. Temporary hull repairs were eventually completed, the agents left carrying explosive residue samples, and a crew of much-relieved Japanese civilian mariners set sail for more peaceful waters. Laboratory analysis later confirmed suspicions that the attack had been enemy initiated.

Only a short time after wrapping up that case, Carr returned to Da Nang, this time because of a counterintelligence lead from Naval Intelligence agents in Japan: a young marine had been photographed entering the Soviet embassy in Tokyo. It was important to know why he had been there.

During the Cold War especially, embassies of countries hostile to Western democracies were carefully monitored, as were the people who visited them. The unauthorized appearance of a member of the U.S. armed forces at the diplomatic mission of the West's main adversary was therefore viewed with alarm. The young marine had some questions to answer. Was he a Russian spy?

Carr shoved the lead sheet and report from Japan and the accompanying high-resolution eight-by-ten-inch print that showed the subject with another young American and a male Japanese national at the embassy entrance into a briefcase and made his way north to visit the marine. At Da Nang Air Base, he changed from civilian clothes into Marine utilities, briefed the command, and set about locating his subject, whom he found standing perimeter guard duty in a large fighting hole. Carr introduced himself and dropped into the hole with him, recognizing the subject as an affable country boy. The young marine was happy to talk about his recent R and R leave in Japan; he and a Marine buddy had seen all the sites together and had a fine time.

Carr produced the photograph taken in Japan at the embassy with everything masked out except the faces of the two marines and the Japanese male. "Yep, that's us," the subject said. Carr then pulled the mask off the photo, saying, "This was taken at the Russian embassy. What the hell were you guys doing at the Russian embassy?" With apparent sincerity he replied, "Well, it looked like an interesting building, and our Japanese buddy asked if we wanted to see it, so we said yes." They had, he said, been received at the door and allowed to look around the large reception area. There had been a large framed picture on the wall, a Russian flag, and a large table. They hadn't stayed long. Carr questioned him carefully as to whether he had been questioned by anybody. "No, they was just nice folks," he replied.

The marine had no security clearance and access to very little that might have been of interest to America's enemies. Carr saw nothing that added to his suspicions during the interview. He wished the young marine well and began thinking about how he was going to get back to Saigon.

A report that a Navy corpsman attached to a Marine rifle company had been using morphine was the reason for Carr's next trip north. Once in I Corps, this time accompanied by a young naval officer, he learned the subject and his company were still at sea but were soon expected to land in an amphibious operation at a beach location. Carr and the officer traveled to the beach in anticipation of the landing, finding it largely deserted. Having been without a shower for several days, the two had a quick swim, then sheltered off the beach. They didn't have long to wait for the marines to come ashore. The suspect was quickly located and interviewed. Though he first claimed that the missing morphine Syrettes had been damaged or lost, he eventually admitted to personal use. While the interview was taking place, the three heard gunfire near a small promontory down the beach, and a while later, they heard much more. Marines returning from the area told Carr two marines had been ambushed and several VC harboring in a bunker there were killed, all within sight of the area where they had been swimming hours before. The experience underscored for Paul Carr the many seemingly innocuous dangers of service in Vietnam.

Carr's last trip to I Corps was apparently the catalyst for major changes in the Naval Intelligence presence in Vietnam. Dispatched to investigate a reported murder involving marines at Da Nang, he arrived after a difficult trip aggravated by an initial absence of available aircraft. By the time he arrived, there was no longer a crime scene, the body had been shipped out, and both the suspect and witness had been flown to Okinawa, where legal assistance was available. While Carr was interviewing the division chief of staff about the incident, the colonel suddenly rose to his feet, Carr following suit. Lt. Gen. Lewis Walt, USMC, III Marine Amphibious Force (III MAF) commanding general, entered, and Carr was introduced to him. "Please see me when you're through with the chief of staff," Walt said to Carr.

Shortly thereafter, Carr and the chief of staff were in the general's office. Lew Walt asked Carr where he was stationed, what area he covered, and how many agents were in Vietnam. Carr explained that the detachment included one senior agent and three others, that their area of jurisdiction incorporated a large tract of Southeast Asia, and that they worked from Saigon. "How the hell can three men cover all that territory?" the general demanded. Carr explained that with available resources, they had to select and work only the major events. Turning to his chief of staff, General Walt directed the colonel to message Naval Intelligence in Washington requesting more agents as a matter of urgency. Big changes were coming. By October 1965 Special Agent Tom Brannon had established a full-time Naval Intelligence presence in Da Nang, and plans were afoot to further increase agent strength and supporting staff in the north.

The activities of dissident Vietnamese elements could have direct bearing on the security of U.S. personnel and the prosecution of the war. For example, in one incident, Nester and his agents together drove into Saigon and were unexpectedly overrun by a crowd of Buddhist monks and students. A bus had been set alight and Molotov cocktails and other missiles were being thrown. Both Navy vehicles were seriously damaged, but the occupants escaped injury. Thus, in late 1965 Navy agents were actively collecting information in Saigon about such dissident activities. John Nester focused the attention of his counterintelligence program on the Port of Saigon and developed a useful working relationship with Vietnamese Navy staff intelligence officers.

During Nester's reign over Navy counterintelligence activities, a scheme headed by an unscrupulous civilian employee of construction consortium RMK-BRJ was uncovered. Military personnel had been asked to purchase postal money orders for a small reward. These money orders, legal tender in U.S. dollars, had found their way to a loan company in Hong Kong, assisted by the American's Indian business partner. From there, a majority of the funds had been dispatched to communist China with the American's share deposited in various California bank accounts. Nester, who covered cases involving U.S. currency—which was highly sought after by the enemy as a means of financing their war effort—led the investigation. As more than $1 million was known to have been transferred in the scheme, it gained a certain amount of notoriety, and Nester was interviewed by two visiting U.S. congressmen. The American civilian was eventually prosecuted for tax evasion.

Meanwhile, on the streets of Saigon, despite the growing emphasis on criminal investigations, Paul Carr's duties remained focused largely on the counterintelligence mission. American troop numbers ballooned in accordance with the military planners' desire to use U.S. troops to take the fight to the enemy and allow Vietnamese allies time to build a fighting force effective against the communist onslaught. Carr expanded a growing network of useful contacts and sources, one of which was retired U.S. Navy Capt. John Pollard, Standard Oil's security officer in Vietnam. Well schooled in the ways of intelligence, Pollard had excellent connections who could quickly supply accurate information about VC activities, particularly as they affected shipping. Pollard was married to a French woman born in Morocco, and his Saigon penthouse was a picture of continental charm and chic. It was a gathering point for some important personages of the Saigon intelligence community.

Memories of the British experience in the Malayan Emergency were still very fresh in April 1966, when Carr received disturbing reports that communist agents had appeared in Vietnam as crewmembers of ships originating in Singapore. Britain had just spent nearly ten years and vast chunks of national revenue in the Malay Peninsula to subdue the insurgency, which was predominantly made up of Chinese guerrillas. Carr, accompanied by Pollard, traveled to Singapore to investigate and initiate changes to remove this security risk.

South Vietnamese Navy sources had periodically reported that Soviet submarines were off-loading military supplies for Viet Cong forces along the coast of South Vietnam. At the time, it was well known that the USSR was supporting North Vietnam with military supplies sent both to North Vietnamese ports and via the Chinese, who maintained road, rail, and sea links with its neighbor to the south. Carr had heard the stories about Russian submarines, but he stumbled across the evidence of Soviet support one day in Saigon, and quite by accident. At a civilian motor pool facility, he met an American communicator manning sophisticated radio monitoring equipment. In the corner of the facility were a number of rifles wrapped in protective paper and grease. These were World War II–vintage German 8mm Mausers. The communicator, a CIA employee, said the rifles were some of the war booty captured by Russians invading Germany in the final days of the war. The Russians had given the weapons and ammunition to regional Viet Cong via a submarine supply drop. The communicator gave Paul Carr one of the rifles; he still has it.

The Soi Rap River, the main tributary and supply line for the Port of Saigon, was always an area of sensitivity for the Navy. Enemy forces were equally conscious of the river's strategic value and skirmishes over it were not uncommon. Perhaps not altogether typical was a report received by Carr that the hull of a Portuguese coastal trading vessel had been punctured on the way to Saigon and was sinking. Enlisting the assistance of Lieutenant Commander Anh, Carr traveled downstream in a Vietnamese Navy boat until the listing vessel came into view. Carr observed that very little was being done to save the ship, and his suspicions were heightened by the presence of VNN underwater demolition team (UDT) sailors in diving gear. While never admitting complicity, VNN soon admitted that it had information that implicated the ship's crew in illegal commerce with the Viet Cong. Carr watched as the ship was vandalized and looted, Vietnamese sailors displaying their disdain for the ship galley supplies by tipping large cans of peas onto the deck. The ship ultimately sank but was later refloated.

Nha Be, on the Soi Rap, was far enough downriver from Saigon to be a safe area in which to off-load dangerous cargo such as ammunition and fuel. This was where the major oil companies had established fuel storage depots, and at the time it was an important venue for unloading ammunition supply ships.

Vietnamese villagers and fishermen shared the river with the larger Navy ships until one day a Navy UDT discovered a strange object attached to the anchor chain of a fully laden ammo ship awaiting unloading. The sailors removed the object and dragged it to the shore, where they disabled the two activated timing devices found on the object. Responding to their call, Carr arrived to find the divers scrutinizing a diabolically clever explosive device, fully capable of sending up the ship it was attached to, and perhaps others in a chain reaction. Viet Cong sappers had packed high explosives into a five-gallon metal container. To this they had attached two partially inflated rubber bladders, one on each end, which had been filled with only enough air to prevent the bomb from either sinking or rising to the surface. Two clocks, waterproofed by the rubber bladders, were configured as primary and fail-safe firing devices. The sappers had made full use of tidal extremes that caused anchored ships to swing on their anchors as water came up the river at high tide and receded with the low. The bomb had been affixed below the surface to a long line from the ship anchor chain. The tidal race did the rest, pulling the negative-buoyancy device back under the ship's hull, where it could do maximum damage. The clocks had less than an hour to go before detonation when the divers disabled them.

A comprehensive report with sketches, diagrams, and photographs was prepared and dispatched to Naval Intelligence and to interested organizations throughout the country. Thereafter, Vietnamese fishermen were unwelcome near ammunition and fuel ships, and soon armed sailors were guarding anchored ships, hurling concussion grenades into the water every few minutes. These grenades produced lethal underwater explosions that could kill any swimmer in the area. The attacks in Nha Be subsided somewhat.

During the early years of the Vietnam conflict, Saigon had been considered a Navy town. The U.S. Navy, through a command named Headquarters Support Activity, Saigon (HSAS), provided Americans with facilities ranging from movie theaters and post exchanges to hospitals. Capt. Archie Kuntze had taken command of HSAS in June 1964, quickly earning himself a reputation as an approachable leader who got things done. Certainly Naval Counterintelligence Support Activity Detachment, Saigon, owed much to Captain Kuntze's support of their mission and his largesse with logistic support—in the form of a villa that served as an agent residence, office spaces, and vehicles. A close, effective relationship existed between commander, HSAS, and the Naval Counterintelligence Support Agency, particularly in the unsettled periods early in his tenure when Naval Intelligence agents provided vital, regular situation reports about enemy activity likely to effect the safety and well-being of naval personnel.

Special Agent Paul Carr held Captain Kuntze in high regard. Carr believes Kuntze, by his lifestyle, created some highly placed enemies in Vietnam, where he became known as the "Mayor of Saigon." An article in an international news weekly focused further attention on claims that Kuntze reigned over Saigon as a king might.

Ultimately, an investigation was launched into a range of allegations against Captain Kuntze. Because of the sensitivity of the investigation, Special Agent Ken Nickel, assistant supervising agent of Naval Investigative Service Office (NISO), San Francisco, was flown in during April 1966 to direct the investigation.

As that investigation proceeded, Nickel was reporting his investigation directly to the NISO Pacific headquarters in Hawaii but also naturally keeping his home office of NISO San Francisco fully informed. There, the executive officer, Lt. Cdr. Bill Manthorpe, kept abreast of the investigation while carrying out his responsibilities as Nickel's military superior to authorize travel and other expenses as well as coordinating with Stateside naval authorities to obtain records and interviews.

As Manthorpe recalls, Captain Kuntze had been accused of a wide variety of offences, which included using the official aircraft to transport a Vietnamese female friend, importing fabric and other items for her, and mishandling official funds by permitting them to be stored in a locked refrigerator. But, it was common gossip at the time that what most irritated the increasing number of Army generals in town was seeing a mere Navy captain driving around town in an air-conditioned car with white-walled tires and other alleged aspects of "high living."

And, it was said that the real reason for the accusations against the captain was the Army's motive to take over the administration and support role in Saigon.

Ken Nickel concluded the investigation and wrote the final report with sensitivity to the situation, emphasizing that Captain Kuntze was more guilty of poor judgment than criminal intent. The captain was punished by a reprimand and the loss of one hundred numbers on the seniority list, enough to end a once-promising naval career.

In addition to official reports, several personal letters from Ken Nickel kept Manthorpe abreast of both the general situation regarding the evolving military command, administration, and support structure in Saigon as well as the personnel situation in the Naval Investigative Service (NIS) office.

Sometime in late May or early June 1966, it was decided to establish a NISO Vietnam to serve as an in-country headquarters to provide more direct guidance and support to the activities of the existing resident agency (RA) and replace its previous subordination to NISO Philippines. Nickel went home to San Francisco to pack his household goods so that he could return to Vietnam and become the supervising agent upon the establishment of the new NISOV. At about the same time, Manthorpe received a telephone call from Capt. Ted Rifenburg, commander NIS, asking him if he would like to be the commanding officer of NISOV. Manthorpe accepted immediately.

Manthorpe recalls that although he did not know it at the time, it now seems that he had been preparing for his tour with NISOV for several years. While serving as the intelligence officer on the staff of the Commander Second Fleet in 1965, he had preceded the Marines ashore into Santo Domingo to work with the naval attaché, a Marine lieutenant colonel. While the attaché was fully occupied conducting liaisons with U.S. and Dominican Republic government officials and trying to calm the actions of the various private militias, Manthorpe's role was to collect intelligence on the location and strength of the alleged communist revolutionaries. That experience, working in a semihostile environment, where one needed to be constantly alert to surrounding people and activities, was good preparation for living in Saigon in the 1960s.

In the summer of 1965, upon completing that sea-duty tour on the staff of Commander Second Fleet, Manthorpe took the then-obligatory tour that every young intelligence specialist was required to have with NIS. As a lieutenant commander, he was offered the position of executive officer at either NISO Norfolk or NISO San Francisco. Manthorpe selected San Francisco.

After receiving his orders to report to San Francisco, Manthorpe was informed that the director of NIS wanted to meet with him. After traveling to Washington, Manthorpe met with Captain Rifenburg, who told him that he was glad that the lieutenant commander had taken the job. Without providing any details, Rifenburg said that it was going to be a tremendous challenge and that if necessary Manthorpe could communicate directly with him. He also said not worry about fitness reports; he would see that they turned out all right. Bill Manthorpe left wondering what he was in for.

Upon arrival in San Francisco, he soon discovered that the commanding officer, NISO San Francisco, and the entire NISO staff were at loggerheads, morale was low, and the case backlog had grown. Both sides were looking to him to bridge the gap and fix the problems.

Lieutenant Commander Manthorpe needed help with ideas and support to improve morale and efficiency. That help came from Ken Nickel, the assistant supervising agent with whom he built a good rapport and worked most closely.

From his experience in San Francisco, Manthorpe knew what a dedicated group of highly professionally qualified people NIS agents and support staff were, how they liked to do their work, and what they needed or expected from the NIS military seniors. His relationship with Nickel and his understanding of the agent force would serve him well in Vietnam. He did not fully understand until later that at NISO San Francisco he had also learned the first lesson of leadership—management is about the processes of an organization and should be left to those responsible, in this case the professional civilian managers, while leadership is about caring for and inspiring the people of an organization and must be the role of the commander.

When given the NISOV command, Manthorpe moved his family back across the country to their home in Springfield, Virginia, and spent several days at NIS headquarters getting background and advice, followed by a week in Coronado, California, undergoing the Navy's standard pre-Vietnam indoctrination. He flew out of California by Military Air Command, 315th Air Division, C141 aircraft, directly to Saigon, arriving July 15, 1966.

The plane touched down at Tan Son Nhut Air Base outside of Saigon in late evening, but still he was met by Ken Nickel, Lt. Bob Dothard, and Special Agents Charlie Baldwin and Milt Steffen of Saigon. The five went immediately to Caruso's, a nice French restaurant not far from the villa that served as quarters for the senior military and civilian members of the office. After a steak dinner, which, Manthorpe recognized, thanks to a previous tour in France, as horse meat, he and Nickel retired to the villa that would be their residence for the next year. The house would also be used for informal meetings with counterintelligence personnel from other agencies, be lent to certain MACV counterintelligence officers for meeting with their contacts, and serve as an overnight billet for NISO and other out-of-town visitors.

This villa was in what had once been the finest section of Saigon. The neighbors were either senior Vietnamese bureaucrats or CIA operatives of various types. Thus, Vietnamese and Army MP protection was supposedly good. The villa sat in the center of a walled lot with metal gates and was essentially a square, stucco-over-cinderblocks, one-floor building. The layout consisted of a large screened room with tile floors that served as living and dining areas, a kitchen, and one bedroom that had been fortified with a heavy door and air conditioned. It was staffed by a Vietnamese maid, Hai, and her young son, who lived together in separate quarters by the back alley. At first glance, and the whole time he lived there, because of the neighborhood and the obvious occupants and neighbors, Manthorpe considered the villa a conspicuous target and a disaster waiting to happen. But it was luxury living compared to the Saigon hotels that served as living quarters for almost everyone else in the city. Besides, those hotels seemed to be regular targets anyway, and fortunately, disaster never came to the villa. The only invasion of the compound came from the geckos, which sat on the walls and ceiling and kept the bugs from bothering the occupants and visitors.

The day after his arrival Manthorpe got to see the office, located at 95 Nguyen Duy Duong Street in the Cholon area of Saigon, which it had its own separate entrance but lay just inside the wall of what was the former HSAS compound. He was impressed with how relatively well housed the organization was and how well provided it was with Navy vehicles, considering that it had just brought about the downfall of the organization that provided those amenities. The rest of the compound was crowded with a number of facilities that the Army had established upon taking over from the Navy: commissary, post exchange, gas station, post office, etc. At the time it was said that the Army had brought in several battalions of people to do what the Navy had done with fewer than one hundred. The compound was crowded.

Thus, in July 1966 NISOV was formed as a headquarters, manned by Lieutenant Commander Manthorpe and Supervising Agent Ken Nickel, two Navy petty officers, a Vietnamese civilian translator, and a Vietnamese civilian handyman-janitor. John Nester continued in the role of senior resident agent, Saigon, and continued to assist in the north as NISO staff suddenly increased in Da Nang to accommodate the buildup.

Soon two RAs, Saigon and Da Nang, were created. Each RA had a lieutenant USNR and an SRA, plus a growing number of special agents as time went on. By early 1967 an agent was assigned to Cam Ranh Bay.

Manthorpe immediately set about the task of molding the NISO headquarters operations. He and Nickel rapidly reestablished their relationship and procedures for operating the organization, which were essentially the same as in San Francisco: Nickel worried about the management of the investigations and Manthorpe concentrated on leadership of the people.

Nickel was known as the quintessential lead investigator. His guidance to the SRA upon the opening of a case was clear and concise; he kept himself informed of the details of every case and its progress by phone without interfering or micromanaging but ensuring that all possible leads had been pursued; and he reviewed the interim and final reports meticulously with a phenomenal memory for the details.

He was like Agatha Christie's Miss Marple in that every case recalled to his mind a similar one from the past, which then suggested additional leads and avenues to pursue and potential results for the latest case. The high standards of investigating and reporting that Nickel expected from the agents ensured continued outstanding performance as the caseload grew. To a man, everyone was glad that NISOV was exempt from the tedious conduct of background investigations. As the Navy and Marine Corps commitment to Vietnam grew, the agents had their hands full with cases of various kinds of personal misconduct, often claims of homosexuality, which may have been malingering; miscellaneous robberies; fraud; and a growing list of murders.

In his leadership role, Manthorpe had no problem keeping in close contact with the agents and staff of the Saigon Resident Agency, which had offices in the same building. He also initiated a Sunday brunch at the villa each week featuring Texas chili cooked by Special Agent Fred Givens. But, to keep in touch with the increasing number of people in Da Nang, Lieutenant Commander Manthorpe flew up regularly and stayed for several days. This close contact soon allowed him to identify a growing problem between the assigned officer and the agents and, eventually, to resolve that problem by having the officer reassigned elsewhere in Da Nang.

In addition to being assigned as commanding officer (CO) of NISOV, Manthorpe served as the counterintelligence officer (N22) on the staff of the Commander Naval Forces, Vietnam (COMNAVFORV). His responsibilities as N22 consisted of ensuring the collection of counterintelligence information of concern to the Navy, then analyzing and reporting it to the commander and his subordinate commands.

Manthorpe interpreted this duty to mean that he was to ensure that the NISO conducted regular counterintelligence activities and investigations in support of the Navy facilities in Saigon and Da Nang and, as possible, in support of other Navy locations. Unfortunately, given the increasing criminal investigation caseload as the number of in-country Navy and Marine Corps personnel grew, very few assets could be devoted to the counterintelligence effort. Furthermore, as agents departed and were replaced by new faces, many of the previous counterintelligence contacts were lost. Thus, most of NISO counterintelligence activities evolved to liaison with the massive Army counterintelligence activities in Vietnam, with contacts that had already been established with the Vietnamese Navy and with the growing Saigon-Cholon-Giadinh Security Committee led by CIA operative Mr. Robert Gambino, in connection with the activities of Mr. William Colby of the U.S. Embassy, Vietnam. In Da Nang, liaison was through Earl Sigg, a Navy lieutenant commander, who was assigned to the U.S. Naval Activities, Saigon, staff for duty with the security committee for that region. The agents maintained the liaison at the working level, gathering information of interest to the Navy from their counterparts and writing up intelligence information reports (IIRs) for distribution to Navy commands in Vietnam and for sending back to headquarters in Hawaii and Washington. Manthorpe maintained liaison at the official level to keep smooth relations and ensure the continued flow of information.

Each week Manthorpe attended the conference led by Bob Gambino and attended by representatives of all counterintelligence and security organizations in the southern region, thus acquiring a good feel for the intelligence threat throughout the southern part of Vietnam. Similarly, he had weekly meetings with Lt. Cdr. Nguyen Do Hai of Vietnamese Naval Intelligence at Vietnamese Navy headquarters and informal liaison with several officers in the Intelligence Directorate of MACV, most importantly Capt. Larry Tracy, USA, and Lt. Cdr. Frank Killilea, a fellow naval intelligence specialist. These officers shared much of the information that MACV had, and in exchange, Manthorpe let them use NISO's villa as a safe house to debrief contacts with whom they met. The resultant information from NISO activities and from the extensive liaison was reported to COMNAVFORV and local commanders by Manthorpe and put into message IIRs for appropriate Navy commands and headquarters.

In an illustration of how close-knit the intelligence community can be, Bob Gambino and Maynard Anderson later served together on the Director of Central Intelligence Security Committee in Washington, D.C. Gambino later became the CIA director of security under Director of Central Intelligence George H. W. Bush.

The NISOV organization worked, as they now say, 24/7/365, but life was not all work. Manthorpe, Nickel, and several agents belonged to the Cercle Sportif Saigonnais, the formerly elegant, but sadly disintegrating, French social and swim club. Nickel was a dedicated swimmer and fitness fanatic. He and Manthorpe tried to get in an hour of swimming and workout each day, either at noon or on the way home for dinner in the evening. In the evening during the early part of his tour, Manthorpe took Vietnamese lessons at the Alliance Francaise, but the language soon defeated him and he found that any Vietnamese to whom he really needed to speak understood French, in which, at that time, he was still fluent after an early four-year tour in Paris.

The year virtually flew by. Before Manthorpe knew it, Ken Nickel had left Vietnam and been replaced by Bert Truxell as supervising agent. Manthorpe quickly became comfortable with Truxell as his roommate in the villa and with Truxell's style at work as well. Shortly thereafter, Bill Manthorpe turned over the reins of NISOV to Lt. Cdr. W. F. Brubaker at the end of his tour in 1967.

Upon reflecting on his tour in Vietnam, Manthorpe has concluded that: "What I learned in terms of dealing with people would serve me well throughout the rest of my Navy career and into my civilian positions with the Navy. I was fortunate that my time in Vietnam was one of optimism and relative safety. I take my hat off to those who came later and had to deal with the disintegration of confidence and security."

# 3

# DA NANG, 1965 TO 1967:
# MARINES AND NIS

**Da Nang—the attractive seaport the French** designed and christened
Tourane—grew along the banks of the Han River, which meanders northward from flat paddy country and terminates in the bay. Da Nang City has
been an important trade center to central Vietnam for more than two hundred years.

Da Nang is possessed of one of those natural harbors for which mariners have searched since Phoenicians ventured into the Mediterranean. The
bay is shaped like a northward-facing cul-de-sac. To the east, an isthmus
called Tien Sa Peninsula protects it, while to the northwest the Annamite
Mountains rise abruptly from the waters, forming a gateway—Hai Van Pass—
to points north.

During the Vietnam conflict, Da Nang was the northernmost deepwater
port in the Republic of Vietnam; its strategic value was immense. Naval construction battalions (SeaBees) ultimately built deepwater piers on the Tien Sa
Peninsula to supply massive amounts of war materiel.

Also facing northward on the sandy flats behind the beach was Da Nang
Air Base, at one time easily the busiest air facility in the world. From sleepy
beginnings, Da Nang ultimately supported a U.S. Marine Corps wing, Air
Force tactical and fighter aircraft, Navy Fleet Air Support aircraft, a myriad
of helicopters from all services, and the VNAF. The commanders knew that
air facility would be critical to the effective prosecution of allied war plans,
especially interdiction of men, war materiel, and supplies, which were filtering down from North Vietnam via a labyrinthine system of trails and crude
roads known as the Ho Chi Minh Trail.

In 1965, facing unprecedented attacks by communist insurgents, South
Vietnamese forces were reeling, prompting genuine concerns they might lose
control of critical assets to the enemy. In response, President Lyndon Johnson
dispatched U.S. marines to protect the Da Nang Air Base. Landing at Red
Beach on the western side of the harbor near the future site of the Force
Logistic Command, marines brought most of what they would need ashore

with them, while other elements were flown in from Okinawa. In a very short time, the marines sent to protect the airfield and other key installations were doing so by active, aggressive patrolling against the Viet Cong.

As Special Agent Paul Carr recalls, Naval Intelligence had not planned an agent presence in I Corps in the early days of the war. As happened in later years in other areas, agent support was requested by affected commands and a permanent presence followed.

Preferring work with the U.S. Marines, Special Agent Tom Brannon became the point man for Naval Intelligence soon after the Marines deployed to the northern sector of the Republic of Vietnam during April 1965.

Brannon had reported to the U.S. Naval Counterintelligence Support Unit, Saigon, on March 7. Transferred from Long Beach, California, he had volunteered to serve a year in Vietnam. At that time three agents were assigned to Vietnam: Brannon, former Chicago police officer Milt Steffen, and Special Agent Paul Carr, all of whom served under the direction of Special Agent Maynard Anderson. Ultimately, they answered to the officer in charge, Naval Counterintelligence Support Activity, Phillipines at Sangley Point, Lt. Cdr. Glenn Fugate.

Two Saigon agents then lived at the 98 Phan Dinh Phoung villa. Others lived in BOQs, converted hotels under military administration. The Five Oceans BOQ, an old Chinese hotel, was situated near the Cholon office, perhaps three hundred yards away. The Five Os, as it was known by all, abutted an especially fragrant Vietnamese market and featured prominently with agents who served in later years.

Soon after Marine elements landed at Da Nang, and later at Chu Lai, requests were forwarded to Saigon, asking for assistance. Brannon and Carr used scheduled military transport to fly north to carry out investigations. The process was cumbersome; the agents carried orders assigning them on temporary duty (TDY) to the requesting element.

In September 1965 the commanding officer of Third Battalion Fourth Marines, Lieutenant Colonel Taylor, requested assistance when he learned one of his young riflemen had been using issued morphine Syrettes from medical supplies. Brannon joined a heavily armed Marine convoy and drove over Hai Van Pass from Da Nang to the 3/4 rear area at Phu Bai, just south of Hue. At Phu Bai, Third Marine Counterintelligence Team personnel provided support and a tent for interrogation purposes. Brannon interrogated the marine, who readily admitted he had been frightened during recent combat operations and had taken the Syrettes, which are to be used to alleviate pain for the seriously wounded. He admitted giving several to other members of the command. He said the morphine had helped ease anxiety in combat. This case is significant because drug abuse was then a rarity; it is also interesting that the drugs were not purchased on the open market.

After several such trips, a full-time agent was requested. In October 1965, following a joint request from the Navy commodore and provost marshal, Maj. Les Barrett, USMC, Tom Brannon agreed to remain in Da Nang. Director of Naval Intelligence (DNI) orders dated November 16, 1965, established U.S. Naval Counterintelligence Support Unit, Da Nang Detachment.

As happened to other agents in later years, Tom Brannon was left to his own devices when the time came to requisition what was needed, even uniforms. Marines, complaining that an individual in civilian clothes stood out and might draw fire, provided issue dungarees.

The Naval Support Activity (NSA) was by then established in the riverside building already named the White Elephant, where it would remain for a further six years. Opposite NSA, Marine command elements were set up at Camp Horn; from there the active war in the north of South Vietnam was directed. Brannon was given a small office cubicle near the commodore at the White Elephant. Not many days had passed before the workload reached horrendous proportions. Men awaiting interview lined up outside the tiny office.

Brannon had little time for anything but work. The Navy provided him a small room in a dingy waterfront building then serving as a BOQ. Messing was several blocks in the opposite direction. A Navy jeep was requisitioned, providing necessary mobility.

No extra agents were available to help in Da Nang, although Special Agent Carl Sundstrom came TDY from Naval Air Station (NAS), Atsugi, Japan, to assist during one particularly heavy welter of activity. Marine Corps Provost Marshal Major Barrett, seeing Brannon's predicament, assigned to him first an infantry first lieutenant, Mike Anderson, and later, Criminal Investigation Division (CID) agent S.Sgt. Dan Buckle. While neither was empowered to act independently, both participated actively in investigations. Anderson, as a junior officer, was especially adroit at finding his way through difficulties in the Marine command maze, while Buckle acted as Brannon's partner in interviews and interrogations. Buckle, a marine with broken service, had initially enlisted in 1947. He was a mature, seasoned marine who was later commissioned and rose to the rank of lieutenant colonel. With no clerical assistance, Brannon typed his reports in the rough and mailed them to Saigon, where the final product was produced and dispatched to commands.

Perhaps goaded on by a seemingly permanent line of shuffling witnesses and suspects with no place to stand but near the commodore's office, the Navy in October 1965 rented a house for its Da Nang office. The house at 20 Duy Tan Street served more than five years in this role. Brannon left most details of the setup to Lieutenant Anderson, who soon moved his gear in. No security arrangements were made for the house, which was located in a central Da Nang neighborhood, but a field phone was soon installed and linked to the Navy switchboard at the White Elephant. Brannon retained his BOQ room.

Two Marine divisions were by then in I Corps. The headquarters element that would control the war effort in northern I Corps, III MAF, was newly established on the east bank of the Han River, opposite the White Elephant.

Telephone communication was undependable. I Corps Navy and Marine Corps commands were still learning about the NIS presence in the region. Command representatives and Marine military police learned to find NISRA Da Nang at their backstreet address. Demand began to increase.

In 1965 agents were dealing with an almost entirely volunteer force. Dissent against the war and authority was minimal, and there were few signs of narcotics usage. In January 1966, however, Brannon began receiving reports that the situation was changing in Da Nang and so began using informants and casual acquaintances to learn more. He suspected there was a Vietnamese drug trade operating through the totally unregulated pharmacies that were a prevalent feature of most settlements—and he suspected illegal drugs were being offered to service personnel who frequented unauthorized bars and brothels in the ramshackle settlements then being erected outside the gates of several important military facilities. As an initial step, Brannon visited the Army Provost Marshal, Da Nang. There he was told the Army had seen no evidence of any illicit narcotics trade in the area; further, he was informed that Army military police did not believe any such problem existed.

Realizing the potential impact of easily accessible narcotics on the battle efficiency of troops, Brannon decided to investigate under cover a notorious shantytown outside the gates of Hill 327, west of Da Nang Air Base and home to Marine headquarters elements. Called Dogpatch by the marines, it was considered insecure and dangerous—but sexual favors and illicit goods nevertheless attracted visitors there. Drawing $100 from the supply officer at Naval Support Activity, Brannon approached the Marine Provost Marshal to request the assistance of a young Puerto Rican marine whose upbringing in a difficult area of New York gave him the precise skills needed to act as a streetwise narcotics buyer. With Lance Corporal Rivera, Brannon went into

Dogpatch dressed as a Marine sergeant, bought narcotics, and took photographs of the transactions as they occurred. They were offered both cannabis and concentrated opium for smoking.

Dangerous drugs were also purchased over the counter at the Vietnamese pharmacy across the street from the Army Provost Marshal. Other purchases in Da Nang confirmed a ready source of narcotics for anybody with a desire to purchase them. An intelligence report was prepared and forwarded to senior command elements; this was very probably the first such report and an indication of what would become in later years an uncontrollable problem in Vietnam.

As Christmas 1965 approached, two events occurred, both of which were pleasant changes in the Da Nang routine: first, Brannon was ordered to the Philippines for a special assignment; then, Bob Hope, with Raquel Welch and the Rockettes, visited Vietnam.

In December Tom Brannon was ordered to report to the Naval Intelligence headquarters element at Sangley Point, Philippines. After the grind of Da Nang, a trip out-of-country was something to look forward to. He wasted no time flying to Sangley, where Supervising Agent Jack Donnelly briefed him: a U.S. Navy sailor named Edwin Ross Armstrong, who had defected to the Chinese Communists at Hong Kong, had been returned. Armstrong, the first defector to the Chinese since the Korean War, had jumped ship from a U.S. destroyer, traveled from Hong Kong to rural Kowloon, and there apparently swam to waiting Chinese sentries. The Chinese had exploited his antiwar sentiments for propaganda purposes, sending him back loaded with presents when his usefulness diminished with time. Brannon was to "maintain a low profile and get him back to U.S. control." His contact was the U.S. defense attaché, a Marine lieutenant colonel.

Flying to Hong Kong on a Navy transport, Brannon checked into a hotel, then made his way to the consulate to contact the attaché. He learned that unspecified U.S. embassy personnel had apparently played a key role in recovering Armstrong, assisted by British counterparts who enjoyed excellent contacts in mainland China at the time. Nothing more was said about the operation. Armstrong was being closely watched in the embassy but was not restrained. The Navy wanted him spirited to the airport and out of the British colony without any members of the public realizing he had been in Hong Kong. Hidden from public view, Armstrong was taken to the airport. Escorted aboard a waiting U.S. Air Force cargo aircraft already loaded with military passengers, he and Brannon were soon airborne, en route to the Philippines.

Armstrong was young, perhaps eighteen, a gangly, fast-growing adolescent. Standing perhaps six feet three, but weighing no more than 150 pounds, he looked like a high school student. Passengers had been told that a defector was being put aboard but not which of the oncoming passengers was the man. Brannon to this day believes most thought he was the traitor, simply because of Armstrong's youthful appearance.

Brig marines took Armstrong into custody as soon as he reached Sangley Point. From all reports, the baby-faced sailor did not have an easy time with his Marine jailers, some of whom were Vietnam vets. He was tried by general court-martial and was awarded a sentence of twenty years confinement and a dishonorable discharge.

To get an easy air connection back to Vietnam, Brannon flew from the Philippines back to Hong Kong, where he gave his wife in California the gift of a long-distance phone call.

Soon after Brannon's return to Da Nang, Bob Hope and his retinue visited I Corps for the first time, entertaining several thousand marines who gathered appreciatively for what was always an unforgettable show. Brannon recalls, "Raquel couldn't have looked better to the men, many of whom had not cast an eye on a round-eye for months." Brannon and Staff Sergeant Buckle, part of the security detail for the group, had an up-close view of all. True to form, Bob Hope returned to I Corps for the next five Christmas seasons, carrying on his tradition begun during World War II of sharing Christmas with overseas troops. He has a special place in the hearts of thousands who were entertained on their first Christmas away from home.

The Da Nang operation remained a single–special agent post until March 1966, when SRA Charlie Baldwin reported. Soon after, several special agents arrived to work for him. Tom Brannon had two days to brief new agents, then flew to Sangley Point to report to his new duty station.

Special Agent Dave Roberts remembers his first morning in Vietnam. He woke up face-to-face with a gecko, arising in fright to the mirth of the housekeeping staff at the ONI villa in Saigon.

On his first-ever trip outside the United States, Roberts had left his home in the Virginia suburbs of Washington, D.C., two days earlier, in the midst of a record snowfall. It was December 1965; he was destined for Da Nang. First he flew cross-country to California's San Francisco Bay Area, and soon after he found himself in a crowded waiting room at Travis Air Force Base, sitting with scores of others destined to fly in a chartered airliner to Saigon and several points between. Following the seemingly endless flight, he was picked up by agents at Tan Son Nhut and driven to the Cholon office. Awed by everything, he saw the wildlife resident on the villa sunporch, where a cot had been set up for him, as just more of the same. On day two, after all the formalities of check-in at Saigon headquarters, he was on a military flight from Saigon, flying north to Da Nang.

Dave Roberts was one of several agents hurriedly recruited to staff the new office in support of a rapidly expanding Navy and Marine Corps presence in northern I Corps. He had been attracted by the opportunities for accelerated promotion and preference in future assignment and by the surety of training in an environment guaranteed to expose an agent to every variety of investigative challenge; this was a major career move. As for nearly every agent who followed, an element of uncertainty accompanied the final arrival at the place that would be home for the next year.

Met at Da Nang Air Base by Special Agent Milt Steffen and 1st Lt. Mike Anderson, USMC, Roberts was driven to the combination office and quarters at 20 Duy Tan Street. Steffen had extended his tour in Vietnam to work in Da Nang after a year in Saigon. Other agents ordered in from various parts of the world were then expected at any time. SRA Charlie Baldwin soon arrived to take over and was followed by Special Agents Jim Levett and Carl Merritt.

Dave Roberts did not have to wait long for his first major investigation, the apparent suicide of the officer in charge of the classified control center. The Navy lieutenant had shot himself in the head; a full crime scene examination was required in addition to in-depth investigation into any apparent motive. In the world of counterintelligence, suicide can be symptomatic of pressures borne by those who have compromised national secrets; that the victim was in charge of scores of highly sensitive documents caused alarm bells to ring and detailed inventories to be carried out in haste.

For Roberts, the tasks were more mundane: detailed measurements and photographs of the victim in a small, hot room in soaring humidity amid blood and spattered brain tissue—followed by a trip with the body to the Navy hospital known as Charlie Med for an autopsy. Roberts felt distinctly unwell by this point, and his discomfort was recognized by a sympathetic pathologist who suggested he wait outside until the critical procedure was complete.

Having returned to the office at dusk after a long and unforgettable day, Roberts had a few extra drinks that night at the officers' club.

Also destined for the new office in Da Nang, Special Agent Carl Merritt was the last agent offered a split tour: one year in the Philippines followed by twelve months in the Republic of Vietnam.

Merritt, with his orders in-hand and a bag of personal effects, joined a C130 Hercules flight at Naval Air Station Cubi Point, Philippines. He and several dozen others crowded into the bowels of the four-engine transport plane, made themselves as comfortable as possible in sling seats and began a flight across the South China Sea to make a late-night landing at Tan Son

Nhut Airport, Saigon. A former marine, Merritt had well-developed skills for making the best of a challenging new situation; confronted on arrival with the vagaries of a sometimes-working Vietnamese phone system, he was unable to communicate with a Navy enlisted man who was to pick him up from the airport and drive him to the supervising agent's Saigon villa for an overnight sleep before beginning the final leg of his journey. On the flight, he'd made the acquaintance of a Navy chief petty officer who guaranteed a seat on the next day's Navy flight to Da Nang. Why not just stay put and have a few beers at the airport bar?

Bier 33, manufactured in Saigon, was not a great example of the brewer's art. It was said tongue in cheek that lawn trimmings were used in the fermentation process instead of traditional hops and barley. Nevertheless, it was wet if not cold. Merritt and the chief drank many through the remainder of the night. Awakening to a brilliant tropical morning, certain the chief had been drunker than he, Merritt learned that the Da Nang aircraft was a World War II–vintage C47 and that the pilot was his drinking partner. The Navy still had a few pilot NCOs in 1966. It was, thankfully, an uneventful flight north to Da Nang Air Base.

Arriving at the 20 Duy Tan address of NISRA Da Nang's quarters and office, Carl Merritt began a memorable year in an atmosphere of anticipation. SRA Charlie Baldwin welcomed him to the fold, as did fellow agents. Hungry and thirsty, a group decided to introduce Carl to Da Nang's very limited nightlife with an evening visit to the NCO club at the air base, called the Take Ten Club. Special Agent Dave Roberts remembers it as an especially warm night. A comedian was scheduled to perform. Merritt had changed into an embroidered white shirt of the type worn in the Philippines. Finding a table, the group ordered drinks and waited for the act to begin.

Unaware, they talked amicably as Viet Cong terrorists outside first shot a sentry and then rolled grenades in through the open door. The resulting explosion injured many, some critically, but the agents were spared. They bolted from the rear of the club and took shelter behind an air-conditioning condenser, anticipating a follow-up attack with either more grenades or rifle fire. None came. Returning to the club interior, they assisted wounded and injured personnel and then soberly drove back to the office.

Charlie Baldwin remembers that his agents returned to the Duy Tan quarters in an atmosphere of tension and excitement. "Some of the tension dissipated when I noticed right in the middle of Carl Merritt's back the perfect imprint of a tennis shoe. In the melee which followed the blast, the wearer had run unnoticed over his white shirt; a combination of grime and beer had stenciled a permanent imprint."

Carl Merrit recalls that agents in Da Nang settled well into their neighborhood. Vietnamese families, few of them with electricity, surrounded agents at 20 Duy Tan. An array of extension cords from the office soon allowed the agents to share the power with poor neighbors up and down the block. One family in particular received regular help from agents. They were the survivors of an ARVN soldier, a veteran of the French colonial force who had been killed. The men adopted the family, who lived opposite on Duy Tan, supplying them with food and other necessities.

Despite the arrival of thousands of American service personnel, vestiges of an earlier, more refined era remained. A few small restaurants in the neighborhood continued to supply high-quality French cuisine. Favored by several of the agents, the nearby Golden Dragon was operated by a black French Algerian who had an impressive wine cellar.

The role of traveling agent roundsman at NISRA Da Nang was created with Carl Merritt's decision to volunteer to manage a growing demand for NIS support in the field. This was a role that other agents continued until 1969, when satellite offices under Da Nang were established at Quang Tri Combat Base and at Chu Lai.

The year 1965 was one of change and transition in northern I Corps as two Marine divisions deployed and redeployed to meet changing tactical considerations. Uniformly uncomfortable with the task they were initially assigned—static defense of the air base—senior marines soon began to extend friendly control by the traditional Marine techniques of patrol and pacification. Communication, particularly to deployed field marines, remained uncertain and transportation to the field was largely a question of an agent's capacity for innovation.

Merritt soon learned he could virtually guarantee himself a seat on any service aircraft by traveling with a colorful mailbag. If asked, he said the bag contained mail "for the troops at [destination supplied]." In fact, the bag was used to carry case files and a horde of trade goods for those willing to provide transport, a shower, or a place to sleep. Liquor was especially effective because marines were then limited to a beer ration. A bottle of Crown Royal would buy just about anything that was capable of being moved.

The mailbag worked with other services too. In Phu Bai, home of the Army Security Agency's secret Eighth Radio Research Station, Merritt permanently assured himself of a shower and clean bunk by leaving a 9mm Swedish K submachine gun with a friendly Army contact. At that point in the war, the station had well-established facilities far better than most other organizations just getting settled in under canvas. The K was a favored weapon in Special Forces units but an uncommon caliber that sounded different enough that, in an armed encounter, fellow allies might interpret its chatter as "nonfriendly" and react accordingly. Merritt elected to stay with the 7.62-caliber M14 rifle, then issued to all marines.

Finding a marine or the scene of an incident always began with the parent unit, either regimental headquarters or the battalion command post (CP). There the situation could be assessed and a plan made to travel forward to do the job. This might involve helicopter travel, a jeep or truck ride, or going on foot, accompanying a sweep. Carl Merritt set the pattern for traveling agent roundsmen who followed in his footsteps over the next two years.

In NISRA Da Nang's area of operation, I Corps, 1966 brought with it the military threat posed by a noticeable buildup of North Vietnamese Army (NVA) forces in the border regions. With it also came more signs of political instability in the fragile Saigon regime, headed by colorful Premier Nguyen Cao Ky. Buddhists remained unappeased by Ky's piecemeal approach to democratic reform, and tensions remained between underrepresented Buddhists and Catholics in power.

Premier Ky regarded I Corp commander Lt. Gen. Nguyen Chanh Thi as a serious rival. Thi was not only a respected military leader, he was also considered an astute politician. He was not above capitalizing on traditional distrust the regional people held for the Saigon government and its policies. Hue had long been a central area of Buddhist unrest; it was also Thi's home. In March 1966 Premier Ky flew to Hue to personally investigate allegations that Thi had been agitating against his government. Soon after Thi was forced to resign. Although he did so gracefully, the people of I Corps reacted with shock. Unrest, demonstrations, and strikes followed in Da Nang and Hue, characterized by the creation of "Struggle Forces" opposed to Saigon.

Despite civil unrest, III MAF commander Lt. Gen. Lewis Walt, USMC, pressed ahead with combat operations in the region south of Da Nang in concert with Vietnamese allies.

After Thi resigned, he returned to his home in Hue. Large numbers of the population rallied to him, creating ongoing political foment. With key military, police, and political leaders in Da Nang also sympathetic to the Struggle Forces' cause, Premier Ky dispatched the Vietnamese Marines by aircraft to Da Nang Air Base.

General Walt was in a difficult position. Wishing to avoid any U.S. involvement in the Vietnamese political process, he nevertheless had a responsibility to prosecute the war against communist forces. Moreover, his professional relationship with Thi had been cordial and effective. Marines did all they could to stay clear of the Vietnamese, hoping matters might be resolved and efforts quickly returned to effective prosecution of the war. In early April, however, an ARVN group from Hoi An, responding to news about the arrival of Vietnamese marines from Saigon, left their barracks south of Da Nang towing artillery, intending to train the guns on the air base, where the Saigon marines were ensconced. General Walt ordered elements of his Ninth Marines to block the force. With the aid of circling, heavily armed Marine fighters and distant artillery zeroed on the rebel position, the rebel Vietnamese were halted at a bridge on Route 1 and, after negotiation, returned to Hoi An.

On April 15 Ky covertly reinforced forces loyal to Saigon and key areas of Da Nang were seized, arrests of Struggle Forces leaders following. Vietnamese Air Force A1 Skyraiders fired rockets and machine guns at positions near the III MAF headquarters, wounding nearby marines—but a full-scale confrontation was avoided.

Three days later General Walt himself played a personal role in regaining control of the strategically critical bridge that connected Tien Sa Peninsula with Da Nang. With opposing forces on opposite sides of the span, Walt confronted a Vietnamese warrant officer to urge that demolition charges be removed. The warrant officer refused, told Walt they would die together, and signaled peers to detonate charges, but the explosives didn't fire. The bridge was quickly cleared by U.S. marines, allowing critical war materiel movement from Deepwater Pier to storage areas to resume.

The NISRA Da Nang office and billet in downtown Da Nang City was surrounded by foment and unrest throughout the troubles. Though U.S. civilians and others had been evacuated, the Naval Intelligence agents remained at their home and office on Duy Tan Street. Other agencies did not stay. Driving to the U.S. Army Military Intelligence Compound to visit detachment commander Maj. Neil Hock, SRA Charlie Baldwin found the compound vacant. The Army had burned their files and taken refuge on Tien Sa Peninsula.

There was palpable tension in the streets of Da Nang as Vietnamese political events unfolded. Factions technically allied to the same cause aligned against each other, and it became difficult for outsiders to know which former allies posed danger to them. Agents went about their jobs with a heightened sense of awareness.

In the home of their Vietnamese language teacher, two agents overheard a heated conversation between some Vietnamese, giving clear indication of an imminent uprising in I Corps and identifying key players. SRA Charlie Baldwin immediately took the information to Da Nang's CIA station chief, who arranged for Naval Intelligence to brief the deputy ambassador in Saigon. At the briefing, the deputy ambassador told Baldwin his report confirmed information developed in Saigon, presumably by CIA (although CIA Da Nang did not have the information). The Navy report added credence and detail to information the embassy had been using to assemble contingency plans for Vietnam.

Agents remained in the small office compound during the periods of high alert when Da Nang City was evacuated. They carefully observed events around 20 Duy Tan for firsthand indicators of developments in the Vietnamese political crisis. The unmistakable sounds of an ARVN tank maneuvering down the street quickly drew the attention of agents away from their confinement one day: the tank was seen to be slowly driving down Duy Tan Street in the adjacent block. As it approached a Buddhist temple, the turret began swiveling to one side, training its main gun at the temple.

Joined by a visiting OSI agent who had braved a multitude of roadblocks to reach the office to trade frozen steaks for C rations unavailable from the Air Force, agents walked toward the tank to observe events at the temple. Taking position on a nearby curb, they sat and waited to see what the response from the temple would be. They didn't wait for long: a Buddhist monk rushed toward the tank screaming at the occupants, climbed up onto it, and doused himself in gasoline. Seeing no further developments in the self-immolation process, the OSI agent offered the monk his personal Zippo lighter. The monk refused and quieted. Some time later, back at the office, the boom of the tank cannon could be heard. Several rounds were fired into the upper part of the structure. There was little damage, but a clear message had been sent.

On a morning in early May 1966, Dave Roberts awoke to find Duy Tan Street quiet, with barbed wire and sand-bagged positions blocking both ends of the street and manned by armed Vietnamese. The agents had a substantial supply of C rations stored in the office. It was plainly obvious that movement outside would be unnecessarily hazardous, and agents stayed at home for more than a week while the sounds of gunfire and unrest could be heard in surrounding Da Nang. A Navy supply truck called periodically to deliver drinking water.

When tensions reached their height on May 15, agents were gathered on the front porch of the house in the midst of an endless pinochle game. There had been more firing than usual that day, but aircraft—single-engine A1 Skyraiders of VNAF—flying over the eastern edge of the city quickly drew the agents' attention. Agents watched with concern as the planes fired rockets and strafed positions that appeared to be in the immediate vicinity of General Walt's headquarters, III MAF.

Isolated and out of communication, Charlie Baldwin decided an effort should be made to reach the Da Nang Combat Information Bureau (CIB) so a determination of the situation could be made. Media reporters could be expected at the CIB; they would have news. Furthermore, CIB might offer a meal other than the C rations that everyone had subsisted on throughout the emergency. Accompanied by Special Agent Milt Steffen, he set off in a jeep. Soon after their departure, rounding a corner in downtown Da Nang, they were confronted by a firefight between Vietnamese National Police and ARVN troops in the block ahead. With stray rounds cracking around them, Steffen turned the jeep around in record time and returned them safely to the office.

Bob Powers transferred to Da Nang to join Charlie Baldwin's team in November 1966. A single agent, Powers had volunteered for duty after serving a stint in Iceland. He enjoyed overseas work. In Vietnam, he was to join his two brothers, one a career Army intelligence officer, the other a young marine assigned to an amphibious tractor unit in I Corps. He would see both siblings during the year that followed.

In December 1966 Bob Powers and Carl Merritt were called out late at night to investigate a reported shooting at a Marine engineer unit on the far side of Da Nang. The city was, as always, locked down tight at night, when "the country belonged to Charlie." Armed to the teeth, they set off in a Navy Ford Bronco, with Merritt in the back, where he could better defend them in the event the worst happened. There were roadblocks everywhere. Powers was new in-country and knew none of the passwords nervous sentries demanded. They talked their way through, Merritt banging on the roof nervously if it appeared the driver was taking a turn that might send them directly into Indian country. They at last found the engineer unit.

The Marine victim's body had been taken away, complicating the crime scene search for forensic evidence. But nine people had witnessed the shooting; they said the suspect had entered a hooch full of sleeping marines and later began shooting. The victim had been trying to get away when he was shot dead. There were indications the suspect had been smoking marijuana and was angry with the marine sleeping next to the victim but had killed the victim when he made a move to escape.

The case was not difficult, but it illustrates the conditions and investigative challenges of the time. All but two or three of the nine witnesses were killed in combat before the case came to trial, but the suspect was found guilty and sentenced to twenty years confinement.

Like Special Agents Merritt and Powers, New Englander Peter Segersten volunteered for Vietnam service while serving at NISRA Newport, Rhode Island. The young, single special agent arrived in Da Nang aboard a Navy C54 on New Year's Day 1966 to join Charlie Baldwin's team.

"Like most of the other agents, my work was almost exclusively with the Marines." Segersten began assisting with supporting forward-deployed USMC units, in particular the Third Marine Division, then beginning a rigorous series of operations designed to rid the area between Da Nang and the DMZ of North Vietnamese Army units and the VC cadre that supported them. The process of getting up to the marines normally began with an aircraft ride, either to Phu Bai or Dong Ha. The aircraft might belong to any of the services, but Marine CH46 and C130 aircraft were the most common workhorses in the livery.

NIS special agents working in the north of South Vietnam were at pains to advise Marine commands that they were in-country and available to assist if required. Segersten and Merritt visited Marine units deployed along the outer edges of South Vietnam, in areas commonly considered Indian country. Agents visited Khe Sanh before the NVA buildup and siege, when it was a forward artillery base; they also flew into Khe Sanh when it was later surrounded by enemy forces and subject to intense artillery and rocket barrage.

Agents working the north soon learned, in an environment of primitive, under-canvas living, that it was always preferable to billet with either a SeaBee battalion or a Marine engineer group. Both organizations knew how to minimize hardship in the field.

Peter Segersten fell heir to an investigation in October 1966 that was to have far-reaching ramifications in legal circles as to how the Uniform Code of Military Justice (UCMJ) applied to civilian employees of the Navy serving in a war zone. Segersten, backed up by Special Agent Howie Dilkes, was called out late one afternoon to investigate a fatal stabbing at a small Vietnamese bar on the Tien Sa Peninsula, opposite Da Nang City.

Segersten found the scene with some difficulty; a nondescript shack made of scavenged material located near the north end of China Beach, it had been erected to take advantage of custom from nearby ship berthing. It housed a few chairs and tables, a bar, and several entrepreneurial females. Marine MPs at the scene told the agents that the victim's remains had been removed to the morgue. They had arrested the suspect, an able seaman civilian employee of the Navy named James Henry Latney—assigned to the Military Sea Transportation Service (MSTS)—and had jailed him in their brig. The investigators found little or no physical evidence, and the Vietnamese employees were less than cooperative.

Realizing that a skilled interpreter would be crucial to successful dealing with the Vietnamese witnesses, the agents drove to the nearby naval advisory detachment (NAD) adjoining Camp Tien Sa. For many years NAD had supported clandestine Vietnamese operations into North Vietnam utilizing fast patrol torpedo boats called nasty boats. At the detachment was a former ONI special agent, then a Marine captain, who made available a Nung interpreter, one of an ethnic group widely used in the shadowy world of the Special Forces.

Back at the crime scene, the Vietnamese witnesses were skillfully interrogated by the NAD Nung, who had learned his skills through contact with captured enemy soldiers. Witnesses said the victim, Beyethe Arthur Trimm, had come ashore earlier in the day while his ship was off-loading fuel at a berth near Tien Sa Peninsula. He had been drinking quietly until Latney's arrival later in the day, when the men had argued and scuffled. A chair was used in the altercation. Latney was seen to slash Trimm several times with a pocketknife, the victim falling to the ground. They said Latney then folded the knife and put it in his pocket. Suddenly, he unexpectedly pulled it out once again and stabbed Trimm fatally in the heart.

Segersten set about learning all he could about both the suspect and the victim, who were crewmembers aboard the bulk fuel transport *Antank*, registered in Wilmington, North Carolina. Latney, he learned, was considered the ship bully by fellow crewmembers. Trimm, a former marine discharged on other-than-honorable circumstances, had recently signed on at Manila, Philippines.

Segersten knew the murder weapon was going to be critical evidence in the case against Latney. The bar proprietor, known to all simply as *mama-san*, said Latney had thrown his knife out the door after the stabbing. After a careful grid search of the beach and water produced nothing, mama-san told the Nung interpreter that a Popular Forces (PF) soldier had later picked up the knife. The Nung began asking Vietnamese in the area about who the PF might have been and later that night found a young Vietnamese soldier who admitted retrieving the bloodstained knife. He took agents to a bush in sand dunes and dug up the murder weapon.

The PF willingly provided a statement, but he would not put his mark on the knife to signify that it was the same weapon he had recovered and buried. Segersten put his own initials on the grip, and the Vietnamese soldier's statement acknowledged what had occurred.

Latney languished in the Marine brig for several months while legal officers and diplomats argued about what was to be done about a trial. The UCMJ stipulates that civilians assigned to a theater of war are subject to the laws of the code, but lawyers were not confident a prosecution would succeed. Finally, the presiding Marine authority ordered that a general court-martial be convened to try Latney. An incident of such blatant criminal behavior could not be seen to go unpunished.

The court-martial ultimately found Latney guilty of murder, and he was shipped to a federal penitentiary to serve his sentence. Ultimately, however, he was released after a successful appeal against the conviction: the appellate court found that a formal state of war did not exist in Vietnam, and thus the UCMJ did not apply to the civilian Latney.

In March 1967 SRA Charlie Baldwin's tour ended. Special Agent Jack Myer, who had just completed three years in Japan, replaced him. Missing his scheduled flight from Tachikawa because of a wake-up call that never came, Myer found a seat on the Air Force C130 that ferried the day's edition of

*Stars and Stripes* newspaper to Saigon. Briefed by the supervising agent, Ken Nickel, Myer began his trip up-country the next day aboard the Market Time shuttle, an aging C47 loaded with Vietnamese Navy personnel and dependents. It was a long trip, made somewhat more tolerable by the fact he was assigned one of ten seats aboard; other passengers squatted on the deck. Jack Myer remembers the flight well because the aircraft crashed on its return leg, killing all aboard.

Myer knew a little about what to expect in Da Nang, the plane crash notwithstanding. As a Japan-based agent, he had carried out investigations afloat at Yankee Station, the off-shore zone where U.S. naval forces were actively carrying out the aerial campaign against North Vietnam. He had flown into Da Nang on a Navy replenishment flight from the fleet on the first leg of his return to Japan. "It was hot and dirty," he recalls. In the few handover days that Myer had with the departing Charlie Baldwin, he was shown the ropes. During a party thrown by the local Army Military Intelligence detachment, a firefight broke out between sentries in the street outside and the VC they thought were infiltrating. It was a suitable baptism for Myer's stay in Da Nang, if a nerve-shaking one.

After his arrival in Da Nang in late 1966, Bob Powers soon established himself as a particularly capable criminal investigator, and this reputation followed him through three decades of service with the organization. Powers holds the dubious distinction of having investigated what is believed to be the first "fragging" in NIS history. Fragging, the use of fragmentation grenades to murder or maim, was usually carried out against disliked superior officers and NCOs.

The investigation began with a call for assistance from a Marine artillery unit deployed along the corridor south of Da Nang, but north of the Marine enclave at Chu Lai. The battery executive officer (XO), a captain, had been very seriously injured by a booby trap rigged outside the tent he shared with his commanding officer. The victim lost both of his legs to the blast by a U.S.-manufactured M26 fragmentation grenade.

Powers was assigned to a month of temporary duty at the Marine enclave of Chu Lai, where he was billeted with Marine military police and CID. A Marine senior NCO from CID accompanied him to the artillery encampment on Route 1 and left soon after dropping him off. Powers began to reconstruct what remained of the crime scene and search for physical evidence. A wooden stake used in gun laying, the process of aiming an artillery piece, had been used to secure one end of the trip wire, the other end connected to the safety pin of the grenade. The stake was one of a set of three. Transparent tape particles were attached to the offending post. Powers carefully preserved the post and its tape as evidence, then began asking questions about battery personnel. As it transpired, one of the unit troublemakers worked in a limited-access supply tent, which was then carefully searched. A broken set of stakes was discovered, with one missing and its packaging tape broken. Forensic laboratory examination later established that the stake used to fashion the booby trap had been broken out of this packet of three. As the supply tent was a limited-access area, this was an important clue.

Powers soon realized that the investigation would not be quickly concluded; he would need to remain at the battery in this forward area. He wore a composite "uniform" consisting of utility shirt, white tee shirt, and chinos, all of which set him apart from every other man at the position and probably rendered him an attractive target. He had no rifle, only his issue .357 magnum. When night fell and there was little else he could safely do, he asked Marine Major Mimmor where he could sleep. Mimmor, who had originally mistaken Powers for an itinerant journalist, was particularly helpful once he discovered a special agent was on hand to carry out the investigation; he offered Powers a bunk in his tent.

The gun battery and battalion areas were separated by Route 1—and at that time the investigation was being carried out among the 155mm gun batteries. The road was an obvious avenue of enemy attack, and Marine defenses reflected this: Powers was led in the dark first past sentries demanding a password, then through an antipersonnel minefield to the highway. On the opposite side, the process was repeated. Powers stayed very close to the major, who later told him it was the first time he'd made the crossing at night.

Interviews in the days that followed all took place in a two-man tent equipped with a table and two chairs. In accordance with regulations for forward areas, all marines interviewed were armed with their issue rifle. Attacks on the gun position could and did occur. Powers's first experienced a mortar attack during an interview of a young marine who bolted from the tent upon hearing incoming rounds. Powers remained, uncertain where to go or what to do, his revolver lying on the table.

Powers interviewed scores of marines. One of them was the troublemaker from the supply tent; although warned of his rights against self-incrimination, he waived them and spoke freely. Bob Powers thought the man came across as a particularly cool and streetwise character, worthy of a careful record check back in Da Nang.

The full investigation lasted several weeks. Interviews turned up a myriad of other offences. Men guarding the perimeter would throw grenades at defensive positions during the night—something they jokingly referred to as War Call—resulting in a general stand-to, in which all marines rush to defend the position against apparent enemy attack. Another marine produced a bag containing thirty pounds of marijuana and admitted he was the main supplier in the battery. Powers burned the dope and never reported it.

While the investigation went ahead, physical evidence had been forwarded to the U.S. Army forensic laboratory at Camp Zama, Japan, for examination. Its report confirmed what agents suspected. Additionally, leads sent to the United States disclosed that the primary suspect had an extensive criminal record; in fact, he had been given the choice of military service or jail at his last court appearance.

Powers decided to interrogate the suspect again. With Special Agent Pete Segersten, he drove from Chu Lai to the battery site, where they conducted the interview in a tent that had been set up as a place of worship. This time, confronted by two agents, the suspect chose to remain silent and was arrested. Handcuffed, he was driven all the way to Da Nang to the Marine brig, despite his protestations that he would be unable to defend himself if attacked en route. Agents were taking no chances with the man.

Another break in the investigation came while the suspect was in pretrial custody. A fellow marine at the gun battery mailed marijuana to the suspect. It was, predictably, intercepted. When the mailer was interrogated, he said the suspect had admitted being out on the perimeter smoking marijuana on the night of the attack. He had been angry, he said, about not having been promoted to lance corporal and so decided to punish the captain with a booby trap. With a stake from his supply tent, he had gone to the tent occupied by his commanding officer and executive officer, then assembled the device, which blew both legs off the captain the next morning.

Witnesses helped build a circumstantial case against the suspect, which was not strong. The suspect eventually accepted a plea bargain and was sentenced to five years in confinement.

Another case for NISRA Da Nang involved a teenage Vietnamese girl who was killed in one of the outlying villages near Da Nang. Marine MPs neglected to report the incident to Naval Intelligence. Their CID investigators began working the case, producing few leads or evidence of value.

Headquarters, Fleet Marine Force Pacific in Hawaii, sent a message to Da Nang agents when advised of the Vietnamese girl's death: Why, they asked, was Naval Intelligence not conducting the investigation? The answer: once again Marine CID wanted this one for themselves. SRA Jack Myer gave the case to Bob Powers.

On the first day Powers interviewed Marine MPs and CID to obtain as much background as possible. There was a good deal of kidding and "good lucks" from the marines, who had yet to produce a useful investigative lead. Physical evidence consisted of one spent .45-caliber cartridge case, inadvertently stepped on by one of the men conducting the crime scene search.

On day two Special Agent Powers, accompanied by a Vietnamese interpreter, traveled to the victim's village to interview her mother. He found the woman to be a cooperative and competent witness who provided excellent information about the Marine suspect. She had obviously not trusted Marine investigators, who wore the same uniform the suspect had worn when he killed her daughter. Inquiries in the village were not without hazard: Powers learned the accused had been involved with the victim's family in a black-marketing scheme but had shifted his allegiance to a family across the street, who had a more accommodating father; the victim's father had not allowed the suspect to have sex with his daughter.

Anxious to obtain further corroboration, Powers was intent on finding other witnesses, including members of the family who were then doing business with the suspect. At their hut, the victim's mother tried unsuccessfully to get family members to cooperate; they would not. Frustrated, the victim's mother attacked the senior male member of the family. This prompted the remainder of his family to attack her. Powers was punched while extricating his witness from the melee. His interpreter had made a fast withdrawal and was not seen until later in the day.

The Vietnamese doctor who had declared the victim dead was then located and interviewed at Da Nang's hospital. An identification lineup was held to allow the victim's mother to identify the suspect. She did. On day two Powers arrested the suspect in this so-called cold case. A general court-martial later found him guilty of murder and awarded a life sentence.

# 4

## SAIGON, 1967 TO 1968: TERRORISM AND TET

**As 1967 began, many signs of the war's escalation** were evident. U.S. forces in Vietnam had increased during the previous year from 180,000 to 280,000; in addition, 60,000 personnel were serving on ships offshore and 35,000, mostly Air Force servicemen, were assigned in Thailand—where air bases supported both the bombing campaign against North Vietnam and the covert war in Laos. American forces were supplemented by allied services: South Korea had 46,000 men assigned, while Australia, New Zealand, Thailand, and the Philippines boosted their forces. South Vietnamese service numbers stood at about 750,000.

The Ho Chi Minh Trail continued to provide communist forces operating in the South with supplies despite constant air attacks against personnel and vehicles threading their way through the mountains and jungles of North Vietnam, Laos, and Cambodia. The Soviets and Chinese kept a regular supply of military commodities and aid flowing to their North Vietnamese ally.

In keeping with the ever-increasing Navy presence in South Vietnam, NIS in July 1967 assigned a lieutenant commander, W. F. Brubaker, as commanding officer, NISOV. Supervising Agent Bert Truxell had taken the reins from Ken Nickel, Nickel having been promoted when the office became an independent command under NIS Pacific.

Truxell had more agents at his disposal than had his predecessor, but he knew immediately they were not enough. Equipped with six years' experience in ONI and two years as an Army CIC agent, Jesuit-educated Bert Truxell nevertheless found himself ill prepared for the chaos of Vietnam at war. Upon his arrival at Tan Son Nhut Air Base, the new senior agent was introduced to that chaos by a rapid trip through Saigon in sweltering heat with car windows all but closed as a defense against grenade attack.

"The unexpected was always the expected in Vietnam. Where else would one's office feature a courtyard with edible bananas and a heavily armed Vietnamese guard?"

The office was set up under an organizational structure typical for the time: Code 20, Investigations, was essentially the domain of the supervising agent, while Code 40, Counterintelligence, was largely under the CO's umbrella. This arrangement was far from rigid and left ample room for cross over of interests, which did occur. With the Saigon senior resident agent across the hall managing cases for the bottom half of South Vietnam, the oversight of the Da Nang resident agency was largely a matter of guidance from afar. Da Nang SRA Jack Myer, a well-seasoned veteran, was known to lose connection on uncertain long-distance telephone calls, a tactic his supervisor understood well and today admits he would have used had roles been reversed.

Agents, often working alone, were dispatched wherever needed. Truxell, with overall countrywide responsibility for their efforts, was constantly confronted with the practical difficulties of their task. "Hopping flights aboard logistic flights and helicopters was a way of life. Time loss was phenomenal; it could take days to get to a case and just as many to return."

Every agent who served in Vietnam was a volunteer. The organization stipulated that the volunteers have a minimum of one year of experience in ONI/NIS. But many had never worked a criminal investigation until their arrival in Vietnam, where there was little else. Truxell and his two SRAs had a further challenge: "How does one supervise an agent in the boondocks of a war zone when reliable communications don't exist?" The agents grew up and learned quickly. If they missed a lead, they were sent back to cover it. There could be no compromise in the quality of investigations; the organization would not tolerate it, nor would the military justice system.

NISOV commanding officer's counterintelligence role at Naval Forces, Vietnam, remained focused on counterterrorism and the protection of forces. At the time, a close working relationship with South Vietnamese National Police authorities provided a regular flow of information about VC activities in the area. These were reports not only of terrorist incidents in Saigon and the Gia Dinh sector of the city but also information gleaned by Police Special Branch in its investigations and interrogations. This information, combined with in-house sources and intelligence provided by ONI's Vietnamese Navy counterparts, the Vietnamese Naval Security Bloc (VNNSB), helped intelligence officers form a picture of enemy activity and, occasionally, the enemy's intentions.

Lt. Cdr. Bill Brubaker furnished the commander of U.S. Naval Forces, Vietnam, with a weekly briefing at COMNAVFORV headquarters in central Saigon. While desk officers briefed on activity in their respective areas of responsibility, Brubaker used a large map of Saigon to illustrate VC activity and its proximity to Navy assets and personnel.

The VNNSB was a valuable conduit of counterintelligence information. A permanent adviser to the VNNSB, normally a junior U.S. Navy intelligence officer, provided the link between the Vietnamese and NISOV.

In June 1967 Lt. Clint Schneider, USN, reported to Vietnam. His job was described as counterintelligence adviser to the Vietnamese Navy. Lieutenant Schneider had been a naval aviator, an A1 Skyraider pilot, until flight surgeons discovered he had developed night vision problems. Uninterested in a career in the back seat, he had opted to leave naval aviation and start a new career as an intelligence officer. After schooling at the Air Intelligence School and a particularly grueling time in escape-and-evasion training, he was dispatched to Vietnam for assignment to VNNSB. It was his first operational intelligence assignment.

Schneider began his assignment as quietly as a very large man who towered over his counterparts could do. Quickly, he learned that the Vietnamese were very competent counterintelligence and countersubversion operatives; indeed, he could learn much from the people he had been sent to advise.

"I figured out the job on my feet," he said. "The Vietnamese primary mission was protection of the regime, though they were often very good at their security tasking too."

NISOV Commanding Officer Bill Manthorpe provided practical advice for the new arrival, but Schneider was quick to decide he would have to use personal initiative to figure out operational aspects of the job and to decide how best he could assist the Vietnamese. He realized that the Vietnamese had the potential to provide good intelligence if he could provide them with basic support requirements in transportation and logistics.

Schneider installed a bunk in his office at the VNNSB compound and spent an increasing amount of time with his counterpart, Lieutenant Commander Hai. "Hai had forgotten more about intelligence than I would ever know. In the first days of my assignment, he was often unavailable to me, but this changed over time as his confidence in me grew."

An impromptu trip to Da Nang via a VNAF C47 was a stark reminder of the logistic challenges the Vietnamese allies faced in running a country-wide intelligence and security program. Schneider and Hai boarded the aging transport together with Vietnamese military dependents, who were accompanied by their worldly goods, including goats and chickens. The aircraft lumbered into the air with its noisy, odorous cargo, diverting its course part way through the flight to avoid a known area of enemy activity. Schneider was prompted to ask his counterpart what he thought might happen if they were to survive a plane crash in this part of the jungle: "You, after all, could strip down to your skivvys and nobody would be the wiser," he offered. Commander Hai smiled and replied, "No, it's not that simple; they'd get me only a little while after they found you. Unlike the peasantry, I've spent my life wearing boots. My footprints would be a giveaway." Although one of the engines was running roughly, they eventually landed safely in Da Nang. But the same aircraft was lost soon after their flight, apparently to an airframe failure.

Knowing he had a lot to learn about the craft of intelligence, Schneider decided he could make the most immediate impact on VNNSB's effectiveness by providing his counterparts with materiel and logistic support. He established relationships with the Army helicopter units who could fly Vietnamese to their field elements, U.S. Air Force, and Air America for longer distance flights. And he utilized NISOV evidence scheduled for destruction, particularly firearms and ammunition.

The Vietnamese provided support to Naval Intelligence also. The VNNSB detachment at the Port of Saigon gathered information about visiting merchant vessels, including crew lists, and provided these to the Americans. And on several occasions, they provided surveillance teams for NISOV, in localities where Americans would have been highly conspicuous. In late 1967 a VNNSB surveillance team assisted in the apprehension of a Chinese gang in possession of counterfeit printing plates.

When VNNSB Port of Saigon agents discovered two Russian-manufactured grenades concealed in the bottom of a metal cookie container in the possession of a port employee, they saw an opportunity to recruit an agent for use in their war against the Viet Cong. When questioned, the Vietnamese man quickly confessed to planting the grenades, telling authorities that his family lived in an area nominally under control of the enemy, at least at night. Viet Cong, learning that he was a port employee, had threatened his family, then offered him a chance to prove his loyalty by attacking Americans with the grenades. He was instructed to use one grenade to destroy something at the port and to use the other against Americans in a Saigon bar they were known to frequent. Schneider was asked to assist in an operational plan to convince the enemy that the port employee was complying with VC orders. A spectacular (but largely nondestructive) blast was staged at the Port of Saigon. Soon after, a Russian grenade was taken into a bar and taped to the leg of a table, where a patron soon discovered it and raised the alarm. U.S. Army explosive ordnance disposal (EOD) soldiers disarmed the device, and the incidents were widely reported by the Vietnamese press. Despite all the hard work, however, the Vietnamese employee eventually told VNNSB he could not operate as a double agent; he was unwilling to jeopardize the safety of his family.

The capture of terrorist team leader Nguyen Van Sam, however, was a major success for VNNSB and their parent command, the Military Security Directorate (MSD). Acting on fresh information, an MSD team snatched Sam in the dingy alleyways of Gia Dinh. Taken to the MSS interrogation facility, the Viet Cong officer soon identified four other sapper cell members, all of whom were quickly apprehended. Because the sapper teams were charged with carrying out terrorist attacks against both Vietnamese and their American allies, the neutralization of VC sapper cells was an important victory.

Intelligence experts were reasonably confident that Sam had told them what they needed to know. A Vietnamese newspaper had reported the capture, saying the VC was being subjected to torture. A decision was made to let the newspaper know that the captive had cooperated fully with South Vietnamese authorities and then been released. Sam was never seen again.

The communists, however, had wins also. A report received by VNNSB in Saigon announced that a crewman on watch aboard a Vietnamese Navy monitor had killed all of his crewmates as they slept, then slipped anchor at Can Tho. The heavily armored vessel was then taken upriver under cover of darkness in the direction of Cambodia. Schneider obtained assistance from an Army helicopter squadron, and a search for the hijacked vessel began. It was never sighted, and the search ultimately was abandoned when the chopper started taking ground fire from Cambodia.

Some time later a Cambodian newspaper article translated from Khmer to Vietnamese appeared at VNNSB headquarters. The article extolled the achievements of the South Vietnamese sailor who had murdered his crewmates, describing him as a true patriot. The crewmembers had been "overthrown," not murdered in their sleep, readers were told. A photo of the seaman, dressed in a chief petty officer uniform, accompanied the article.

Because the Cambodian press claimed that U.S. advisers were absent from the VNN ship during the takeover—allegedly ashore "to get women"—Schneider received orders from the U.S. senior naval adviser to investigate the true circumstances. No evidence that the allegations were anything other than propaganda surfaced.

Bombings continued, as did individual attacks against vulnerable Americans. One young Navy lieutenant, in the habit of walking to work from his Saigon billet in dress whites, fell victim to a notorious VC assassin known as the Dragon Lady. He was shot and killed on the street by a young Vietnamese woman riding as a passenger on a motorcycle. Intelligence agencies concentrated their attentions on the mystery killer as the list of victims grew until finally Vietnamese National Police apprehended a twenty-four-year-old Vietnamese woman of Chinese descent after she made an unsuccessful attempt on the life of a Nationalist Chinese intelligence officer. Clad in traditional *ao dai*, Phung Ngoc Anh had used a .45-caliber pistol to shoot her victims at close range. Some witnesses had described her as having long hair, while others said she had short hair, which she covered with a red or blue scarf. When police arrested her in her apartment, they discovered both wigs and scarves matching this description. Anh admitted killing three of her victims, including two Americans. Ballistic tests tied the weapon seized at the time of her arrest to five killings.

Acts of terrorism characterized the war in Saigon as 1967 drew to a close. Both the Americans and their South Vietnamese allies continued search-and-destroy missions against Viet Cong forces and North Vietnamese regulars. Staff officers in the rear areas created charts and diagrams reflecting various means of measuring military activity: body counts, villages and hamlets wrested from enemy control, rice harvest statistics. The war's progress was not static, but neither could it be said that either side was obviously winning.

In North Vietnam, the architect of France's defeat at Dien Bien Phu in 1954 had hatched a plan to turn the tide in the communists' favor. Gen. Vo Nguyen Giap and his staff conceived a strategic concept that relied on assistance from the general population in South Vietnam to swing communist fortunes toward victory. The General Uprising Plan was as clever as it was ambitious: it relied heavily on insurgent Viet Cong elements to spearhead coordinated attacks against South Vietnamese and U.S. installations and personnel.

In 1967 Viet Cong infrastructure remained a viable military and political force. Northerners marching hundreds of miles down the Ho Chi Minh Trail bolstered the ranks of southern communist elements and provided direction from the Hanoi Politburo. Southern communists, sensing opportunity in a defining military event, were ready to join their brethren in attacking South Vietnamese and their American allies. General Giap's comprehensive strategy called for coordinated attacks against several hundred targets ranging from small provincial outposts to the American embassy in Saigon. Timing for the operation was set to coincide with annual celebrations of Tet—the lunar new year—the most important religious holiday for Vietnam's overwhelmingly Buddhist majority.

What has become known as the 1968 Tet Offensive was a largely well-kept secret until the communists launched raids all over South Vietnam. Commander Brubaker received a general warning from his National Police sources intimating that VC attacks were expected against allied installations in Saigon. This he included in his regular staff briefing at Naval Forces, Vietnam, headquarters in the days before January 1968 drew to a close. In the same briefing, he advised the staff chaplain not to expect his Vietnamese driver to show for work: he had been arrested as a Viet Cong overnight.

Brubaker concedes that the warnings he got from Vietnamese police were not taken as seriously as they might have been. Such warnings were almost routine and were sometimes accurate and sometimes otherwise. He pondered on the fact that VNAF Gen. Nguyen Ngoc Loan had not mentioned intelligence about potential Tet attacks at a recent pre-Tet luncheon hosted by U.S. Air Force counterparts, OSI. The VNAF general who commanded the seventy-thousand-man police force later gained a degree of notoriety in a Tet Offensive photograph of his street-corner execution of a captured Viet Cong implicated in the slaughter of National Police dependents. The .38-caliber revolver Loan used to fire a bullet through the man's head had been a gift from OSI.

At VNNSB headquarters in Saigon Lieutenant Schneider noticed an increased level of activity among Vietnamese counterintelligence personnel as Tet grew closer. "Something was in the wind. The Vietnamese were busier than usual in the final days before Tet. The enemy couldn't keep something that big a secret forever." They prepared for festivities but also issued nonspecific reports of impending enemy activity. The Vietnamese at naval headquarters in the Saigon River were ready for an attack.

The information passing through Vietnamese Navy channels and forwarded for translation at NISOV was out of date because of the time it took to produce and find its way through channels. The reports were, in the main, about enemy buildups in certain areas.

In Da Nang, CIA agent Foster Fipps provided marines with a clear warning before attacks broke out. Brubaker characterizes Fipps as the exception to the rule: he got his own information. Others depended heavily on Vietnamese allies. Fipps and NISRA Da Nang representative Lt. George Wheeler met almost every day, so the bases in I Corps were covered at least.

Brubaker used Vietnamese police information only once before or after Tet: in a warning to NAVFORV staff.

"I thought it was important. The defense of Saigon had been turned over to the Vietnamese in the month before the offensive, with the redeployment of the U.S. Army 199th Light Infantry Brigade. I knew the ARVN were planning to give upward of half their troops leave to go home for traditional Tet celebrations; that left only the National Police and a few Army Military Police to defend all the pencil-pushers . . . "

With Tet celebrations formally beginning on January 29, 1968, a round of receptions began. The American embassy held a well-attended social function. The same night Bill Brubaker, Supervising Agent Bert Truxell, and a Navy Reserve commander, in Saigon for his two weeks of annual active duty, were invited to the home of Saigon's police chief, Col. Nguyen Van Luan.

"If the police knew something specific about enemy intentions, they hid it well. Luan passed nothing of this nature to me or the others," Brubaker says.

The colonel's guests at the party were entertained by his six-year-old son, who rode his miniature motorcycle around the yard, which was protected by the high concrete fence separating the chief's quarters from central police headquarters. (Luan was killed days later when Vietnamese Army Rangers mistakenly guided a U.S. Army helicopter gunship strike to an incorrect target, a high school serving as a command post during the offensive. Several other ranking Vietnamese officers were also killed or wounded in the incident.)

We now know North Vietnamese planners scheduled the offensive to begin on the night of January 30. Communication problems meant that not all the communist units involved received the same information; some attacks occurred on January 29, mostly in northern areas, while others came twenty-four hours later. Alerts were posted after the initial attacks, but NISOV personnel were not warned. At 2:00 AM on January 31 a large explosion woke Brubaker and Truxell at the villa, several blocks from the American embassy. Brubaker believes this explosion was caused by satchel charge used to breach the wall. They discovered the villa phone to be inoperable, and the maid, Hai, made an appearance to ask whether another coup attempt was afoot. The men decided to drive to the NISOV office in Cholon, Truxell driving and Brubaker riding shotgun cradling the villa's carbine. They found the streets remarkably quiet.

At the office, an agent standing guard at the entrance greeted them. The Vietnamese guard was nowhere to be seen. Truxell immediately took stock of the strategic situation at the office, particularly in view of information received that enemy units were nearby and an attack on the compound was anticipated. "The compound may have withstood attack by marauding Indians, but there was little chance it could repulse heavy weapons. I thought we were doomed if faced with a concerted attack in force. It appeared we were facing scattered elements of the VC and/or armed sympathizers."

The office had an ample supply of small arms and ammunition. The compound's surrounding wall would be pivotal to the defense plan; the enemy had to be kept far enough back that grenades could not be thrown over it. "A couple of well-placed grenades in the courtyard would likely injure everyone inside. Also, we had to keep the enemy clear of the next door service station, as blowing that up would almost certainly do us in and give them entry into the compound."

Had the enemy breached the wall and sent grenades through the only two window fire points available, NISOV would have been completely overrun. The central issue seemed to be whether the compound could hold out until another force could relieve them. Truxell began drawing up an evacuation plan, in full knowledge that there were no "friendly" compounds or military elements anywhere near Cholon.

Next, a hasty plan for watch duty was drawn up with four men assigned to each watch of two hours. Truxell cannot recall whether the office came under fire on the first night, but the next day three or four Australians were caught by heavy fire outside the office and made their way inside. Those Australians provided much needed military experience and gave the defenders a big lift in morale.

"It became apparent that our watch-standers had little understanding of fields of fire. The enemy were diagonally across the street in the upper floor of an apartment building. At one point, a .30-calibre machine gun manned by U.S. Army troops in another sector of the compound tore into the building with return fire. Some of the guys would not fire because they couldn't see anyone to shoot. I could hear the AK47s and see puffs of smoke from windows. When I pointed this out, they replied that it might be a little old lady making tea. I told them that if they didn't fire soon, that little old lady making tea was going to shoot their ass off."

The composite force of agents and sailors was relieved on day three, and things in Vietnam were never the same. Agents started wearing greens and carrying military weapons. "So much for noncombatant status," said Truxell.

"I found that the thing that generated the most fear was the unknown—and we knew almost nothing about the situation surrounding us. Would we have surrendered had we started taking casualties? Not while I was still alive. I thought that solution assured a bullet in the back of the head for all survivors."

There were casualties of a different sort, however. NISOV YN1 John Springer, himself a defender of the compound, was abruptly ordered from Vietnam before Tet hostilities were concluded. Springer had served three continuous years as an intelligence yeoman, had developed scores of useful contacts, and had fallen in love with Miss Cang, a Navy employee in Saigon. They had two daughters in the years together that followed. Refused permission to extend his tour into year four, Springer had only enough time to collect his things from the house he had shared with his Vietnamese wife and two small daughters before bidding a tearful goodbye to her and his children. Springer survived several firefights en route to Tan Son Nhut Air Base for his flight out of Vietnam. In the circumstances, both Springer and Cang were sure that they would never see each other again.

Tet '68, as it became known, was a milestone in American involvement in Vietnam. It was not the only occasion the enemy chose this all-important holiday period to stage attacks around South Vietnam, but although allies virtually destroyed the Viet Cong infrastructure during the offensive, attitudes toward the war changed both within South Vietnam and in the United States, as support for the war waned.

Supervising Agent Bert Truxell was relieved in March 1968 by Bob Morrice. Texan Royce Logan became senior resident agent, Saigon. Several months later Lt. Cdr. Bill Armbruster replaced Lieutenant Commander Brubaker. Despite personnel changes, Tet left an active legacy. In the counterintelligence shop, NISOV executive officer Lt. Jim Law, USN, headed up initiatives to acquire as much information as possible about the tactics and organization of the enemy sapper units that had spearheaded many of the attacks against U.S. facilities during Tet. Working with counterparts at the VNNSB and COMNAVFORV intelligence staff, Law looked actively for an opportunity to conduct in-depth examination of sapper tactics. Much could be learned to assist the Navy in devising defensive tactics. Law was rewarded for his patience in early 1968 when U.S. Army troops captured a North Vietnamese Navy sapper during operations near the Cambodian border, an area known as the Parrot's Beak.

Law and his team drove through miles of rubber plantation and open country considered by all to be Indian country and successfully recovered the prisoner from the Army. The drive back to Saigon was considered hairy by all but was without major event. The prisoner was successfully interrogated over several days. The information gained was shared widely within U.S. naval commands in South Vietnam.

NISOV also ensured many successes by developing information about arms caches left buried by the enemy during Tet. Designed to arm the masses during the anticipated mass uprising, the loss of the weapons further weakened Viet Cong ability to regain strength after the offensive.

# 5

# DA NANG, 1967 TO 1968:
# AGENTS IN THE FIELD

**Lt. George Wheeler, USN, did a good job** when he sought out a suitable billet for NISRA Da Nang in 1967. The original office at 20 Duy Tan Street and the billet were situated on parallel streets in the center of Da Nang, accessible to commands serviced by NIS but independent of all.

The billet that housed all NIS personnel was on a corner at 23 Doc Lap Street. A former hotel of three stories, it was surrounded by a wire-topped brick wall and metal gate. Front gardens had been concreted over providing an excellent if unforgiving surface for jungle-rules volleyball matches. On the first floor was a foyer with a rather graceful stairway. One room doubled as a library and lounge, with several years' collection of well-worn pocket books graced wall bookshelves, revealing the most common recreation at NISRA Da Nang. Decor was worn contemporary Vietnamese. The senior resident agent and the representative (a Navy lieutenant reserve intelligence officer) bunked in a sandbag-protected room off the first deck porch, and a second room was situated off the foyer. The top two decks had similar rooms, each shared by two men. A central arms locker on the first deck housed long-arms, but each man had helmet and body armor and at least a handgun in his room at all times.

The billet at 23 Doc Lap was renowned for its bar, which was carefully constructed by an itinerant SeaBee with superb carpentry skills to resemble a small German *hofbrau*. It had stained rustic benches, false beams, and a gabled bar, which was considered unique in Vietnam. Christened the Boom Boom Room by the troops (but called the Blue Elephant among more genteel company), the bar enjoyed the status of a military club, offering discounted liquor and soft drinks. Significantly, the billet became an important social gathering place for guests from other agencies and of course Marine compatriots traveling to and from the bush. Navy lawyers, the American consul, and even occasionally German nurses from the hospital ship *Helgoland* were eager visitors.

Da Nang had an after-dusk curfew and remained off-limits to military personnel throughout most of the war, meaning those who could not demonstrate a legitimate reason for being there were subject to arrest by Marine MPs. Da Nang City was dusty, dirty, and noisy, but its accommodations were a vast improvement on billeting elsewhere, especially in the cantonments and the field. Large tamarind trees populated street verges and vestiges of lawn, and behind some high fences were hibiscus and even some bougainvillea blossoms.

The office at 20 Duy Tan Street, which had originally served simultaneously as a billet, was a converted Vietnamese residence rented to the Navy. By 1968 a high security barrier with a gate had been erected, in front of which a U.S. Navy sentry was posted at all times. Vehicles were parked next to the sentry, where they could be watched. A tiled walkway led to the porch, which doubled as a reception waiting area and had a connecting door to the office occupied by the yeoman chief petty officer. Three former bedrooms housed, respectively, the senior resident agent, the representative, and three or four special agents. A converted garage held the balance of special agents, and there were also spaces for interrogation and an office for the Vietnamese interpreter. Little excess room was to be found anywhere, and were it not for agents traveling away almost constantly, the office would have been as claustrophobic as a warship.

Opposite the office on potholed, muddy Duy Tan Street were houses of the Vietnamese citizenry. Their children and pets played in the street through the day and seldom missed the early arrival of the chief, who passed out apples and oranges from the chow truck on morning breakfast rounds for the sentries. NISRA Da Nang looked like most of the better houses on the street, except for its fence and sentry, and by Da Nang standards it was in one of the better neighborhoods. Around the next corner on a cross street, which ran through to the NIS billet, was the American consulate. Guarded by members of the Marine Security Battalion, it maintained a lawn and gardens and large tropical trees.

Although the walk from office to billet may have been only five hundred yards, few chose to travel on foot because of concerns about personal vulnerability. Smart Americans moved quickly and without regular pattern if they wanted to improve their chances of getting home. There was ample rolling stock for the trip and meals to think about before the drive.

The Navy officers' club in Da Nang was called the Stone Elephant. Conveniently situated at the top of the Da Nang Peninsula just a few blocks from the NIS billet, it was an eating spot and favored watering hole. Agents began their day at the Stone Elephant, where a smorgasbord breakfast was the norm and Vietnamese waitresses in *ao dais* rushed around with pots of steaming black Navy coffee. By evening, the atmosphere at the bar changed with happy hour—with beer and cocktails at give-away prices and often a floorshow presented by visiting bands. Most common were Filipino and Korean bands but the favorites were Australians. Packed with Navy officers and Marine aviators from Marble Mountain Air Facility, the Stone Elephant crowd showed real enthusiasm for their entertainers, particularly if they were Westerners. Without doubt, the most popular song—always guaranteed to have patrons enthusiastically join in—was "We've Gotta Get Out of This Place." The British band The Animals created a Vietnam classic with this song.

Unlike Saigon, Da Nang had no authorized town nightlife, meaning men who worked together every day under often high pressure had no place to go on liberty. Except for the occasional night at a Navy club, playing it safe meant personnel were inside the guarded billet gate by dusk. Surprisingly, there was very little friction between men—but there were some memorable "horror shows" in the hofbrau bar, where patrons were known to pour mixed drinks and popcorn into a roaring twenty-four-inch fan to top off an evening's celebration. Jungle-rules (meaning "no rules") volleyball was another favored after-work activity, always pursued with aggressive spirit. Body blocks and net pull-downs were favorite winning tactics.

Nearby neighbors were Vietnamese National Police families, who were billeted on the adjacent corner in a two-story former French villa, resplendent with a balustraded tower. Farther along in the block, Vietnamese Lt. Gen. Hoang Xuan Lam, ARVN, had his quarters. Lam commanded all ARVN forces in I Corps, making him a prime target for enemy guerilla attack. Thus, virtually every night an ARVN armored car would position itself opposite 23 Doc Lap. Far from making the billet occupants feel more secure, it instead kept them aware of the potential effects of the .50-caliber machine gun on the flimsy masonry walls of the old building.

Therefore agents had little to do at NISRA Da Nang but work; a seemingly endless caseload occupied everyone's attention. With responsibility for more than one hundred thousand Marine and Navy personnel deployed throughout I Corps, NISRA Da Nang answered regular requests for assistance from commands faced with serious incidents such as murder, rape, fraud, and theft. This caseload was supplemented by lead requests from global NIS components and federal agencies without representation in Vietnam—and the demands of a counterintelligence program. Agents were asked to locate individuals and conduct on-the-spot investigations about things as diverse as an individual's activities in the Black Panthers, a stolen or missing government check, and matters pertaining to the transmission and safe custody of classified material.

NISRA Da Nang shared central Da Nang with Commander Naval Support Activity, Da Nang, where the command remained in the imposing waterfront colonial structure known by all as the White Elephant. The admiral had responsibility for a command that oversaw most of the supply and support function for the northern end of South Vietnam, I Corps. Camp Tien Sa, sprawling around the base of Monkey Mountain at the head of the peninsula, housed the majority of NSA's personnel—who manned the Deepwater Pier, ship repair facilities, and warehousing facilities.

By 1968 NSA detachments had also been established at key points along the coast where resupply was often carried out by lighters and landing craft. Rivers in the northern part of I Corps served as secondary highways, carrying supplies to inland dumps—especially large-caliber ammunition.

Behind the white facade of NSA's command headquarters was a courtyard surrounded by a warren of offices and workspaces, none of which ever seemed large enough. The daily mail pickup was made at the White Elephant.

One street back from the waterfront, Da Nang Cathedral stood to remind all who passed of the more gentile times of the 1920s, when French settlers erected the church and adjoining convent. Packed in opposite, a mass of commercial storefronts supplied every imagined need. All this was considered off-limits to U.S military personnel, and it was a temptation to many.

A little farther upstream, the Han was bridged by a critically important structure constantly guarded by roaming sentries who fired at every bit of floating detritus that might shield an underwater swimmer/sapper intent on blowing it up. Barriers, including a cage of concertina wire, surrounded pylons, and concussion grenades were frequently thrown in their vicinity as a further defense. The bridge was the only viable link to Tien Sa Peninsula, whence all material—including ammunition—from the port originated.

On the Da Nang side of the bridge, a ship-landing ramp had been constructed especially for use by Navy LSTs and heavy landing craft. Known to all as Bridge Ramp, it was a hive of activity at any time of the day or night. Sweating sailors atop bellowing loaders and industrial forklifts jockeyed huge pallets of ammunition and other supplies into the waiting maws of the berthed ships, under the glare of floodlights at night. Intelligence indicated that Bridge Ramp was a favored enemy target for long-range rocket attack. The presence of large volumes of explosive and volatile cargo was attractive for its potential to damage ships and men. Attacks were normally carried out with a barrage of Soviet 122mm rockets, fired from a point far to the southwest, well outside the Marines' perimeter. They did periodically cause serious damage—and always concern. Vietnamese civilians, often crowded into makeshift improvised housing, undoubtedly suffered the most casualties.

Peter Reilly flew into this scene to assume the senior resident agent post from Jack Myer in March 1968. Reilly, a linguist who specialized in Chinese and had begun his Navy career in the Naval Security Group (NSG), had just completed a four-year stint in Taipei, Taiwan, before volunteering for the Vietnam post. To the consternation of the NIS command element in Saigon, he used a regular Marine Corps C130 logistic flight to travel direct from Taipei to his new duty station, without the usual entry formalities and briefings at NISOV in Saigon. Peter Reilly was demonstrating, and not for the first time, the independence and direct action that would characterize his thirty-year career in Naval Intelligence. Jack Myer had already left Vietnam; Peter Reilly, made aware of his error, boarded a plane and flew to Saigon to meet his new supervising agent, Bert Truxell.

Former Tucson police officer Mike Nagle came to Vietnam in July 1967 after completing his probationary year of service as a street agent based at Pasadena, California. Nagle had completed his degree at the University of Arizona while serving with the Tucson Police Department, and as his graduation date neared in the spring of 1966, he began looking for federal law enforcement career opportunities. He submitted applications to both ONI and the FBI.

Mike Nagle had never known his father. Ens. Patrick Nagle, USN, trained in Pensacola, Florida, as a Navy fighter pilot in the dark days before Pearl Harbor, participated in the vanguard of America's first attacks against Imperial Japan—the storming of Guadalcanal in the Solomon Islands. As war loomed, the senior Nagle had been part of the Navy's accelerated training program. Returning from a mission on August 8, 1942—the day after Maj. Gen. Alexander Vandegrift's First Marine Division waded ashore into the tropical hell of Guadalcanal—Ensign Nagle's aircraft ran out of fuel while en route back to his carrier. Telling his wingman that he could go no farther, Nagle ditched his F4F Wildcat in the dark waters of the Solomon Sea. He was never seen again. Mike Nagle's only link to his lost father was a trunk containing his father's treasured personal effects and photographs of himself as a newborn in the arms of his uniformed father.

Despite the prestige of an FBI career, Mike Nagle really wanted to serve his country overseas. When in early 1966 the FBI came to him with an offer to become a special agent, Nagle telephoned ONI to determine the status of his application. ONI responded with their own offer. Mike Nagle was soon a special agent, ONI, working personnel security on the streets of Los Angeles. By the time he received orders in February 1967 to attend Agent Basic School at headquarters in Washington, D.C., Nagle had volunteered for duty in Vietnam. He was told while at Basic School that he would be assigned to NISRA Da Nang, his transfer scheduled for July 1967.

Mike Nagle was one of the few agents dispatched to Vietnam via commercial aircraft rather than via the charters most personnel endured. He boarded a Pan American flight to Saigon at Los Angeles International Airport, joining Special Agent Dick Ryan, who also held orders to Da Nang. Ryan, a former Los Angeles police officer and veteran of the Watts Riots, had volunteered for Vietnam service with Nagle. Their flight traversed the Pacific with stops at Hawaii, Wake Island, and Guam before crossing the bomb-blasted red soil of coastal Vietnam at high altitude.

"As we neared Tan Son Nhut, Saigon, the pilot pushed the aircraft nose down into a steep descent; this was not really reassuring for a new guy," Nagle remembers. Once safely on the ground, they were enveloped in the hot, muggy blanket of a July day in Saigon. After meeting a few NISOV personnel, Nagle and Ryan were driven to the office to begin in-processing. Nagle recalls saying to himself upon seeing the office for the first time, "My God. What have I got myself into?" Very little could prepare anybody for the initial shock of immersion in Vietnam at war.

The new agents were issued the identification necessary to get along in Vietnam: modified credentials that excluded the word "intelligence," a Vietnamese identity card issued by MSS (guaranteed to frighten any sane Vietnamese citizen), a MACV identity card showing the bearer to be an engineer at the Office of Civil Construction, and a PX ration card. Two days after their arrival, Nagle and Ryan boarded a USAF C130 for the flight to Da Nang.

"I remember very well my first night in Da Nang. The air base was hit hard by VC attacks, and men were killed. Rockets were hitting the base and falling in the city too. One of the agents, who will remain anonymous, was in a skivvy house enjoying the company of some Da Nang ladies of the night when the first incoming rounds hit and he found himself marooned. The supervising agent in Saigon somehow got wind of it and tried to find out who it was, but none of his fellow agents were going to give him up."

Nagle quickly learned that many forms of excitement were available in Vietnam's I Corps. He joined a team of agents under the capable control of SRA Jack Myer: his roommate Peter Segersten, already an old hand; Bob Powers, even then considered one of the organization's most capable investigators; and Howie Dilkes, also already well seasoned. In the fall of 1967 Special Agent Joe Rodriguez, also a former Tucson PD officer, replaced Powers.

The new agents settled into the routine of a six-or-seven-day work week. It didn't take long for Mike Nagle to realize that the residence that housed the American Red Cross girls was a mere three blocks away. "I got into a little trouble. Jack Myer came and got me one night, reminding me about Da Nang's curfew hours."

On the work side, the agents were exposed to professional jealousy and obfuscation by some members of Marine Corps CID. Investigations were grudgingly given over, sometimes after having been legally compromised by zealous but untrained MP investigators. Mike Nagle began to share the caseload that required agents to travel alone through northern I Corps.

As 1967 drew to a close, agents working the north along the DMZ, like combat forces deployed in the region, began noticing increased enemy activity. The NVA were on the move, particularly pressuring Marine outposts defending the border area between North and South Vietnam.

Nagle found himself at Khe Sanh Combat Base, near the Laotian border, in the final week of December. The reason for his journey has been lost to time, but he still remembers the fighting at and around the base as the communists built up in the hills around the outpost, intending to besiege the marines.

"I had flown into Khe Sanh with M.Gen. Tompkins, USMC, in his helicopter, from Phu Bai near Hue. I was hoping to get back out on the same day, but it didn't happen. My work was done; there just were no seats available on any of the aircraft." This was Nagle's first exposure to life at the front. He could hear Russian 122mm rockets being fired from the mountains and hills surrounding them, followed by a distinct double detonation as they struck the ground. "We were taking incoming rounds constantly."

Men were dying at Khe Sanh, while increasingly the enemy probed hilltop Marine bases. A fairly constant stream of wounded came in by helicopter for the attention of the Navy medical team on the ground.

Generous marines found a spot for the special agent—who really just wanted to get out of Khe Sanh—in a deep underground bunker festooned with a sign that announced simply, "The Womb." Here Nagle slept in a hammock like the other bunker occupants to keep away from the menace of rats. "The damned rats were huge. The grunts entertained themselves by shooting them with a pellet gun, and by keeping a Rat KIA tally sheet on the bulkhead."

The worst part for Nagle was having nothing to do. Marine defenders all had tasks; they seemed to be on the run constantly. Nagle stayed out of the way and attended intelligence briefings, at which it was reported that thousands of North Vietnamese were around them. Between briefings, he hung out with Marine aircraft control personnel at the airstrip, ever hopeful of a ride to the rear. "There was a lot going on at the airstrip. C130s and C123s were touching down, kicking cargo out on the run, then turning and trying to take off before enemy incoming rounds could find them on the ground."

After four unforgettable days at the busiest combat base in the north, Special Agent Nagle was able to hitch a ride on a Marine helicopter heading to Dong Ha. With considerable relief he flew away from the cauldron that would soon be called the Seige of Khe Sanh.

Finally back in Da Nang, Nagle learned that his former Tucson Police Department colleague Joe Rodriguez had arrived in Vietnam and been promptly sent north to Dong Ha to run a case. "That was a hell of a fast introduction to the life of a special agent in Vietnam for Joe Rodriguez," Nagle recalls.

As January 1968 drew to a close, agents in Da Nang were conscious of preparations around them for the celebration of Tet. But they failed to realize that the VC was building up its forces near Da Nang until the communists actually launched the ill-fated Tet '68.

"As I recall, we first got word that Saigon had been hit—and that the compound where NISOV offices were situated in Cholon had come under attack. Soon after, we heard that Hue was being attacked, and we started making hurried preparations to defend ourselves at the Da Nang billet."

Agents retired to 23 Doc Lap Street, began filling sandbags to enhance the billet defenses, and stocked up on drinking water, rations, and ammunition. The office at nearby 20 Duy Tan Street was closed and left in the care of Navy sentries.

Agents didn't have to wait long for the war to come to downtown Da Nang. The night reverberated with the sound of small arms, mortar, and rocket fire. Allied red and communist green tracers arced through the sky, and the schoolyard on the opposite side of the street became a rallying point for VC attackers and, later, the scene of an intense skirmish. South Vietnamese tanks were deployed nearby, probably to defend General Lam's quarters.

"We all had issued rifles, flak jackets, and helmets at the ready. We were very careful to keep lights down at night; we really wanted to keep a very low profile."

The agents were on their own in Da Nang as VC and allied forces fought at night for control of the city. Communication was irregular, and the tactical situation was unknown. The men began to consider what they would do if the billet were attacked and overrun. "The Marines at III MAF were our closest help. Some of the guys actually planned to swim the Han River if the worst happened." Nagle himself had no such option: injured in one of NISRA Da Nang's infamous jungle-rules volleyball matches, he was sporting a cast on his broken foot. There would be no evasion and swimming with that cast, he knew, and he began seriously to think about sawing it off.

After two or three days behind the walls of 23 Doc Lap, the situation normalized enough that the men were allowed to leave during the day. All were glad for hot meals after the steady diet of C rations.

To their north beyond Hai Van Pass, U.S. Marines fought on at Khe Sanh while the media tried to draw parallels between their defense and that of the French at Dien Bien Phu. Communist forces tried to encircle Khe Sanh just as they had done in the North, where the French were finally defeated. Marines, however, were never in danger of being starved in an extended siege at Khe Sanh. Massive, extended air strikes by B52 bombers kept the communists at bay, though the base was subject to many days of artillery and rocket attacks, and Marines fought desperately for the mountaintop bases that defended the base approaches. Ironically, the North Vietnamese Army was itself drawn into a massive meat grinder as allied airpower systematically eliminated troop concentrations. Air strikes and artillery, both by design and by volume, searched out and destroyed the enemy by the hundreds.

Hue, symbolically important to most Vietnamese, had been largely overrun in audacious attacks by VC and NVA units. The Citadel was taken by the enemy, who were quick to raise the National Liberation Front (NLF) flag atop the flagstaff overlooking the Perfume River. VC troops captured a number of Americans, including civilian government employees. They also began a program of systematic execution of suspected Southern sympathizers, the magnitude of which became known months later when hundreds of bodies were exhumed from shallow graves in the sand.

Marines, from their Phu Bai enclave south of Hue, began a drive northward, fighting house to house to reach the Perfume River. After days of bitter, costly fighting, they joined in an allied offensive that finally saw communist forces pushed out of the Imperial City. Hue and its inhabitants were bled white by the 1968 Tet Offensive. Many U.S. troops died giving it back to them.

Dave Hall's regular exposure to Marine Corps rifle companies made him the logical choice to manage a counterintelligence investigation into reports of U.S. personnel sighted with VC or NVA troops. One such case was code-named Salt and Pepper. Two men, believed to be marines, were alleged to be cooperating with the enemy. It had even been reported that the men—one black, the other white—had been seen carrying Eastern-bloc pattern military weapons. Hall came to the case ably assisted by the ongoing work of a select group of nearby Marine Corps counterintelligence specialists.

Across the river from NISRA Da Nang in the old French military compound that housed Lt. Gen. Robert Cushman and his III Marine Amphibious Force headquarters was a small file-filled office. Here Maj. John Guenther, USMC, III MAF staff counterintelligence officer, directed Marine counterintelligence initiatives in I Corps.

Major Guenther and his counterintelligence marines formed a highly trained group of professionals who served as the eyes and ears of the commanding general, collating and analyzing information from many sources. Most came from counterintelligence teams deployed with Marine rifle companies in the field, where interrogations of both enemy and friendly Vietnamese produced important information on an almost-daily basis. A strong spirit of professional cooperation existed between the counterintelligence marines and NIS, and in this instance, the marines held a majority of the intelligence dealing with alleged defectors, missing in action (MIA) personnel, and prisoner of war (POW) marines.

Capt. Ken Klem, USMC, assigned to Major Guenther's staff and assisted by Gy.Sgt. Galayzin and Sgt. Davis, maintained extensive files on missing marines, made up of sighting reports, interviews, and prisoner interrogations as well as relevant reports from other intelligence agencies. Klem could recite from memory the names and histories of any captured marines and the known circumstances of their loss. Moreover, the Viet Cong often paraded captives through villages for propaganda purposes, thus providing indicators of the general area of the camps in which they held the prisoner. Many of those marines taken in Da Nang and points south were marched to a remote area in far-west Quang Ngai Province for incarceration in horrifying, primitive prisons. Those captured farther north, in Thua Thien or Quang Tri Province, seemed more likely destined for ultimate internment in North Vietnam—after prolonged captivity in the desperate circumstances of a jungle holding camp and a grim trek up the muddy Ho Chi Minh Trail.

Klem recalls, "Two marines were lost in 1964 while sightseeing on a motorcycle outside Da Nang. Garwood was lost in September 1965 outside of Da Nang. Other marines disappeared after being enticed into Vietnamese hooches in the Da Nang area during 1966. . . .

"One marine escaped from the III MAF Brig in late 1967 and was subsequently captured by the VC. Later, another was scooped up by Viet Cong while in a restricted liberty area and ended up in captivity. The U.S. Army also had a few I Corps personnel grabbed by the VC while engaged in nonauthorized activities."

Besides the pressing information about captured Americans, Major Guenther's marines had been receiving multiple reports from different sources alluding to sightings of a tall Caucasian operating with Viet Cong in various enclaves within I Corps. These came both from allied South Vietnamese military sources and from interrogations of captured Viet Cong. Physical descriptions of the defector's garb, hair color, and eye color varied considerably. Moreover, attempts at identifying the missing personnel from photographs were equally ambiguous.

Special Agent Hall became involved in the uncertain—and so far secret—investigation because the Salt and Pepper case had apparently been compromised by the appearance of a series of wanted posters. Command was concerned that information leaked about possible defectors and persons known to be held by the enemy could endanger U.S. prisoners of war and provide the enemy with intelligence that would hamper ongoing efforts to free Americans. A classified program managed by MACV called Brightlight used Special Forces personnel to target possible VC prisons to free American and allied prisoners.

Hall, assisted by another intelligence agency, succeeded in locating and retrieving the remaining wanted posters. As he had been told, the poster carried grainy, distant images of two men: one was black, the other Caucasian.

The press corps, always hungry for a bad-news story, never was able to make much of this one. Hall continued following up every lead that came his way, but a satisfactory identification of the two men was never made, nor were they captured. Major Guenther's counterintelligence marines became convinced that many of the reports they had received of the pair assisting and training the enemy were actually Viet Cong proselytizing and propaganda feeds.

NISOV commanding officer Thomas A. Brooks, longtime intelligence officer who rose to become the director of Naval Intelligence, remembers that both Salt and Pepper were identified as Marine deserters but that most of the allegations about their activities could not be proved. It was concluded that many aspects of the reports had been exaggerated. Commander Brooks, who later interviewed the war's most infamous alleged defector, Marine Robert Garwood, had an intimate knowledge of information about men believed to have switched sides. He does not know whether either Salt or Pepper survived the war.

The Garwood investigation had been far more definitive than Salt and Pepper. Not only were Vietnam-based counterintelligence marines involved, but at Headquarters Marine Corps in Washington, D.C., the Counterintelligence Branch worked closely with the Casualty Branch on all matters pertaining to missing and captured marines. They monitored intelligence and open source reporting for information about American MIAs in an effort to confirm whether they were alive and, if captured, their health and overall condition in captivity.

Capt. Chuck Bushey, USMC, then assigned to the Counterintelligence Branch, Headquarters Marine Corps, recalls, "In the case of Garwood, propaganda leaflets purported to have been written and signed by him were found in South Vietnam and forwarded to HQMC, usually through Marine Corps channels. Thus began the compilation of a substantial file regarding Garwood. Perhaps noteworthy, we would hand carry the leaflets to the FBI laboratory for handwriting analysis in an effort to confirm they were written by him. It took several leaflets and several handwriting examinations before the FBI finally confirmed they were his. If I recall correctly, Garwood was listed as a deserter in 1969. Also, around 1969, POW releases in South Vietnam indicated that Garwood was cooperating and working with the VC. His dossier at HQMC continued to grow."

Later reports indicate that CIA analysts had also independently evaluated propaganda material believed to be written by Garwood on behalf of his captors. Agency analysts reported that they believed at least six documents had been written by Garwood and that they additionally profiled personality traits based on their document examination.

In part, the Garwood file was growing because more released prisoners of war had observed him at enemy detention camps and could describe his activities, some conversations with him, and his relationship with the Vietnamese captors. Captain Bushey and fellow counterintelligence marine Robert Wingfield interviewed returned marine Lance Cpl. Jose Agosto Santos at Bethesda Naval Hospital after his release from a VC jungle prison camp. "We gleaned a great deal about Garwood's activities at that time, including information about his collaboration with his captors. As I recall, he was living separately from the other prisoners," Bushey recalled.

It has been reported that Agosto Santos asserted in his debriefing that not only was Garwood billeted separately from other U.S. prisoners but that he had "crossed over" to the enemy, refusing repatriation to U.S. forces and actually accepting a commission in the North Vietnamese Army. Other released U.S. Army prisoners said that Garwood had carried arms and ammunition for the enemy, was billeted with enemy guards, and assisted in U.S. POW interrogations by virtue of his understanding of the Vietnamese language. Finally, in late 1969 a repatriated U.S. Army captive related a conversation with Garwood in which Garwood said he would soon be traveling to North Vietnam to meet with leaders of the U.S. Black Panther and Black Muslim parties. The evidence suggests that he made the trip to North Vietnam four years after his capture.

Garwood was not returned to the United States following the formal release of POWs by Hanoi in March 1973. He did not return until 1979, with many unanswered questions as to his intentions and loyalties.

As for the possibility that Garwood was the elusive Salt of the duo, Captain Klem said, "I do not doubt that Garwood did a lot of moving about the countryside, but while remaining under VC control. Many sightings and broadcasts have been attributed to his movements from 1967 to 1970. To my knowledge, there has been no known connection of his movements with another person that could be construed as being Pepper."

Many years after he had returned to the United States from Vietnam, Dave Hall met a former recon marine who had served in I Corps at the same time as he had; their conversation touched on the topic of Marine defectors to the North Vietnamese side. The marine said he had firsthand knowledge of Americans joining enemy units and related a strange story: He had been part of a four-man reconnaissance patrol operating in contested country outside of Da Nang. The group stopped to eat a short distance away from a stream. Sitting back-to-back, facing outward, and silently eating their meal, they were surprised when an enemy group appeared, preparing to cross the stream. Among the lead elements in the group were several Caucasians. The marines took them under fire. At least one Caucasian had dropped face first into the stream, causing the marine to believe he had been killed along with several enemy Vietnamese. Seriously outnumbered and aware that they had completely compromised what should have been a clandestine reconnaissance, the patrol then moved as fast as they could for their scheduled extraction point, where a helicopter picked them up.

In 1968 NISRA Da Nang's caseload remained overwhelmingly the investigation of criminal activity. Nonetheless, the organization's intelligence mission was not overlooked, and when NISOV was tasked with a particularly sensitive collection mission, it fell to Dave Hall. A global positive intelligence operation aimed at compromising Soviet intelligence operations had been initiated in Washington and required a suitably qualified agent to carry out tasks in Southeast Asia. Civilian Special Agent Hall met the requirements of Washington spymasters. He would work alone and independently of even his own immediate superior. The command structure of NIS made this arrangement workable, while perhaps it might not have been with other intelligence organizations active in Vietnam.

Hall received orders which took him to remote areas—wherever a particular person or information source was—and there he developed the information his masters desired. All went to fill in the gaps of a global chessboard plan designed to compromise the Russian bear and his intelligence-acquisition apparatus. As is typical of such operations, the men controlling information requests provided no feedback to agents on the ground; they had no need to know the master plan, and what they didn't know couldn't hurt them.

In addition to a seemingly never-ending supply of leads and investigation on the criminal side of the house, NISRA Da Nang's agents managed sources in the city capable of providing intelligence of a more immediate nature. Attacks by enemy sappers and rocket artillery were a constant concern because of the concentration of U.S. forces in the Da Nang City area. Rockets were a particularly indiscriminate weapon that killed many more innocent Vietnamese civilians than Americans. Enemy ability to launch attacks from well outside the perimeter was a continuing thorn in the side of U.S. commanders. Thus, when Special Agents Fred Beatty and Dave Hall received reports from informants about Viet Cong plans to attack Navy shipping, they reported known facts as soon as possible.

Agent reports are by their very nature uncertain. Many factors govern the amount of credence they receive from intelligence analysts and responsible commanders, including how reliable the informant has previously been and how credible his information seems in the context of known factors. Hall and Beatty's informants told them that a team of enemy swimmer sappers planned to target U.S. Navy shallow-draft vessels using the Da Nang Bridge Ramp to receive and discharge cargo—much of it ammunition destined for artillery units deployed along the coast and waterways of I Corps. Their reports filed, Hall and Beatty could do little more; it became the duty of Naval Support Activity, Da Nang, to decide what countermeasures should be taken. Appearances suggest none were taken. Agents sleeping at 23 Doc Lap in early 1969 were abruptly awakened in the predawn hours by a massive explosion that broke panes of glass from billet windows. The blast originated at nearby Bridge Ramp.

When dawn finally came, NISRA Da Nang agents were witness to a scene of devastation at Bridge Ramp. A beached landing craft, utility (LCU) loaded with ammunition had exploded, laying waste to nearby vessels and supplies. Divers were in the water attempting to recover bodies. More than seventy men were believed dead. Naval authorities speculated that an errant enemy rocket had scored a direct hit on the vessel, but a below-water examination of the hull suggested an audacious underwater attack.

In mid-1969 a 122mm rocket barely cleared the third floor of the NISRA Da Nang billet at 23 Doc Lap Street, slamming into a Vietnamese National Police billet housing mainly dependent wives and children. Penetrating the roof of the old French villa across the street, the midnight explosion killed many occupants and left shrapnel marks on the Navy house. Americans could do little to assist the victims, most of whom were beyond help.

Few secrets are more closely guarded by governments than those that relate to communication security. The U.S. government has a huge apparatus designed both to protect its own secrets and to learn those of other nations. The weakness in the system is simply that few sensitive messages are passed by safe hands; rather, they are encrypted at various levels of sophistication and transmitted as electronic signals.

The continuing struggle to safeguard secrets while attempting to learn as much as possible about those of others is not a new one. During World War II cryptographers breaking enemy codes gave their commanders a very substantial advantage in decisive military engagements. If anything, the business of signal intelligence had grown even more important in the years since World War II.

When NISRA Da Nang SRA Pete Reilly received information that a certain U.S. Marine Corps officer assigned to a sensitive communication facility in Da Nang had been trying to sell classified communication equipment to Russian agents, his reaction was swift. The first lieutenant, a U.S. Naval Academy graduate, had apparently intended to sell the equipment to a Russian agent while on leave in Bangkok. Other U.S. agencies had prevented him from doing so in Thailand and quickly bundled him aboard a military flight back to Da Nang.

Special Agent Dave Hall was given the case. His objective was to learn as much as possible about "Ivan" in Bangkok and the circumstances of the marine's contact with him and also to build a criminal case. When the lieutenant arrived in Da Nang, Hall was there to meet him. Hall decided to arrest the accused, then launch his investigation with an interrogation. While this at first seemed a logical progression, Dave Hall very quickly learned that the first step in an officer arrest is the presentation of the accused to his commanding officer. The communication facility commanding officer was unimpressed with the young agent's oversight. SRA Pete Reilly successfully calmed those concerned at Hall's breach of military law and etiquette, and the agent continued interviewing witnesses.

The investigation was not yet complete when, about a month later, an informant called Hall. The same officer, he reported, had once again tucked a piece of sensitive communication equipment under his arm and was at that moment on a military aircraft bound for Saigon. His destination was again Bangkok—and presumably a certain Ivan. Agents met the plane when it arrived at Tan Son Nhut Air Base in Saigon and turned the young man around on a return flight to Da Nang.

Once again, Hall was waiting at Da Nang Air Base when the aircraft taxied up. Seeing the agent waiting, the accused—still carrying the equipment—tried to escape. Hall again arrested him and took him into custody, and again he endured vehement protests from his commanding officer. This time, Senior Resident Agent Reilly was less conciliatory with the upset marines. Two such serious breaches clearly underscored substandard security practice at the communication station, the CO had to agree. Authorities, however, determined that the young accused was mentally unbalanced and returned him to the United States. Procedures at the communication station underwent a major overhaul, and Naval Intelligence knew the identity of one more Russian agent lurking in the fringes of the Vietnam War in Bangkok.

Special Agents Dave Hall and Frank Orrantia, who served at NISRA Da Nang in 1968 and 1969, were among the last established northern roundsmen. Introduced to the north by Special Agent Joe Rodriguez, Orrantia soon was joined by Hall, assigned by SRA Pete Reilly to learn the ropes. Hall and Orrantia would often pair up to travel to a particular area and then split to run assigned leads. Both were improvisers, especially with transportation. Frank Orrantia developed a useful contact in an Army aviation unit at Da Nang Air Base, a captain who could often fly them directly to a northerly unit. The aircraft was a single-engine DHC Beaver. Air Force and Marine C130s flew regularly, but over time the agents grew to prefer a trip by sea. Via contact with Navy staff at Operation Market Time headquarters on Tien Sa Peninsula, space would be found for them aboard a northbound Swift boat or Coast Guard cutter. Frank Orrantia had made the trip before, disembarking at Cua Viet, the last stop before the DMZ began.

Cua Viet had been little more than a remote river estuary until the war focused on its strategic value. The Cam Lo River debouched into the South China Sea next to the dunes and broad sandy beach where Cua Viet was established. Though subject to attack from NVA units ranging south of the DMZ and to frequent mining, the river was a vital logistic link. Most supplies for Third Marine Division units defending the northern border were boated up the river in LCUs or LCMs (landing craft, medium). Agents needing to access marines rode the landing craft upstream to the hardstand ramp on the riverbank at Dong Ha, adjacent to National Highway 1.

Naval Support Activity Detachment (NSAD), Cua Viet, was established at the river mouth to facilitate the movement of war materiel inland to the Marines. Fuel, ammunition, and rations were mainstay items. Within easy rocket and artillery range, it was one of the most dangerous Navy duty stations, despite deep, protective bunkers and thousands of sandbags. Sailors worked every day, and they worked hard. Other than a Marine amphibious tractor battalion and other ground security elements, they had the area to themselves.

In late 1968 NISRA Da Nang received a desperate plea for assistance from NSAD Cua Viet: Death threats had been made against an officer there. The threats were of such credibility that command believed a homicide might be imminent. Dave Hall and Frank Orrantia were given the case.

The request arrived during the monsoon, at a time when typhoons were ranging around the South China Sea. The weather was foul, even at protected Da Nang. Winds were up, visibility down, and rainsqualls had grounded aircraft. Logically, the agents first approached the Navy for transportation north; operations staff at Market Time told them no vessels were sailing except for combat essential missions. Taken aback, they next approached the Coast Guard, who operated cutters in support of the Navy's Operation Market Time surveillance and interdiction mission. Here it was a different story: told of the threat at Cua Viet, the duty officer reached for his radio and summoned a cutter for an immediate emergency mission. Soon boarded, the agents joined the small crew of the cutter, and they began pushing their way northward through surging seas. Once they were clear of Da Nang, conditions improved markedly: seas smoothed, and they made good progress. Dave Hall wondered why the Navy hadn't gotten the word.

As the cutter pushed its way northward with long, sweeping miles of beach to its port side, an alert lookout spotted a motorized Vietnamese junk navigating the shallows between a sandbank and the beach. The junk was ordered to heave to but ignored the order and took evasive action. Local mariners had an intimate knowledge of the rules in these waters. Similar vessels had long been used to bring arms and supplies from the North to insurgent groups fighting in South Vietnam. The Vietnamese were taken under fire with a single high-explosive round from the breach-loading 81mm mortar mounted on the after deck. The round struck the bow of the vessel, which quickly began to sink in the shallow water. The sandbar was more than a mile long, and given the urgency of their mission, the cutter commander elected to continue on course.

Soon after, a critical pump failed, and they had to slow the vessel down. As they were then nearing Thuan An at the mouth of the Perfume River, the commanding officer decided to seek Navy assistance. They sailed over the bar and made their way up the river to Hue.

Navy personnel at Hue were not, at first, particularly interested in the Coast Guard's mechanical problem. Concerned at the impasse, Frank Orrantia quietly took a Navy chief petty officer aside, identified himself, and explained the nature of the mission. It would not, he patiently explained, reflect well on Navy Hue if a threatened officer was killed while the Coast Guard waited for assistance. The chief saw the wisdom in Orrantia's comments. Parts were found to repair the pump, and Navy mechanics assisted with a record-time installation. The cutter was soon under way again.

Several hours later the cutter approached the many shifting sandbars at the river mouth of Cua Viet. A combination of extra runoff in the river from the rains and the huge tidal range had transformed the river mouth into a mass of churning white water and boiling current. There was concern on the bridge as the captain conversed with his helmsman about the best way into the river. Both Hall and Orrantia were alarmed at the conditions, which they had never seen before. After several minutes delay, the helmsman suddenly gave the cutter full throttle, and after a bumpy ride over the bar, they were suddenly into the river and reducing headway to avoid anchored vessels. The agents disembarked moments later and the coastguardsmen wasted no time turning around and getting back into open water.

There was palpable tension in the air at NSAD Cua Viet, but the threat to kill the commanding officer had not been carried out. Word quickly spread of the agent presence. They first interviewed the CO, who said he had been in his quarters the night before, lying awake in bed, when he heard the distinctive sound of the spoon flying off a thrown grenade. He dove to the deck of his sandbagged hut and was lying prone when the fragmentation grenade exploded outside. The hooch was damaged, but the commander was uninjured. He had not, he said, been threatened in any way before the attack and had no idea who might wish to harm him.

No clues remained other than the spoon from the exploded grenade. Hall and Orrantia made much of having recovered it, then began to interview everybody who had been in the area, both to determine their movements and whereabouts and to see if there were undercurrents of dissention. The many interviews failed to produce even one logical lead. Finally, announcing the grenade spoon would be forwarded to the FBI lab for development of latent fingerprints, the agents announced they would return to Cua Viet to arrest the offender as soon as results of the scientific examination were known. As every member of the U.S. armed forces is fingerprinted upon induction, this was perhaps something more than an idle threat. Both agents by this time were of the opinion that there had not been an intentional threat on the CO's life; rather the explosion had been the product of carelessness in an area where sentries were routinely heavily armed and had access to all manner of weapons and ordnance.

The next day they boarded a landing craft loaded with ammunition bound for the Marine logistic bridgehead upriver at Dong Ha. This was always a slow, anxious voyage as the LCM battled currents and hidden sandbars as crew watched very carefully for mines in the muddy waters. There was a history of mayhem and minings on the Cua Viet, and so Hall and Orrantia walked down the sloping ramp and onto the steel matting at Dong Ha with some relief. They walked up to nearby National Highway, put out their thumbs, and were soon hitchhiking to Dong Ha Airstrip. Finding seats on a Marine C130 returning to Da Nang, they were back in their own quarters that night.

The origins of the threat, if there had been a threat at all, were never identified.

# 6

# DA NANG, 1969: A YOUNG AGENT'S LESSONS

**What would induce a young man to volunteer** for service in Vietnam, particularly in 1969—the year after America's press had transformed the Tet Offensive from a tactical victory to a strategic defeat? In hindsight, I would have to say it was a cocktail of ambition, spirit of adventure, and a sense that it was time for me to serve, as my father had done before me.

I was born on April 1, 1945, the day U.S. Marines stormed the beaches of Okinawa, one of the deadliest campaigns in the corps' history. Dad was then a junior naval officer in a destroyer escort, the USS *Joseph Conolly* (DE450), in the buildup to the anticipated assault on the Japanese homeland. He returned home from the Pacific in 1946 and took up an appointment to begin a career as a park ranger in the National Park Service.

My early childhood was spent in the idyllic surrounds of Hawaii National Park. Dad, in his uniform, set off each morning for the walk through rainforest to park headquarters, while we children spent long hours exploring among towering fern trees and the nearby volcanic crater. We enjoyed occasional trips with Dad into the Kau Desert in his GI jeep. One of my favorite spots was a practice range used by marines during the war. It was strewn with the sort of refuse a young boy finds very interesting, including unexploded ordnance. There I first fired my dad's 1903 Springfield rifle at the tender age of four.

Transferring to Yosemite National Park in 1952 was a shock for my siblings and me. Gone were the gentle tropical climes and the equally gentle Hawaiian folk, the fat mammas who would feed me *poi*, and most particularly my very close friends. Yosemite was a community of perhaps fifteen hundred souls nestled around the fringes of one of the most beautiful valleys on the planet. Cliffs that started, quite literally, one hundred yards behind our home rose vertically two thousand feet. The base of Yosemite Falls was a ten-minute walk away, and when the spring thaw of high country snow came, it rattled the windows in the National Park Service homes clustered near its final drop.

Here I attended Yosemite Elementary School and later commuted to high school in Mariposa, California, some forty-five miles away. I had completed two years at Fresno State, and a four-month trek across the South Pacific, when Dad was transferred to Washington, D.C., where he had an office in the Interior building. It must have been a shock to him after nearly twenty years as a field naturalist and interpreter.

I was a criminology major at Fresno State, working part-time and focusing simply on getting a degree behind me as soon as possible. There were no frills to my existence. The folks helped me when they could, but getting the necessary education was certainly my own responsibility. I thought the California Highway Patrol (CHP) might be a good organization in which to begin my career in law enforcement, and I successfully passed both the written and the oral examinations. The CHP Academy accepted me in the summer following my graduation.

When I did finally complete my degree in the summer of 1967, I took up my parent's invitation to visit them in Washington. Soon after my arrival, Dad suggested I might like to talk with people in federal law enforcement to consider what career options they might also offer. This seemed like a good idea. I had a job, I was saving money for a car, and Washington was an exciting place. But what I really hoped for was a job that would allow me to serve overseas. When I explained this to a Secret Service colleague of my father's, he referred me to people he knew in State Department Security and at the Washington, D.C., field office of the Office of Naval Intelligence (this field component had recently been renamed the Naval Investigative Service). I applied for special agent billets at both agencies and began the long wait while a detailed background investigation was conducted.

In the meantime, I applied and was accepted for Officer Candidate School at the U.S. Army Military Police Command. I was hedging all my bets, I thought.

I also continued my job as a butcher in Springfield, Virginia, while my background investigation slowly went forward—doubtlessly complicated by my 1965 travels through French Oceania, Fiji, New Zealand, Australia, and New Guinea. The State Department had the means to do checks in each of these countries; the Navy did not. But as the domestic phase of my background neared completion, NIS obtained State's investigation reports. State Department Security in early 1968 was battling with a funding freeze and could not hire until the new fiscal year. The Navy was not so fettered. In the first week of March 1968 the commanding officer of Naval Investigative Service Office, Washington, interviewed me in his office in building 200 of the Navy yard. He told me that my background investigation and screening had been successfully completed and that he was prepared to offer me an agent appointment; he would, however, expect me to promise not to leave NIS if State made me an offer later in the year. I promised, as requested, and we shook hands. I was on board. In July State called me and asked me to accept an appointment. Feeling a strong sense of obligation to NIS, I declined.

NISO Washington, my first assignment, was established in one of the massive buildings that had once been part of the Naval Gun Factory, within the confines of Washington Navy Yard. The historic yard, constructed on the waters of the Anacostia River, was and is a hodgepodge of eighteenth-century brick buildings and others added during the two world wars. On my first day, wearing a new suit, I reported to Special Agent Cecil Boggs in his office in the bowels of building 200 and began in-processing. At the Naval Dispensary, I discovered that the documents I presented listed me as a research analyst. Obviously, the medical arm of the Navy had no need to know that I was in fact a fledgling special agent. Temporary credentials identifying me as an agent and thus cleared to top secret were issued, and I was then ready to hit the streets for the Navy.

New agents invariably learned their job by conducting background investigations. In March 1968 the Naval Investigative Service was charged with the conduct of all of the services' background investigations (BIs), which were used to determine a candidate's suitability for exposure to classified material. In the Washington office, we had a massive workload of BIs. All agents did at least some BIs; a lucky few got the criminal investigations, and a couple of counterintelligence specialists did liaison work and were often seen snipping newspaper articles for their files.

I quickly learned that every background investigation followed a clear matrix of what we called "leads." What these were depended on a variety of factors, in particular the level and type of access the candidate required: a Marine officer candidate attending the Communication School at Quantico might need only a secret clearance to complete initial training; on the other hand, a cryptographer at the Nebraska Avenue headquarters of the Naval Security Group would require periodic upgrades and a number of coworker and neighborhood interviews to establish suitability for continued exposure to some of the nation's most closely-guarded secrets.

The starting point in a BI was normally a local agency check, literally a check of any agency in the area in which the subject had served or resided in during a particular period. At NISO Washington, a dedicated staff did little else. Later, I learned to run checks in the old courthouses of Stafford and Fredericksburg, Virginia.

When I was handed my first background investigation lead sheets, I was patiently told what was required, then paired up with an experienced agent. This was Special Agent Ralph Robillard, a retired U.S. Air Force OSI major with two decades of experience running BIs. I soon assimilated the elements that were required to be covered in any BI interview: how long the subject had been known to the interviewee and in what capacity, whether the subject had any questionable foreign connections, whether the subject was considered to be honest and trustworthy, whether the interviewee was aware of any reason why the subject should not be grated a position of trust and responsibility, and whether he recommend the subject for such a position.

I was soon running leads in the decaying halls of the temporary buildings erected along Constitution Avenue—and known to all as Main Navy—and to a lesser extent, the labyrinth Pentagon. In the afternoon, to beat rush hour traffic, we would do neighborhood checks—interviewing the subject's neighbors, past or present. Neighbor interviews were often a good opportunity to identify what was called a developed informant by asking the interviewee to identify another person who could supply information about the subject. The results were sometimes startling and could lead an investigation down a derogatory path. A "derog" BI demanded detailed interviews, statements from interviewees, and a detailed report. That report would be used by command to decide whether the subject should have continued access to classified material. In many instances investigative results had a direct bearing on a person's job assignment.

Although the Washington military and civil environment was very interesting, I never really enjoyed doing background investigations and could not contemplate a career centered around this type of work. In May 1968 I was ordered to NIS headquarters, then located in the Hoffman Building in Alexandria to attend Agent Basic School. This marked a real turning point in my career.

Basic School classes were quite small. Several experienced street agents who acted as mentors were assigned to students in each course. My mentor was Special Agent Jack Renwick, a likeable highly capable man just back from a one-year assignment at NISRA Saigon. Renwick sat at the table through the lectures, answered questions, and provided guidance.

Holding Basic School at headquarters was wisdom at work. We had regular exposure to the men who led and drove the organization. If they were not on the same floor as our classroom, they were a short elevator ride away. Thus, we were exposed to counterintelligence specialists, received briefings on the communist bloc's current activities against the free world, and were taken step by step through major espionage cases. We were frequently reminded that our primary mission was to be spy catchers. At Basic School, I developed a far clearer concept of the NIS mission and some idea of how I might participate in it.

Although the hippy revolution had its liberalizing effects, the United States was a different, more socially conservative country three decades ago. Because a good number of the agents at Basic School had had previous careers in street law enforcement, there were not any prudes in the group. As we were exposed to more case histories involving espionage and attempted espionage, it became increasingly apparent that sex, perhaps even more so than greed, was an underlying issue in many cases. The Western nations had learned to their detriment that homosexuals could be particularly vulnerable to manipulation by foreign agents, that so-called aberrant sexual behavior could be the weakness our enemies might exploit to learn national secrets, and that even a healthy libido could spell trouble in certain circumstances. Thus, NIS took sex cases seriously; they were all managed and monitored from a vault known as the Cat 8 shop. Its overseer had dossiers guaranteed to make the most seasoned agent blanch.

As Basic School drew to a close, I began to consider carefully what I had learned from Jack Renwick. He had never tried to sell the concept of Vietnam service to any of us. I soon discerned, however, that duty with NIS in Vietnam could immediately expose me to just about every type of investigative challenge on the books. Agents who successfully completed their year tour were permitted to take the promotional exam to full journeyman level, were given preferential assignments, and were sought after because of their well-rounded vocational experience. Vietnam service was clearly a short cut to the top. I was twenty-three; the world was my apple. I volunteered and was told I would be eligible after my year of probationary service was up in March 1969. I specified Da Nang as my choice of duty station.

In 1969 the First Marine Division, headquartered at Hill 327 west of Da Nang Air Base, had battalions actively deployed in an arc beginning at the northern boundary of the area of operations (AO), Hai Van Pass, extending westward and especially to the south. This was the An Hoa Basin, beyond which was Que Son Valley. Both areas had been bitterly contested for the entire period of the U.S. involvement in Vietnam. Not only was there a strong Viet Cong infrastructure presence there, but An Hoa Basin was also a natural exit point from mountains to the west and the extensions of the Ho Chi Minh Trail beyond. Marines spoke of seeing small units of NVA marching in step out of the mountains on their way to valley battlefields.

In more peaceful times, a coal mine had operated at An Hoa, and the French had constructed a serviceable airstrip there. This made An Hoa one of several important strong points selected by Marine command from which to embark on operations focused on finding and destroying the enemy. The area was not, unfortunately, in an ideal location for resupply by land. To address this problem, SeaBees and Marine engineers constructed a large bridge, later christened Liberty Bridge, across the Thu Bon River. The northern approaches to the bridge were muddy roads not much better than cart tracks, which were originally built to access the village of Dai Loc and during the war passed a series of Marine firebases: Hills 55, 37, and 65. Overlapping artillery "fans" allowed the guns on call on these hills to drop massive firepower virtually anywhere in the area. Tank-escorted convoys, preceded by engineers checking for mines, regularly trucked large amounts of materiel into this hostile environment. Supplying ammunition alone for the scores of artillery pieces in the area was a major logistic headache. Once completed, Liberty Bridge was a considerable focus of the enemy's interest. It was fortified with mortar pits, concertina wire, and dozens of marines, who endured endless monsoon rains observing the rushing waters, watching for enemy sapper-swimmer attacks.

Manning armed strong points is the antithesis of Marine Corps practice, which emphasizes going to the enemy. The hills and bases were considered protected venues for the artillery, logistics, and command. Marines patrolled and came to grips with the enemy on his own turf. Marine command also had a strongly developed belief in the value of civic action and pacification, prompted by hard lessons learned in the Banana Wars of Central America earlier in the century; Marine combined action groups (CAGs) were made up of volunteers who lived in villages with Vietnamese to assist them with basic needs such as security, medicine, and hygiene.

All of this could make it difficult for a NIS agent to go directly to a command venue and expect to find a particular individual. Agents who worked an area normally had a good idea which units were operating in what area. This knowledge was supplemented by good contacts in the Marine postal system, who could usually ensure accurate information about where a subject's battalion was receiving its mail and supplies from. After obtaining information from these sources, an agent could sally forth to the command rear and start asking questions.

Flying to the base areas was always preferable to driving, except perhaps in the case of Hill 55, which was the nearest to Da Nang. This well-fortified hill overlooked surrounding paddy fields and their villages, its eight-inch howitzers staring down the throat of the An Hoa Basin to the south. As with the other hill strong points, Hill 55 was an important rear area for battalions and small-unit groups screening the country, putting in ambushes by night, and hurting local VC doing their rounds. By 1969 the Viet Cong around 55 were finding tax collection and intimidation far more difficult than they had been in earlier years. Marine patrols were taking their toll, as were the high watchtowers at the hill where Marine snipers with rifles and night-scope-equipped .50-caliber machine guns accounted for a mounting casualty rate of nocturnal VC. Life may have been easier for the enemy in the southerly rice fields, called the Arizona territory by marines, but it was not improving around Hill 55.

Fragging was most common in the later years of the Vietnam War. After Bob Powers's first 1967 fragging investigation, the practice became more prevalent. By 1969 commands were looking more carefully at deaths caused by grenades. Most victims were NCOs or officers. When a Marine staff sergeant was blown in half, apparently while asleep on his cot in a hooch at Hill 55, the First Marine Division requested assistance from NIS.

Special Agent Larry Coleman was officially Da Nang SRA Don McCoy's assistant. A solid, mature agent and highly skilled investigator, Coleman was respected by his peers and was a quiet source of advice to the less experienced. He took over investigation of the Hill 55 fragging, starting with a careful examination of the scene. The victim, a cook, was assigned quarters in a Southeast Asia (SEA) hut—a lightly framed rectangular building with a metal roof and sides of plywood and screening. Initial indications were that the culprit had cut fly screen immediately adjacent to the victim as he lay sleeping, introduced the grenade through the cut, and quietly placed it adjacent his abdomen. The blast had disemboweled the victim but caused surprisingly little damage to the upper torso and, in particular, his face.

A postmortem examination provided little additional information except to confirm that death had been caused by the blast and unique stainless-steel wire fragments utilized in the manufacture of the M26 fragmentation grenade. The screen panel with its cut was removed for scientific examination. Sentries were interviewed to see whether any had seen movements around the victim's hooch that night. Neither sentries nor colleagues were able to provide substantiation; nor were footprints or other scientific evidence discovered around the building's exterior.

But clues discovered during the detailed search of the victim's personal effects pointed more to suicide than homicide. And, when the scientific examination of the screen definitely confirmed it had been cut from inside, those suspicions became stronger. It was hard to imagine anybody creeping unnoticed across a squeaking plywood floor and then, after managing to place the grenade, making good an escape. Agents in the United States followed up leads in an attempt to learn about the victim and his possible state of mind at the time of death. Ultimately, it was determined that he had indeed wished to kill himself, but not in a way which would preclude an open-casket military funeral at which he could be interred in his Marine dress blue uniform. The only doubt lurking in Larry Coleman's mind related to the fact that the safety pin from the grenade that killed the victim was never found.

Later in the war, Hill 55 was the scene of several intimidation efforts using fragmentation grenades. Disliked NCOs, called "lifers" by the discontented, were targets for expressions of defiance of instructions and orders. Grenades were placed to act as warnings, although any could have unexpectedly detonated. Trip wires were attached to a gunnery sergeant's desk chair and the other end connected to the safety pin of a grenade affixed to the desk interior. Another intimidation effort involved an M26 frag with its safety pin removed and a length of electrician's tape wrapped around the striker lever (which a spring throws loose when the grenade is thrown, causing the delay fuse to arm). The holding tape rendered the grenade safe temporarily—until it was placed in a can of gasoline, intended to provide a time-delay explosion: the solvent would gradually dissolve the adhesive on the tape, then allowing the striker lever to spring out and strike the detonator, starting the short fuse burning. An explosion could be expected three to five seconds later.

The perpetrators of this intimidation could never be brought to justice because of a lack of evidence and a carefully maintained code of silence and intimidation in the ranks. But those responsible were eventually identified, and judicious transfers by command neutralized the problem.

Often, a NIS special agent would go to forward areas to conduct investigations initiated by leads and requests sent from other NIS components. U.S. postal inspectors were a frequent source of referrals. Mail in Vietnam was always treated as a high-priority item and deliveries occurred daily in many instances. There was a large volume of return mail and parcels destined for home, in many instances items purchased from excellent PX facilities. Injury, attrition, and death produced opportunities for a few to mail arms and other stolen property home, items perhaps lost in the unit weapon accounting system or acquired through barter with a Vietnamese ally. Although they were disassembled in most instances, mailers hoped goods would pass scrutiny at the point of entry and be waiting at home for their homecoming.

Even more common, particularly from 1969 onward, were cases of narcotics mailed in various guises. Tape cassettes, a favorite communication medium between Vietnam and the home front, were a common receptacle for these. Forward Marine commands in particular were disturbed when a special agent visited them carrying a report alleging narcotics use and exportation by men who might have been functioning as riflemen in the field. Many grunts, who depended on each other to stay alive, had a code of conduct that forbade narcotics, at least while on operations, but a responsible commander could not rely only on an informal code of conduct when his troops' effectiveness and welfare were concerned.

A trip I took in 1970 illustrates the unreliability of this code. Carrying three cases involving members of the Fifth Marines, I embarked on a Marine CH46 resupply mission early one morning. I shared the bird with five or six enlisted men returning to their units, and we flew southwest across rice paddies and the choked, dusty road that led to Dai Loc and the Arizona territory. On that day the road streamed with tanks and trucks carrying marines returning to Da Nang. Interspersed among them were Vietnamese pedicabs loaded to the bursting point with people, pigs, chickens, and other rural impedimenta. Even more prevalent were small motorcycles and pedestrians balancing huge loads on carrying poles bouncing rhythmically as they shuffled to the next village. Beyond, the mountains rose above verdant rice paddies. It might have been a peaceful picture were it not for artillery bursts on the slopes and the impatient convoy surging along below.

Hill 55 was the first stop for the resupply mission. Several men got off, taking personal gear, weapons, and cargo with them; then they moved away from the big chopper shielding their eyes and grasping caps in the rotor wash. Clouds of red dust carrying loose detritus blew from the landing zone (LZ) through wire entanglements; nothing grew on these firebase hills and dust was ever-present.

Taking off, the CH46 gained elevation and continued a southwest course skirting the massif on the right known to Marines as Charlie Ridge, whence artillery fire had earlier been observed. Ahead, the Vu Gia River curled down from the mountains and across the paddies and plains to the south before joining the Thu Bon. Hill 65, overlooking the river and situated near the base of Charlie Ridge, was the next destination. Skimming over hooches and upward-pointing muzzles of momentarily quiet artillery batteries, the CH46 landed slightly down-slope on the metal helipad. I got off, moved away, and watched the helo take off again and clatter off over the Vu Gia in the direction of An Hoa Combat Base, a smudge of smoke and circling aircraft far in the distance on the opposite side of the Arizona.

Up the hill at the battalion CP, I was redirected to the battalion executive officer, who read official NIS reports indicating that one of his men had attempted to mail a disassembled M16 home. The XO knew the accused, describing him as a fairly quiet, young country boy originating from a town in the Deep South. He sent an NCO to find the marine and arrange a suitable location for the interview. Obviously surprised to see an agent, the marine confessed. The weapon, probably issued to a man wounded in the recent operation, had been unattended at an LZ following the operation. The marine had taken the rifle, fieldstripped it into pieces as small as possible and mailed them home in several packages. "I just really wanted it for next deer season at home," he said.

The interview completed, I briefed the battalion commander in the presence of his sergeant major, promising that I would forward a complete report to assist with any disciplinary procedures soon. It was late in the day. In the charge of the sergeant major, I had been escorted to the hooch normally used for transient officers when my host said he had a spare bunk in his hooch; would that be suitable? I had been around marines long enough to know that battalion sergeants major are a force to be reckoned with: smart, astute, and all knowing, they are the eyes and ears of their commanders. I gratefully accepted the invitation and settled into a small private hooch with panoramic views of the position and the villages and fields beyond. The hooch included a private shower, replenished by a young marine toting water in five-gallon jerry cans—as close to luxury as is possible in a war zone.

As the shadows lengthened, a squad quietly walked down the base access road and through the perimeter fence to set up a listening post and lay ambush for errant enemy. Soon after the squad exited the perimeter, three batteries of 105mm howitzers fired together at a distant tree line where a contact had been reported. The fire was supplemented by an eight-inch howitzer battery on Hill 55, which dropped a string of rounds with uncanny accuracy across the tree line where it faced the paddy fields. Massive explosions tossed full-sized trees into the air like so many toothpicks. It was perhaps not a wise thing for Charles to take pot shots at marines with this sort of reactive firepower on call.

Marines had several tall sandbagged observation towers that were used both to monitor surroundings and to provide fire support. A 106mm recoilless rifle's business end pointed northward from one tower, its breach open to the elements. Commands were shouted and the 106 spotting rifle was fired, sending a red tracer arcing out into the growing darkness, quickly followed by a huge blast as the main gun fired support for a patrol skirmishing on steep slopes above. It was, the sergeant major said, a fairly routine evening at Hill 65. The war went on as it had for several years, but there was little doubt that friendly forces were gradually gaining advantage in this traditionally hostile region. Batteries fired through the night as the rains fell over the Arizona. I could not help but wonder what sort of a miserable night the grunts were having outside the wire; the answer was, "Another just like the last one." Marine riflemen and their leaders had it hard in the bush.

Needing to travel on to An Hoa Combat Base to conduct my next investigation, the next morning I walked to the CP to learn what air movements were planned for the day. The hills had regular helicopter visits, but they were certainly not events one could set his watch to. Low cloud ceiling and continuing drizzle were currently causing delays for all air missions except the most urgent. "Maybe this afternoon," I was told. Knowing by then the unpredictable vagaries of Vietnamese monsoon weather, I opted to join a Marine Roughrider convoy to An Hoa expected within the hour at the nearby village, Dai Loc. A jeep from Hill 65 was scheduled to join the supply trucks. I joined the driver and his shotgun escort, winding down the road to Route 4 and their rendezvous. The convoy was waiting; perhaps twenty heavily loaded five-ton trucks and several tractor-trailers, each with a gunner manning a coaxial .50-caliber machine gun. Drivers were out kicking muddy tires, doing a last-minute check of their charges before the journey into the Arizona territory. Gunners wearing radio-linked headsets wiped weapons and checked ammunition. Slotting into the procession, the jeep moved off in convoy, navigating water-filled ruts and seemingly bottomless holes, seldom shifting above second gear.

Outside the village and paddy fields, terrain adjacent the road became increasingly barren and inhospitable. This was the Arizona territory, a scene of virtually continuous conflict between marines and the enemy since NVA/VC control had been challenged. Flashes from artillery round impacts and columns of smoke rose in the distance. Approaching the northern banks of the Thu Bon River, the convoy passed a squad of marines preparing to march from an overnight defensive position. With water-filled holes nearby, hooches made from ponchos and shelter halves provided cover from the rains and a place to sleep. Young men all, the marines had the skinny, hard-staring look of the men who spent their lives in the field. They ignored the convoy, either intentionally or because of preoccupation with their next task and the march ahead.

Slowly, the trucks began to drive across Liberty Bridge, recently constructed by SeaBees and Marine engineers of U.S. timber imported for the job. Song Thu Bon is a wide river, even when there is no rain; in the monsoon, it rises rapidly, the brown waters carrying branches, logs, and other detritus with it—a challenge to the integrity of any timber bridge. Sentries constantly watched the waters as they approached the bridge. Flotsam was not harmful only when it hit the bridge but also when it hid enemy swimmer-sappers. Sentries enduring seemingly endless rain fired into the water at anything looking suspicious.

A heavily fortified outpost had been constructed on the far side of the bridge. The position was the subject of major attacks, and its marines had repelled several attempts to overrun it and then destroy the bridge. Without the bridge, supplies for the scores of artillery pieces at nearby An Hoa would have to be ferried across. As we approached An Hoa, Marine artillerymen readied an 81mm mortar for an imminent fire mission.

Tanks from An Hoa and several wet, tired engineers who had swept the road for mines awaited the convoy to escort it the remaining distance. Mud-encrusted and festooned with antenna flags, they would precede the trucks, to protect the convoy in the event of ambush. Rumbling off ahead, the convoy trucks began following in trace under leaden skies. The road carried them past a school and the German hospital from which, I recalled, the Viet Cong had abducted a nurse. Vietnamese pedestrians made haste to leave the roadway and the splashing bow waves of convoy trucks.

An Hoa's artillery could be heard long before the watch towers and perimeter defenses hove into view. Guns continued to fire as gates were opened for the convoy trucks. An Hoa, headquarters of the Fifth Marine Regiment, was a hectic, claustrophobic hive of soggy tents, SEA huts for the fortunate, duckboard walkways, and ever-present mud. Conversations were routinely interrupted by the huge blast of a nearby howitzer or a helicopter landing. To use the jargon of the age, An Hoa was not considered a "garden spot" to any but the field marines.

I quickly located the commands to which I believed the subjects of my cases were attached. One had been injured and medevaced out of country to the naval hospital at Yokosuka, Japan. He was not expected to return to his command, so I would have to pass the case to Japan. The subject could expect a ward visit from an agent dressed in conservative civilian attire within a few days. A NIS investigation originating in the United States implicated the second subject in importing narcotics by mail utilizing a tape cassette. Though the subject was then in Da Nang, his personal effects were nevertheless in a hooch at An Hoa. Armed with a command-authorized search authorization, I searched the accused's locker and soon discovered cannabis traces in several items of clothing bearing his name. He would later be interrogated in Da Nang. Soon after completion of the command briefing about the results of the search, the first sergeant approached with the news that a late-afternoon CH53 flight was inbound; there might be room on the return flight to Da Nang. Heartened by this news, I moved quickly to the cargo handling area adjacent the helicopter landing pad, joining perhaps thirty-five Marine infantry, still fully-equipped after a stint in the field. Soon, the huge helicopter appeared high above and began a steep spiral to land within the circular fan of outward firing guns.

The Marine riflemen were tired and dirty. Sitting patiently, leaning against packs or each other, most dozed or slept. They were well used to waiting for the Big Green Machine to tell them what to do next. Arrival of the CH53 prompted a few to shift their gaze to a young forklift driver jockeying his machine up to the chopper rear ramp, his head feet away from the certain death of a whirling tail rotor. Pilots kept their machine running at full power. Moments after the forklift had removed a pallet of cargo, passengers were urged to load. I joined the grunts. All were quickly sandwiched in, squatting on the deck, as pilots taxied a short distance then hauled controls back to begin a steep, tight spiral climb out of small arms range. It was cool at elevation, when the helicopter leveled out. Nobody tried to speak over the rotor din. It was almost peaceful.

I was on the ground at Marble Mountain Air Facility twenty minutes later, calling NISRA Da Nang for a ride home at the end of an eventful day.

While the Fifth and Seventh Marine Regiments battled the enemy in the mountains and An Hoa Basin, their sister division, the First Marines, was fully engaged in the slice of coastal land to the east. Immediately east of the An Hoa Basin AO was a section of country known to marines as Dodge City. Combating incursions by NVA units and resident VC was the task of the First Marine Division, as was effective control of the heavily populated country northward to Da Nang. Through it ran the Han River and many

tributaries. This was rice-producing country dotted with picturesque hamlets, paddy fields, and bamboo tree lines. It is said that an army marches on
its stomach; control of the rice harvest was thus a hotly contested issue
between communists and marines with their Vietnamese allies. That control
was extended both by civic action programs and aggressive patrolling.

A First Marines outpost had been established at Tu Cau Bridge, both to
guard the vital bridge from enemy sapper attack and to project an allied
presence into surrounding countryside. It was one of several such posts. By
day marines and hospital corpsmen visited villagers to assist with basic im-
provements in health, hygiene, and security. At night they watched roads and
trails for evidence of visits and intimidation by Viet Cong anxious to wrest
control from the allies. Marine ambushes and patrols were paying dividends
in the hearts-and-minds stakes at Tu Cau Bridge and in surrounding villages.

Marines were billeted in tents within a wired perimeter on the west end
of the span that covered Song Tu Cau. They were regularly resupplied by
road from Da Nang. The camp defenses reflected the fact that pacification
had been quite successful in the region—and the Marine philosophy of
taking the war to the enemy rather than defending ground. Tu Cau was a
small but important enclave in the strategic plan that defended vital Da
Nang facilities.

On an evening in August 1969, a squad led by a junior Marine NCO
moved out of the Tu Cau perimeter to begin a patrol down the river, where
an ambush site was to be established. Marines were hoping to find Viet
Cong infiltrating by night into houses and villes set back from the fields.
After several hundred yards of eastward movement, the squad turned north
to enter a small peanut patch, immediately beyond which stood a modest
two-room masonry farmhouse. The patrol was jumpy. The lance corporal
leading the patrol had a squad made up largely of newcomers. The area was
known to be rife with booby traps making night patrols unpopular—and
the group decided to sandbag the patrol. They would wait out the night in a
relatively safe location, sending periodic radio transmissions back to the
bridge base; these would give false positions to the operation center. A Vietnamese household had previously allowed marines to use their farmhouse,
and the patrol was guided there. The squad radioman set up next to one
room of the farmhouse and lit a cigarette. Vietnamese occupants remained
in a second room.

In the meantime, another Marine patrol approached the house, not knowing other marines were nearby. Nearing the room from outside, the point
man saw a cigarette glow and the outline of the sandbagging Marine radioman
through the window opening. Surprised and certain he had seen a Viet Cong
soldier, he opened fire. The fire was returned, and in the melee that followed, grenades were thrown and a vast number of rifle shots exchanged.
In an instant, four Vietnamese peasants were dead. All were women and

children. A second squad was at the scene moments later. There were no Marine casualties.

The second lieutenant platoon commander responded from the bridge position within a few minutes. What he saw caused him to believe homicide might have been committed. He isolated all squad members and began the pitiful task of collecting scattered remains and calming Vietnamese, who remained convinced they had been attacked by Viet Cong. Marines stayed on the scene through the night, relaying a request for assistance to the First Marine Division staff judge advocate. Judge Advocate General (JAG) in turn requested investigative support from NISRA Da Nang.

Assigned to lead the investigation, Special Agent Lance Arnold gathered a small team of agents to assist with early, critical periods in the inquiry. He was joined by agents Frank Orrantia, Ed Hemphill, and me. We hurriedly left the Da Nang office in a Navy gray twin-cab Dodge truck, still dressed in civilian clothes and carrying an assortment of rifles and equipment. Arnold drove through the teeming streets in Da Nang, finally emerging on the gravel thoroughfare that had once been the highway from Saigon to Hanoi, Route 1. Sharing the busy road with Marine convoys could result in delays, but Route 1 was far safer than the coastal road. Some miles south, we reached the turnoff and drove east until a clutch of antenna masts and barbed-wire entanglements announced Tu Cau. There, at the sandbagged command post, we were met by a sleep-starved platoon commander. After a short briefing, we joined him to walk eastward toward the village and the possible crime scene. Along the graded dirt road, squatting in the red dust, sat members of the offending patrols, each stationed well apart to prevent possible collaboration.

Children led us to a tiny Vietnamese house set back a short distance from the bridge road. We found it at the end of a path that wandered through a modest peanut cultivation field that continued up to the farmhouse front verandah. An inverted wicker basket sat incongruously along the path. Agents were warned to stay clear of it because an unexploded 40mm grenade from the night remained uncleared. A slight jar, we were told, could detonate it.

As was so often the case in Vietnam, curious villagers and shy children followed the group to the crime scene. Perhaps expecting more hostility after the deaths, the peasants were gracious to the Americans new to the ways of rural Vietnamese. To me it seemed as though they had accepted the terrible violence of the previous night as unavoidable—another legacy of a long, painful war.

By the time NIS agents arrived, the platoon commander had methodically sifted through the wreckage and detritus and found all the victims' body parts.

Controlling agent Lance Arnold first inspected the interior of the house, noting shrapnel and bullet-strikes in the plastered brick walls. The evidence suggested that the deceased had been clustered in the small northern room and in a modest underground shelter at the time of the attack. Grenades had shattered the room and its contents, reducing the material to a collage of burnt, broken matter.

While others sifted through evidence in and around the Tu Cau farmhouse, I drove back to Da Nang and met Special Agent Larry Coleman at the NSA morgue. The victims' remains had been taken to the hospital mortuary, where a medical examination had been requested.

I walked from the hot, dusty sand dunes of the Tien Sa Peninsula and through the door of the Quonset hut that housed the morgue, entering a cool, wet blanket of air clearly tainted with the scent of death. Coleman, standing over a crude red wooden coffin, turned to me with a look of overwhelming sadness. A man who had witnessed much death and destruction, Pops Coleman was clearly moved and a little overwhelmed at what had taken place. I glanced down at the box at his feet, filled with violently rent body parts. In a few seconds I had taken in the details of the tragedy: on top, next to a severed foot, was the scalp and partial cranium of a young Vietnamese woman, her long tresses shrouding what remained of her and her family. Averting my eyes, I walked past Coleman and the coffin, crossing the room to speak with the medical examiner. Small, dapper Dr. Bill Buck told me simply that the victims' remains all reflected the effects of modern high-explosive ordnance on the human body. Little else could or needed to be said. Vietnamese family members waited nearby to take the bodies back to Tu Cau for burial that afternoon. We let them get on with their sad task.

In the meantime, interviews of witnesses at Tu Cau had begun to develop a story suggesting two Marine squads had been involved in the incident, not just the squad that initiated the attack. Special Agent Coleman recalls that interviews of Vietnamese peasant witnesses conducted via a local interpreter had prompted suspicions because of the uniformity of their recollection of events. Too many people seemed to remember similar, sometimes obscure facts. Coleman closely questioned his Vietnamese interpreter and discovered that their too uniform statements were the product of willingness to both ask and answer questions in a way they assumed would please investigators. Interviews were halted, many witnesses had to be reinterviewed, and all testimony was then subjected to careful scrutiny by agents.

By the time interviews and interrogations were complete, it was apparent that the attacking squad had strayed from the area they were to have patrolled. The "enemy" they had seen and fired on were actually other marines from the patrol who had approached the farm house from the opposite side. The attack lasted only seconds before the error was realized and the action halted. The defendant squad leader was not charged with murder but with a lesser offense and found guilty. He had taken his squad into another squad's area of operation. It was a tragic error.

It was then—and still could be—argued that oversight and error had caused these civilian deaths. There seemed, in the final analysis, to have been more negligence than malice. But the Marine command, sensitized by then-emerging reports of a massacre by U.S. Army troops in the Quang Ngai village called My Lai, wanted no hint whatever that Vietnamese civilian deaths were not being thoroughly and professionally investigated. We had done a good job of investigating a ghastly event that never should have happened.

In May 1969 NISRA Da Nang received information from the First Marine Air Wing that the body of a Marine sergeant had been found in a disused bunker at the air base. The victim had been stabbed.

SRA Don McCoy assigned the case to Special Agent Vern Oakum. An experienced investigator, Oakum was nearing the end of his tour in Vietnam and was well established with marines at the wing. I was assigned to assist him; it was my first homicide investigation.

The body had been removed when we arrived at the scene, a sandbag defensive bunker near a recreational area where the victim had been drinking the night before. The bunker was not in a good state of repair, probably because there was little need of firing points within the perimeter area. In it we found bloodstains and evidence of a struggle. The murder weapon was an issue bayonet.

The scene was carefully processed for forensic evidence, though we assumed that contamination had occurred by those who discovered the body and by military police. Later that morning we drove to First Medical Hospital at Hill 327 to visit Graves Registration, where the deceased's remains were held.

Graves Registration at Hill 327 was behind the hospital. It consisted of several refrigerated vans and a covered work area with examining tables and was manned by marines from Force Logistics Command. As one might expect, the marines were individuals, both in their conduct and appearance. I thought to myself that I really didn't care what anybody at the unit looked like, considering the nature of the job they were called upon to do.

As we walked into the covered, screened area, two black marines dressed in shower thongs and shorts were finishing the processing of a dead aviator officer whose body had remained strapped into a crashed helicopter for several weeks before the site was discovered. The sight of the aviator was neither pretty nor something my olfactory senses care to recall. Finished, the men zipped the dead man into a body bag, dragged it onto a stretcher, and jogged to the refrigerator where bodies were stored prior to transportation to the Da Nang mortuary for processing. "That'll be a closed coffin," the rear stretcher-bearer said. "Whew, that one stinks!"

I said nothing. Oakum spoke to the NCO in charge and told him why we were there. The sergeant pointed to a body bag lying against the wall and said, "That's him." After what I had just seen, I experienced a degree of dread as I pulled down the zipper on the bag, not knowing what to expect. What I saw was a young black man, dressed in camouflage utilities. A cursory examination showed he had been stabbed many times. We hoped that a medical examination would tell more. For now, we took receipt of the clothing after searching it carefully.

Our inquiries then sought to trace the victim's movements before the murder. Oakum determined that he had been drinking with a group of marines the previous night. We moved as quickly as possible to locate and interview these witnesses.

The next day I drove across the Han River to the NSA hospital opposite Marble Mountain Air Facility. There, I attended a postmortem examination of the victim's remains. The hospital mortuary was housed in one of many Quonset huts at the rear of the wards similar to the others except for a sign on the door. I parked my vehicle and entered. A partition with a partly opened door was straight ahead, the stainless steel examination table glaring back under the lights. To my right, a large, whirring walk-in refrigerator took up most of the room. The concrete floors were spotless. The strong odor of disinfectant didn't quite cover the smell of death. Hearing the door, a Navy hospital corpsman wearing a surgical smock came through the partition door. I showed him my credentials and explained why I had come. "Dr. Buck will be doing the PM," he said. Then he opened the reefer door. Inside, on shelves, were the remains of Marine dead removed from the field on medevac flights. "I've got fingerprints to do—but not on this one." The bottom half of a torso lay there, the victim perhaps of a very large booby trap.

I saw the doctor moving around in the examination room, so I went in and greeted him. An intense young doctor, he taught me much in the months ahead, not just about human physiology but about the multitude of ways the body can be made to cease functioning on a permanent basis. We spoke for a few minutes about the investigation and what was then known about the deceased and his movements. Then the doctor's corpsman assistant rolled the deceased in from the refrigerator on a gurney. The body bag was hoisted onto the metal table and unzipped, and the examination was begun.

The victim was a slight, almost delicate African American. He had been stabbed many times in his torso and face. As injuries were noted on a medical chart, the hospital photographer arrived and began making a photographic record. Measurements of the wounds indicated to Dr. Buck that only one weapon had been used in the attack. Very few of the injuries were defensive; this caused me to wonder if perhaps somebody much stronger than the victim had swiftly overpowered him. Most injuries were on the front side of the body. The back of the body was also carefully examined. Dr. Buck checked the anus and then commented that the state of the sphincter suggested the victim had been a practicing homosexual. This was an aspect we had not yet considered. Swabs were taken for possible semen traces.

Once the body was opened and vital organs were examined, it was verified that several of a total of thirty-seven stab wounds would have been fatal.

Having survived my first autopsy, I drove back to the office in Da Nang. The other agents had in the meantime been reconstructing what the victim had done at the club on the night of his death. They had located witnesses who said he had left in the company of another black Marine NCO. Oakum interviewed the man. A big, jovial sergeant, he very candidly said he had been drinking at the club, admitted he knew the victim, and acknowledged they had left the club together. Warned then about his right to remain silent, he told agents he had nothing to hide.

We began to think we had very possibly identified the murderer. He was obviously a street-smart man, but never seemed to make any attempt to hide facts from his interviewers. Asked what he had done after he and the victim walked out of the club together, he said, "I don't know where he went; I went on a leg run to the ville. There's a place we can get through the wire." He was claiming he had left the victim as soon as they exited the club to seek the sexual pleasures of a Vietnamese prostitute in a skivvy house near the perimeter. This was against the regulations, but it was not murder.

There were no other apparent avenues of investigation. Vietnamese witnesses tended to tell interviewers what they thought the interviewer wanted to hear. The finger still pointed to the big black marine with a penchant for through-the-wire forays into the ville.

Before this investigation concluded, Oakum had completed his twelve-month assignment and was bid farewell by envious agents in a boozy send-off back to the United States. I became control agent of the homicide case. SRA Don McCoy and I discussed the options with Marine JAG staff. The question of the NCO's guilt remained unresolved. None of the scientific evidence from either the autopsy or the crime scene examination linked him to the murder. It was time to consider a polygraph examination.

Reinterviewed, the suspect readily volunteered to take a polygraph test. So-called lie detector results are seldom used as evidence in court, but they can be invaluable guides to the direction of an investigation. We needed to know if this man had told us everything he knew about the victim's death.

Tom Brannon, the very man who had opened up NISRA Da Nang in 1965 and acquired our office at 20 Duy Tan, was the Western Pacific polygraph operator, then stationed in Taipei. We sent a request for his services; several days later, Tom was in Da Nang with us.

Brannon was a polygraph natural. Blessed with great memory and the gift of gab, Brannon had skills honed by years of intense interrogation experience. He was welcomed back into the fold after more than a year away from Vietnam.

Our suspect was delivered to the office early one morning. Brannon escorted him to the rear where the air-conditioned interview room was located with its purpose-built polygraph examination chair. He emerged less than an hour later with some startling news: we had the wrong man. "This guy is clean," Tom announced to us.

I had hoped to be able to clear my first homicide, even if I had inherited it from another agent. We had run every logical lead to ground and in Vietnam, where operational staff often changed daily, this didn't auger well for a resolution. On the other hand, we had cleared a heavily implicated but innocent man. He would not endure the rigors of a general court-martial because no charges would be laid against him. We sent him back to the First Marine Air Wing.

The case was never solved. I have often wondered what might have triggered the rage that snuffed out that young marine's life.

# 7

# DA NANG, 1969 TO 1970: MAYHEM, MURDER IN I CORPS

**The summer of 1969 was a busy time at NISRA Da Nang.** In addition to the usual caseload of leads, narcotics, and fraud work, several incidents were of such import that all office resources were directed toward their resolution. One such event was the murder of Australian entertainer Catherine Anne Warnes.

Miss Warnes, who used the stage name Cathy Wayne as a member of the musical group Sweethearts on Parade, had been shot while performing with her troupe at the staff and officers' club at the First Force Reconnaissance Company's base camp, Camp Reasoner. The Australian entertainers had proved very popular at earlier engagements in Vietnam, so a good crowd had assembled in the small, thatched building to see the show. Sydney television personality Warnes was the lead singer. As blond, mini-skirted Miss Warnes, twenty years old, finished singing her last song, she bowed to the crowd. As she straightened, a muffled shot was heard. Grasping her left side, Warnes spun and fell to the floor. A .22-caliber bullet had penetrated her body striking vital organs and her aorta. Death was almost instantaneous. The spent bullet exited the right side of her body and dropped to the floor with not even enough momentum left to puncture her dress.

The entry point of the fatal bullet was quickly located in a fly screen to the left rear of the victim. Seated in a row of chairs immediately in front of Miss Warnes had been the company CO, Maj. Roger Simmons, USMC, and it was conjectured that he had been the target of the attack. A search of the compound for a possible enemy sniper was begun. Company personnel were ordered to remain in their hooches.

SRA Don McCoy received a late evening call for assistance at the 23 Doc Lap billet. It was well after curfew, a time when all personnel were expected to be in a secure, recognized compound within Da Nang City. Marine

MPs manned jeeps festooned with light machine guns. They prowled the streets watching for signs of suspicious persons who might be VC infiltrators or attackers. But NISOV agents made a point of answering calls for help, particularly those from the Marines, at any time. Marines seldom made requests that were not genuine; nor did they take unreasonable risks with agents' safety.

McCoy placed his assistant, Larry Coleman, in charge of the investigation. Tom Stallings, so near to transfer at the end of his tour, volunteered to accompany the agent team that was to drive to Camp Reasoner to conduct the preliminary investigation. They piled into an aging Chevrolet Suburban and began threading their way through roadblocks manned by heavily armed, jumpy Vietnamese soldiers and police out past the air base to the western perimeter of the Da Nang enclave, where First Force Recon made its home. At the late hour, agents carried out hasty interviews aimed at determining the whereabouts of everybody in the compound. All men had been ordered to return to their SEA huts in the minutes following the shooting. After the first round of interviews, the agents crosschecked stories for those that did not fit the pattern of normality or seemed implausible. Coleman and his colleagues had suspicions—but they could do little before daylight came and detailed searches of the scene could be conducted. The camp was buttoned up tight. Agents returned to the billet in town for several hours of badly needed sleep.

The next day an alert marine assigned to search the area found a strange-looking handgun lying in a ditch. Rusted, missing both its grips and magazine, but equipped with a permanent silencer, the weapon was identified as a High Standard pistol of World War II vintage. These weapons were believed, but never verified, to have been manufactured for Office of Strategic Services operations. This was certainly not an issue weapon; in fact, no .22-caliber weapons were on issue to recon marines.

While Coleman's team aggressively pursued every potential angle of the investigation that morning, I was told to attend an autopsy of the victim. They drove back to Camp Reasoner, and I made my way across the river to the NSA hospital and the small windowless Quonset hut that was the morgue. The body of tall, slender Miss Warnes was already on the stainless-steel examining table when I arrived. Postmortem examinations of females were not a normal occurrence. Miss Warnes's status as an international personage also added significance to the event.

The Navy had that morning assigned its chief pathologist to conduct the autopsy. A senior commander, the graying doctor quickly made me at ease with small talk about the discipline of pathology as it applies to post-mortem examination. I soon discerned that he was broadly experienced in forensic medicine, as he spoke of examinations he had carried out on crewmembers of the USS *Pueblo* whom the North Koreans had killed when the Navy spy vessel was captured on the high seas. Their remains had been returned along with the survivors after prolonged negotiations.

We knew the murder weapon was small caliber. The entry wound under her left armpit was minute, almost like a blemish. Opposite, the exit wound was scarcely larger. The doctor aimed to confirm Warnes's cause of death and to look for any other evidence that could assist with the investigation. He carefully removed and minutely examined every organ in the body cavity, taking microscope samples as he went. He asked me if there appeared to be any sexual aspect to the investigation at that point; I said that I did not know of one. The victim, he said, was sexually active, but there was no evidence of any trauma or unexplained body fluid. The tiny bullet had penetrated her aorta and heart. Death was nearly instantaneous.

Several hours later the examination was complete, and Cathy Warnes was returned to the olive drab body bag and wheeled into the adjacent refrigerator. As I walked outside into the fresh air and tropical heat, I found myself pausing to consider what Warnes's family in Sydney was enduring as they received the news of their daughter's senseless murder.

Marine combat engineers, armed with a surveyor's transit, used information supplied by the Navy pathologist to start the search for the point from which the weapon had been fired. Agents followed the trajectory of the bullet that had killed Warnes to a parked jeep in the low rise. A search of the vehicle disclosed a spent cartridge case and a .22-caliber misfired round on the ground next to the rear wheel. Crime scene assessment led by Special Agent Larry Coleman established that the weapon had been fired from a parked jeep, the bullet traveling about thirty-five yards before entering the club fly screen and striking Warnes.

Agents approached the investigation from several angles. They continued checking all persons with whom Warnes had had contact of any type. Band members assisted in lineups of marines, who marched past, uncovering for inspection. The agents also investigated the dynamics within the band to determine if any tensions had existed between members. A major effort continued to determine the whereabouts of all personnel within the confines of Camp Reasoner when the murder occurred. Coleman identified a good potential witness and spirited him away from the camp. The young corporal, a very capable armorer, was found in a bunk at the NIS Da Nang billet, where he disassembled and serviced the entire arsenal of rifles and submachine guns to while away hours between interviews.

Coleman had concerns about the safety of the witness and for good reasons. Camp Reasoner was home to recon marines, the eyes and ears of the force. These men regularly went into the most dangerous, insecure areas of Vietnam, in particular the border region with Laos, where contacts with large North Vietnamese Army units were common. They lived by wits, determination, and an unsurpassed level of physical fitness. Most accepted daily death as part of the job description.

While the agents searched for the suspect, ongoing investigations disclosed that the murder weapon had been stolen from the company operations office the month before. It was determined that two marines had been handling the weapon in their hooch on the night the murder occurred. That night they had been approached by Sgt. James W. Killen, who had asked to borrow the weapon. In later testimony, Killen said he had wanted the weapon to shoot feral dogs in the area, but as he had found none to shoot, he had returned the weapon to the marines' hooch.

When interrogated, the two marines alleged to have supplied the weapon to Killen said the sergeant had returned to their hooch soon after the shooting, while the camp was being searched for an enemy sniper. The two . . . asked Killen why he had "done something like that". . . and Killen had replied, "She was just winged."

As the Marine Corps prepared to try Killen, NIS sent leads to Camp Lejeune, North Carolina, the sergeant's previous duty station. What, the lead sheet asked, could agents find out about the man who had apparently killed a woman unknown to him without any clear motive? The report came as Killen sat awaiting court-martial in the III MAF brig not far from the murder scene. It did not provide legal staff with additional ammunition for the trial—but it contained disturbing, unconfirmed indicators that Killen had somehow been involved in the Camp Lejeune murder of his late wife.

Killen was convicted for murdering Miss Warnes. A motive for the shooting was never developed. He was released from custody in 1971 after a retrial in the United States. His enlistment had expired in 1969, and upon his release, the well-decorated Killen was immediately discharged from the U.S. Marine Corps. He had served two years and nine days in confinement for murder.

Fragmentation grenades were feared and respected by all who used them or had seen their lethal potential. The small M26 frag packed a huge wallop. Its high-explosive charge was wrapped by strands of serrated stainless-steel wire, fragments of which traveled at several thousand feet per second on detonation—providing a kill radius of about fifteen meters. It was an effective weapon when deployed properly by infantry either in defensive or offensive operations.

At Chu Lai, marines from the Seventh Engineer Battalion shared with other organic units the responsibility for guarding the base perimeter defenses. Although later in the war grenades were taken out of circulation in many units, in 1969 they were issued to sentries standing watches at Chu Lai.

Late one evening a sentry completed his watch on the perimeter and began walking across the white sand upon which the base was constructed. As he approached his hooch, he could hear a card game under way among fellow engineer marines. This seemed like an excellent opportunity for a practical joke on the marines, then so absorbed in their poker hands. He turned and went some distance away and, taking a grenade from his pouch, unscrewed the detonator assembly from the body. (The assembly incorporates the fuse, cap, and detonator necessary for initiating the grenade's main explosive charge and might be roughly equal in power to a blasting cap used to initiate commercial dynamite.) Pulling the pin on the assembly and then quickly covering the fuse and detonator with a nearby sandbag to muffle sound and explosive force, he then reassembled the grenade without the vital, already-fired internal detonator. The grenade was inert, but without disassembly, this was not obvious.

Grenade in hand, the marine entered the hooch, pulled the safety pin, and placed the device in the middle of the table. The cardplayers didn't wait for an explanation; they bolted in every direction, including through fly-screen openings. Well-satisfied with the reaction and hysterical with laughter, the perpetrator retrieved the grenade and its parts and walked away.

Some time later, the dummy grenade again reassembled to look and act like a live one, the jokester returned to the poker game and tried his trick for effect a second time. This time the cardplayers didn't charge insanely away from the table, and seconds later there was a shattering explosion. Two marines lay dead and several were seriously injured, among them the sentry with a sense of humor.

At the scene, agents carefully checked the equipment that the perpetrator carried. They discovered a deactivated grenade, the one he had used in the first ruse, in among other live grenades. He had selected the wrong grenade for his second "joke on friends."

The location at which the detonator was fired under a sandbag was soon found, together with other evidence that clearly supported what the few witnesses capable of speaking said. Some of the marines had injuries so severe that they required medical evacuation from Vietnam. Most were flown to the U.S. Naval Hospital at Yokosuka, Japan, for treatment.

A postmortem examination of the deceased at Naval Support Activity Da Nang Hospital confirmed what everybody assumed: they had been killed by tiny particles of stainless steel traveling at supersonic speeds to penetrate vital organs—in this case, the brain and heart.

NISRA Yokosuka agents interrogated the grenadier when his condition had sufficiently improved. His story basically confirmed that he had made a deadly mistake. Manslaughter charges were prepared.

Old hands were occasionally heard to comment, "There are so many ways to die in Vietnam." A true statement; never refuted. Not only were there many ways to die, but many of these fell into nonglorious categories like "stupid" or "stupid accident." Nobody wanted to go home in a body bag after being run over, killed by careless weapon handling, or overdosing on drugs.

The entire city of Da Nang and its outskirts were off-limits to all military personnel. Driving through the city required authority, and stopping was not allowed. These rules made a marine's search for narcotics, contraband, and sexual favors slightly more difficult, but certainly not impossible.

Vietnamese entrepreneurs were well aware of the rules and were skilled at flaunting them if it meant improving business with Americans. Outside Hill 327 and the First Marine Division area, the shantytown called Dogpatch thrived, providing vice-of-choice options for those driving through. At several important intersections arterials from vital tactical areas joined others, and knowing these locations would bring plenty of traffic from the field, Vietnamese hustlers and prostitutes targeted them also.

On the southwest edge of Da Nang, one such intersection was the exclusive domain of a ten-year-old pimp and general trader known to all as Charlie. Wiry, wily, streetwise Charlie spoke fair English and knew how to bargain with his American clients, whatever their requirements. His girls, certainly not known for their beauty, had been imported from paddy fields far away. None could speak English. Charlie attired his stable in black peasant pajamas, cotton blouses, and the Vietnamese peasant conical straw hat. Lipstick, rouge, and eyeliner were liberally applied, covering a multitude of defects.

Into this domain, a marine and his SeaBee buddy entered late one afternoon, after enjoying several hours of drinking at an enlisted men's club. They wanted a woman. Charlie quickly concluded arrangements for them to share one of the girls. Taking their money, he showed them to a small thatched hut away from the road, where the woman was waiting. They entered the hut, and Charlie pulled a dirty curtain across the doorway. Facilities were basic. The bed was actually a pile of discarded shipping pallets that served to elevate a sleeping mat from a muddy dirt floor. Having received instructions from Charlie in Vietnamese, the prostitute shed her trousers and hopped up on her "bed." This initiated a lively discussion between the marine and the SeaBee about who was going first. To emphasize his point, the marine unholstered his .45-caliber pistol and waved it at his buddy. It fired, striking him several inches below the armpit. His last words were, "You shot me, you bastard."

The U.S. model 1911 pistol had been in service many years. The chunky .45-caliber bullet was renowned for knockdown lethality. In this instance, the projectile struck lobes of both the victim's lungs and ruptured his aorta before bouncing off ribs and lodging under a scapula. Death was nearly instantaneous.

His ardor cooled by the incident, the shooter was soon in military police custody. NIS followed up with a thorough investigation. The accused claimed the shooting was accidental. Senseless might also have been a suitable adjective. An agent was heard to say, "Who's going to try to explain this one to the victim's mother?"

NISRA Da Nang investigations did not always illustrate our investigative talents in the best light. Such was the case of the mysterious obscene phone calls that were made to nurses' quarters at the NSA hospital.

It would not be entirely correct to say that Da Nang's Navy nurses lived in a cloistered environment, but it was certainly cosseted. Like just about everybody else in-country, the nurses worked long shifts, and they worked virtually every day. A nurse commander was in charge, and all were housed together in a secure area within the NSA Hospital. They were surrounded—not just in the hospital but in the geographic region—by men desperate for even a look at a real Western woman, even if she were an officer. Marine officers stationed across the road at Marble Mountain Air Facility paid careful attention to nurses whenever an opportunity presented itself. Navy nurses did not want for attention.

When nurses started receiving obscene late-evening anonymous phone calls at their quarters, their commander took the complaint directly to SRA Don McCoy. I inherited the case and was, frankly, not particularly enchanted with the prospect of possibly spending days identifying the perpetrator, given the seriousness of the rest of the NISRA Da Nang caseload.

Special Agent Mike Quinn, a lieutenant junior grade who had been agent-trained, was assigned to assist me. We began our inquiries at the nurses' quarters, where it was confirmed that nurses were getting calls featuring heavy breathing and suggestive comments.

From there, we visited the Navy's telephone exchange on Tien Sa Peninsula and spoke with the duty chief about our problem. He told us that, because the calls were being made at night, the exchange could monitor the nurses' quarters phone line. He was confident the calls were originating within the area serviced by the exchange; otherwise, he told us, an operator would be involved in connecting the calls. He agreed to call us with reports about activity on the line.

Two days later he called our office, and Mike and I drove across the river to see him. "What have you got for us, Chief?" I asked as we walked into the exchange. The chief had both hands buried in a mass of colored wires in one of the rows of exchange links. He turned, grinned, and said, "There are some real popular ladies in those nurses' quarters." "I can just imagine," I replied. "You got a heavy breather too?" The chief acknowledged such a call had been placed the night previously; he had traced the call to a barracks telephone at First Light Antiaircraft Missle (LAAM) Battalion on Monkey Mountain. This was a marine antiaircraft missile battalion positioned on the mountaintop from which they could best defend Da Nang from an enemy airborne attack. The LAAM marines had been there on standby since 1965. I could readily imagine idle minds were finding ways to create mischief.

It was time to tell the battalion battery commander he had a problem. Quinn and I returned to our quarters at 23 Doc Lap Street and there changed into camouflage utilities. Quinn put on the silver bars of a lieutenant junior grade, and I borrowed brown ensign insignia. We reasoned that we would attract far less attention at the marine outpost if we wore utilities rather than civvies.

Monkey Mountain is a conical mass situated at the northern end of the sandy Tien Sa Peninsula, a natural position both for navigation aids and antiaircraft defenses. A narrow, winding road had been built to its crest, and the drive up the road was spectacular. Below in Da Nang Harbor perhaps a dozen ships rode at anchor. Beyond, behind the beach, the air base swarmed with all types of aircraft: helicopters, cargo aircraft, and bomb-laden fighters blazing off on their missions. Behind the sprawling town rose the Annamite Mountains and Hai Van Pass's northern blockade. Where the road finally leveled out at the top, the tail plane of a crashed Navy A4 protruded from the hillside immediately below. Stenciled across the bent fuselage were the letters, FUBAR. Quinn told me that in Navy parlance this meant "fucked up beyond all repair." I had to agree.

First LAAM had very well-established positions on the mountain crest, extending down the southern side. Barracks, messing facilities, and offices were comfortable by Marine standards and the defensive positions were carefully maintained with fresh sandbags. The barracks in which the offending telephone was located was a two-story timber-frame structure built on the very steep hillside below the administration area. A timber ladderway connected the barracks and the administration building. We reasoned that our only possible hope for apprehending the culprits was staking the barracks out and having the telephone exchange communicate with us when the barracks phone was used to call the nurse's quarters.

The command was anxious to assist. They suggested we use a small office near the head of stairs leading down to the barracks area. This would provide us with a place in which to conceal ourselves; it had an operating telephone and was reasonably near to the barracks phone. It looked fine to us. We said we'd plan to come back the next night.

The following night we were back, concealed in the office and confident we had gained entry unseen. Everything seemed normal. It was one of those spectacularly clear nights that offered unobstructed views of the entire Da Nang area below, even the paddy fields to the city south, where we could see a continuous display of pyrotechnics. At least twelve illumination flares were in the air at any time. The jet engine afterburners of aircraft taking off on bombing missions carved blazing arcs from the air base across harbor waters. And we could see artillery missions being fired outward into Indian country. Somewhere out there, marines were skirmishing with the enemy.

On Monkey Mountain, life was far more peaceful. But relative peace notwithstanding, the marines lodged there, being marines, were not of a pacific nature. Unfortunately for us, First LAAM decided to have a stand-to, a base defense exercise, on the night of our operation. Quinn and I heard orders being shouted and the heavy tread of men in boots running on the double. We crouched low in the office to avoid being seen should illumination give away our presence in the office. Then somebody threw a CS grenade—CS is an improved form of teargas—outside the office, and the air conditioner began sucking in the gaseous fumes before we were able to shut it off. It became difficult to find untainted air to breathe; we were both very uncomfortable.

Some time later the office phone rang. The telephone exchange announced that our quarry was at that moment doing heavy-breathing exercises for one of the nurses at the hospital. Quinn and I dropped the receiver and ran as quickly as we could out the door and down the long ladderway to the barracks.

Ours was not a covert approach. We were both wheezing from the effects of CS gas, and the timber stair treads drummed out each of our footfalls down the stairs. When we burst into the barracks, the pole-mounted phone was not in use. Marines in the squad bay feigned sleep or acted as if nothing had happened. Assisted by a senior NCO, we noted who was present. But, short of coming back again and subjecting each man to interrogation, we knew we had blown our chance to catch the caller in the act.

I briefed command about the events of the evening. "I think we might be able to manage this," I was told. Seeing the glint in the top sergeant's eyes as he heard his CO speak, I was perfectly confident the problem would be solved very quickly and effectively, and it was. The nurses never got another obscene phone call, or at least none they wished to complain about. Neither Mike Quinn nor I was particularly impressed with how the case was resolved but we managed to rationalize: we decided we had achieved a reasonable result even though disaster had never seemed far away.

A short ferry ride across the Han from the White Elephant, III Marine Amphibious Force headquarters was housed in a picturesque former French

Army compound, a pleasant spot when compared to other areas under U.S. military control. There were trees and even some lawn, undoubtedly a legacy of the Gallic generals who made it their home in the 1950s.

III MAF was home to the senior Marine general in Vietnam, normally a lieutenant general. Names like Lew Walt and Herman Nickerson are synonymous with the command, which included two operational divisions and logistic support. Control of the First Marine Division, defending Da Nang and points south—and 3 Mar Div along the DMZ—emanated from here. A site of many high-level briefings and conferences, III MAF had an important intelligence component that provided information of a most sensitive nature to commanders making high-level decisions about the conduct of the war. Some of that information originated from radio intercepts and other electronic warfare initiatives; these have always been the most closely guarded secrets.

The guardian of communication intelligence for the Department of the Navy is the Naval Security Group. A close-knit body of highly proficient cryptographers and analysts, the NSG has a proud history that began in the early days of World War II, when a Pearl Harbor office headed by Cdr. Joseph Rochefort broke Japanese naval codes. This success enabled Admirals Chester Nimitz and Raymond Spruance to formulate the audacious operation plan that resulted in a defeat for the Imperial Japanese Navy at the Battle of Midway, a defeat from which it never recovered.

Much of the role of NSG in Vietnam remains classified, but we may assume it was important. Nor can much be said about its presence at III MAF, but it certainly was represented.

In early 1970 a senior Marine Corps NCO working with the Army Security Agency (ASA) facility at Phu Bai boarded a twin-rotor Marine CH46 helicopter for the hop south to Da Nang. In violation of security regulations governing such things, he carried extremely sensitive top-secret documents intended for III MAF. Neither the master sergeant nor his documents made it to Da Nang.

The ASA station at Phu Bai, just south of the old imperial city of Hue, was a highly secure facility that carried out a range of electronic intelligence activities. Massive radio towers and high fences marked the station, but little was known about what occurred within. Their documents and personnel unaccounted for, some very concerned marines launched a search for the missing aircraft when it became overdue.

Central coastal Vietnam is largely sandy, flat country. Farther inland, the Annamite Cordillera rises suddenly from the flats and paddy fields to form a formidable mountain barrier. Often shrouded in cloud and mist, the mountains become a serious hazard to the unwary aviator, and for this reason, normal flight paths from the Marine Air Group at Phu Bai stayed on a course close to the coastline and at an elevation sufficient to avoid ground fire. The only danger point between Phu Bai and Da Nang is Hai Van Pass, north of the city but within view of the airport. Here the Annamites crowd eastward to the ocean, creating a natural barrier. In these mountains, the marines began their search.

III MAF alerted First Marine Division operational staff to the possibility that the missing helicopter might have come to grief in the Hai Van area. As it happened, a rifle platoon was patrolling the pass area. Hai Van has been a favorite site for ambushes for several centuries; it was prudent practice to aggressively patrol the ridges above the road to keep the enemy off-balance if possible. Alert marine infantry were first to discover the crash site, as darkness, mist, and rain halted aircraft-borne rescuers. The grunts reported no survivors, as the chopper appeared to have impacted head on at full speed with the steep slope.

Potentially serious security implications surrounded the disposition of the top-secret documents aboard the crashed aircraft. Most important were the questions: Had the contents been compromised? Who had actually seen what they were? NISRA Da Nang SRA Don McCoy was cleared to read documents of this special classification on a need-to-know basis. Because this was clearly a NIS investigation, McCoy elected to undertake it personally, with my assistance. McCoy and I rendezvoused to meet a CH46 piloted by the squadron CO, who was overseeing efforts to recover bodies and investigate the crash of his aircraft. Loaded aboard with their gear was a team of marines from First Marine Air Wing with expertise in aircraft crash recovery operations.

The takeoff from Da Nang was routine. It had been raining, but the ceiling was reasonable on the low areas, and the chopper made its way around the seaward side of Hai Van to the northern slopes where a distinct, heavy cloud ceiling surrounded the slopes in their upper elevations. The recovery crew was a cheerful group lead by a sergeant named Brown who was in-country on his second tour—having made his first as a grunt with a rifle platoon. Brown was equipped to make the first descent into the site when it was located. Bedecked in goggles and combat webbing and carrying a PRC25 radio on his back and an M79 grenade launcher in one hand, he smoked with his free hand and joked with his crew.

Don McCoy did not like to fly. He stoically endured the first minutes of the flight, strapped into his spartan sling seat and chain smoking while considering how the day might unfold. The pilot was in the meantime following a bearing up the mountain slope, staying just feet below the cloud ceiling as it very slowly receded upward. For long minutes the bird hovered motionless over the jungle below, clouds unexpectedly cleared revealing the crash site ahead. Pilots eased the chopper upward, hovering over the marines and wreckage below.

Wash from the huge double rotors spinning overhead blew leaves, branches, and helmets from the men crouching in jungle below, revealing the compacted wreck, which had accordioned into a mass less than a quarter of its original length. What identified the wreckage was the distinctive rear ramp and wheels, now facing skyward. Expecting the rescue crew to assist them, marines below cleared material from atop a huge boulder immediately below the crash, a logical landing point for men descending from above. Others formed an outward perimeter in the certain knowledge that all the activity would have alerted every enemy soldier on the mountain as to their whereabouts. The platoon commander then reported by radio that all bodies had been located with the exception of the two pilots and that several had been removed. Importantly, the master sergeant and his valuable briefcase were there.

The Boeing Vertol CH46 Sea Knight is equipped with an amidships floor hatch, called the hellhole by marines, which enables men and material to be winched in and out via a ceiling-mounted apparatus. Sergeant Brown scrambled onto the waiting jungle penetrator—a metal pod with folding legs to form a seat—and through the hole for the ride downward, the crew chief urging him to hurry because of worsening weather. Brown dropped through the hole, swinging in the wash and trying to target the large boulder as a landing spot. Marines grabbed him off the penetrator. The crew chief reeled cable back into his winch as fast as he could and then sent a second marine down.

The weather was worsening. With the penetrator back aboard, the pilots had to withdraw down the slope to stay under clouds. Don McCoy and I had a quick conference about possible courses of action. I said I would go next, recover the documents, and carry out the necessary interviews; McCoy reluctantly agreed. It was unlikely we would both get to the ground and far more unlikely that a ride off the mountain would be forthcoming. That agreed, we talked about developments on the ground: it appeared that the lieutenant platoon commander had seen the secret documents to confirm their existence, but that others had not. Platoon commanders do not often have top-secret clearances, and this one was no exception. Don McCoy smiled upon hearing this, saying, "The lieutenant is a lucky boy. He's just spent his last night in the bush, and I'd guess will soon be winging his way far to the rear where they can keep a close eye on him."

Twenty harrowing minutes passed without the cloud ceiling retreating. I sat with my gear zipped and buckled waiting to make a hurried descent. But it didn't happen. Getting low on fuel, the aircraft returned to Da Nang. By the time it returned, refueled, worsening weather dictated against a second attempt. On the slopes of Hai Van Pass, a cheerful young marine lieutenant was packing his gear for a walk out and pick-up, with thoughts of hot chow, a clean rack, and cold beer on his mind. The investigation would have to be carried out from a different perspective.

Battered but intact, the papers that had sparked so much angst and concern were returned to the crypto facility at III MAF amid sighs of relief. There was no indication they had been compromised or even seen during the short period they were out of Marine control, albeit uncleared Marine control. The young marine lieutenant platoon commander was soon after abruptly transferred to Okinawa, out of harm's way. McCoy and I finished up the investigation in Vietnam with an uneventful trip to the ASA station in Phu Bai to verify outstanding leads, and the case was closed.

# 8

# THE NORTH, 1969 TO 1970: STREET WITHOUT JOY

**When an international conference at Geneva** divided Vietnam along the eighteenth parallel in 1954, what was formerly central Vietnam became the far north of the new Republic of Vietnam and a DMZ became the republic's northern boundary. At the Ben Hai River Bridge where Route 1 and the railway to Hanoi crossed, communist northerners of the Democratic Republic of Vietnam faced off with their Southern brothers and awaited elections they were certain would amalgamate the entire country as a communist state. The elections never came; the South Vietnamese and their Western supporters believed the communists would use intimidation and non-democratic tactics reminiscent of the days following World War II, when the Soviet Union swallowed up Eastern Europe.

Until the DMZ was created, the country from which it was formed had been of little account to anyone but the peasants who lived on the lowlands and tribal Montagnards inhabiting the high country. The South China Sea swept onto miles of white sandy beach on both sides of the boundary, providing a source of livelihood for scattered villages of fishermen. Agriculture was difficult in most areas of the flat, sandy, and largely infertile plain that extended westward from the sea. In the hills and mountains of the Annamite Cordelera, hill tribes practiced slash-and-burn agriculture and kept largely to themselves. Vietnamese had never been popular with Montagnards.

The creation of a new border did nothing to change the fact that the country south of the DMZ from Quang Tri to Hue had been hardcore communist since the early 1950s, when French soldiers christened Route 1 on the stretch Street Without Joy. Black pajama–clad main force troops had sprung a series of highly successful ambushes from fortified villages along the route, imposing heavy casualties on French convoys.

The 1965 buildup of communist forces, which had so alarmed U.S. officials in the South, consisted of ever-increasing numbers of NVA regulars who had marched from their northern homeland down the Ho Chi Minh Trail. Communist leaders were confident enough to formulate a strategy that called for NVA units to draw U.S. troops into conventional battle and there inflict maximum casualties. The U.S. Army in the autumn of that year faced an overwhelming communist force at Ia Drang in the Central Highlands and beat them back into nearby Laos after fierce fighting.

The commander of MACV, Gen. William Westmoreland, was watching developments in the north, believing Hue to be an irresistible target for communist planners desiring control of the old imperial city that to many symbolized Vietnamese unity. Tentacles of the Ho Chi Minh Trail extended into remote valleys in the area, allowing for large-unit buildup. In early 1966 the Special Forces camp in the Ashau Valley, inland from Hue, was overrun by an enemy of at least a reinforced regiment. Surviving Montagnard irregulars and the Special Forces officers fought running, rear-guard actions until Marine helicopters based near Hue at Phu Bai rescued the fortunate ones. This was unsubtle evidence that corroborated ongoing intelligence collection in the region. The buildup of Marine forces, centered on their positions at Hue/Phu Bai, began shortly thereafter.

Although northern I Corps was assigned important U.S. Army combat elements—and was home to some of the better ARVN commands—the DMZ and points south were to be Marine territory until the end of 1969. In that three-year period, marines carried out almost continuous major operations against the NVA along the DMZ, established firebases in critical areas, fought the NVA and VC at Hue, and drove them from the city during the 1968 Tet Offensive—and fought a very successful campaign in the west, which culminated in the Siege of Khe Sanh. Third Marine Division headquarters ultimately moved from Phu Bai north to Dong Ha, within enemy artillery range, and remained there.

In difficult, fluid conditions, NIS had a continuing responsibility to the Navy Department as well as all Marine commands needing investigative support. Until 1969 contact with northern commands and their marines was accomplished by agents doing circuits of key installations. Investigative and other lead requests forwarded by NIS components elsewhere in the world and from other federal agencies found their way to the senior resident agent's desk in Da Nang, where they were farmed out to traveling agents for action. Typically an agent assigned a case would visit the Marine field elements to brief the command and then carry out investigations to satisfy, if possible, the requests contained in the lead.

Leads constituted a majority of the caseload handled by agents traveling in the far north, but requests for investigative assistance in very serious incidents also required response and often long complex investigations that started from scratch.

The process of getting to an active combat component could be very challenging. The agents who did this work were all volunteers; some agents would not work in the difficult field environment outside the Da Nang command headquarters, and others were not suited for the work. Perhaps the most important element a bush agent had to have was a comprehensive knowledge of what command elements were located where, what transportation would likely be available, and where to find that transportation.

The Marine Corps had its own fleet of C130 transports; these, supplemented by Air Force aircraft, operated from Da Nang to airports at Phu Bai and Dong Ha. So, air transport was an option, weather and the enemy situation permitting. Marine Roughrider armed convoys left Da Nang regularly for the difficult, often-dangerous trip over ambush-vulnerable Hai Van Pass to Phu Bai. Navy and Coast Guard patrol and logistic craft plied the waters of the north, and there were less-predictable helicopter flights from Da Nang for those who knew the ropes. The good operators planned their work around rides they knew they could find and shoved off. Typically, nobody heard from them again until they turned up perhaps a week later, tired and needing a ride to the billet from an airport or helipad somewhere near Da Nang. In their gear was a sheaf of lead sheets and reports, most complete, they hoped.

On the ground at forward areas, Marine counterintelligence teams often provided support to agents who turned up needing transportation, hot chow, and a place to sleep. The cordial professional relationship engendered in Vietnam between NIS and counterintelligence teams continues to this day in naval commands around the world.

There were certainly dangers present throughout these trips for the agents concerned. Enemy rocket and mortar attacks were prevalent, and it was not unusual to hear the "crack-thump" of a shot coming nearby while traveling by road in what was never a very secure environment. All of the traveling agents understood and accepted these risks: they were certainly minor when compared with the daily existence of the young Marine riflemen with whom they had daily contact.

An additional danger that worried every agent who ventured out into the ever-fluid tactical world in the Vietnamese countryside was the danger of capture. All special agents carried leather-bound credentials printed at the U.S. Mint, identifying them with a photograph and a unique number. These credentials were necessary for most official contacts and all interviews. For agents on duty in Vietnam, an alternative top leaf was printed without the words "naval intelligence," and their originals were stored in a safe with the issued badge until the tour of duty in Vietnam was complete. None thought it would make much difference if the worst happened, especially if they had a sheaf of cases and leads in their bag and a Vietnamese identity card that identified the holder as an agent of military intelligence. Agents thought carefully about where they took the Vietnamese identification, which was useful when dealing with difficult ARVN soldiers at roadblocks. Fortunately, no member of the NIS command was ever captured. But credentials were lost in forward areas. An incident of this type normally sparked a detailed investigation because presentation of credentials provides legal authority for access to highly classified information (on a need-to-know basis, of course). Allowances were made for the difficult working environment, but nobody at headquarters ever devised a means for quickly disposing of credentials in the field.

In mid-1969 NISOV directed that satellite units (SUs) be established in two areas serviced by the Da Nang field office: to the south, NISSU Chu Lai was set up at the naval facility there and NISSU Quang Tri Combat Base was accommodated by a construction battalion maintenance unit, CBMU 301, directly opposite the Quang Tri Airstrip. Thus, agent roundsmen became redundant in the north. The lone agent assigned to Quang Tri was supplied with a radio-equipped jeep and an office in the plywood SEA-hut headquarters building, which had a telephone that could be patched through a myriad of bored signalman-switchboard operators to major command components.

The establishment of NISSU Quang Tri was a response to a growing caseload and the desire of the command to establish a permanent presence near Third Marine Division so that an agent could be available for serious incident response. The Marines had a CID section that handled misdemeanors and occasionally more serious cases, but NIS rationalized that there was less risk of legally jeopardizing a critical case if a special agent could respond immediately.

A growing caseload was symptomatic of the rot that was fast setting into most U.S. commands in Vietnam and that grew alarmingly until the last troops withdrew in 1972. The incidence of felonies, fraggings in particular, was rising throughout NISRA Da Nang's jurisdiction, and narcotics violations became an increasing burden. For an outfit of some twenty thousand men, the Third Marine Division, whose area of operation included most of northern I Corps, ran a tight ship. They were a fighting outfit, and to a large extent the field marines looked after themselves; certainly, they were not the problem for NIS that they might have been without strong internal leadership.

Quang Tri as an established small city had sprawled along the south bank of the Thach Han River for probably two hundred years. South Vietnamese colors flew over provincial headquarters buildings built many years previously by the French; the city had a railway station (not functioning), markets, and schools—and even a few gardens. It was an important commercial center, which had adapted itself to war footing. A few advisers were stationed in Quang Tri City, but the majority of U.S. contingents were in cantonments on the north of the river, connected by a fine old railway bridge with a French engineer's plaque on it inscribed with the name "Eiffel."

Quang Tri Combat Base was the antithesis of the old city across the river. It had been hastily constructed in 1967 on the territory between the inoperative Saigon-Hanoi railway line and the meandering river. A U.S. Marine Air Group with utility and medium helicopters occupied the revetments of an airstrip, and other Marine units had rear-area administration housed in plywood SEA huts. Opposite the airstrip were two cantonments housing SeaBees: these were CBMU 301 and slightly north, a camp used by rotating SeaBee battalions. Westward were U.S. Army elements, including a medical evacuation hospital adjacent the SeaBees. This supplemented the U.S. Navy's Third Med, a full-sized hospital situated to service Third Marine Division. When further medical help was needed, hospital ships were never far away.

Quang Tri was a large base area, surrounded by wire and defensive works to protect its inhabitants from an active enemy. Roads were oiled to keep down dust, but it was hot and dusty all the times it was not either raining or bracing for the next typhoon. Over it all hung a pall of burnt fuel from the numerous vehicles—and of course the unforgettable odor of burning waste from latrines. "Shitters" were a feature of life in remote military cantonments; waste was collected in drums, doused in diesel fuel, and burned each day. No one who ever served in Vietnam will ever forget the stench. "Not a garden-spot" was an apt description, but conditions at Quang Tri were still much better than those endured by field marines living on firebases or in the bush.

Special Agent John Schlictman opened NISSU Quang Tri in 1969. An experienced agent who had volunteered for Vietnam duty from NISRA Jacksonville, Florida, he was a World War II veteran with twenty years of service in the U.S. Army CIC, from which he had retired as a warrant officer polygraph operator. He was a logical choice for SRA Don McCoy to send north.

Standing six feet six inches tall, Schlictman stood out in a crowd. He was well liked by his SeaBee hosts at the battalion wardroom where the commanding officer gathered his officers at the dining table. The wardroom was an oasis of sanity at Quang Tri Combat Base. Constructed of windowless eight-inch reinforced concrete walls, the air-conditioned building was impervious to all but direct hits, and it boasted the only flushing toilet in northern I Corps, table linen, and service by Navy stewards. Schlictman quickly learned the ropes, unit deployments, and other useful information.

Special Agent L. A. Gonzales, a former Marine infantry captain, and I frequently assisted Schlictman. He organized a small office in CBMU 301's headquarters SEA hut, containing two desks, a small filing cabinet, a wall locker, and a fan. An old Vietnamese woman agreed to come daily on her rounds of headquarters to sweep accumulated sand off the plywood deck. Agents bunked in a SEA hut at the end of the CBMU street with two SeaBee officers. By local standards, it was very comfortable, with an internal shower, urinal and sink, and a private two-holer nearby. Because the SeaBees operated a large asphalt-production plant in the base, they had an ample supply of the empty fifty-five-gallon tar drums that could be filled with sand and stood on end around the hut walls for shrapnel protection. A telephone-equipped bunker for protection during rocket and mortar attacks stood a few feet away from the front door.

Most of the caseload was lead requests—other NIS offices asking that persons or specific information be gathered. Schlictman quickly learned his way around the headquarters elements at Quang Tri and at Dong Ha, ten miles to the north. Dong Ha Combat Base housed Third Marine Division and SeaBee brigade headquarters. Other than several forward firebases in very hostile country, Dong Ha was the last stop before the DMZ and was within range of the NVA's hidden 130mm Soviet field guns to the north. Working cases had become less time consuming because NISSU Quang Tri had its own new M151 jeep. For the first time, agents had the flexibility of a radio-equipped vehicle, which was serviced weekly by CBMU 301's mechanics.

The drive from Quang Tri north to Dong Ha took only a few minutes, but it entailed a stop at the MP checkpoint on the perimeter edge, where travel documents were checked and a quick inspection made to ensure that flak jackets (body armor) were being worn and suitable firearms were being carried. A radio check with either MPs or the SeaBee command post would have ensured communications were available if the worst happened out on the Street Without Joy. A narrow two lanes, Route 1 had been widened and improved by successive deployments of road building SeaBees, who worked twelve-hour days, seven days a week, during their eight-month tours of duty. Agents shared the road with tanks, ammunition trucks, and huge tractor-trailers hauling armor—as well as military and civilian Vietnamese driving everything from trucks to bicycles. Accidents were a regular occurrence. When they happened, traffic stopped and drivers began to feel vulnerable.

The small weapons NIS special agents carried in the north varied depending on preference and individual weapons handling abilities. They were issued with Smith and Wesson Model 19 Combat Magnum, .357 magnum caliber, but 9mm Smith and Wessons and short-barreled models were used too; it depended on circumstances. For travel in an open jeep in northern I Corps, 40mm M79 grenade launchers, .45-caliber Thompson submachine guns, and M16s were all carried.

As leads began to take Schlictman, Gonzales, and me farther westward from Dong Ha on Route 9, the jeep took on a load of sandbags over the floorboards. This was a largely cosmetic step, meant to offer a degree of protection from mines. Soon after we started carrying in extra sandbags, a Marine artillery officer at Cam Lo related to agents how an ARVN officer traveling by jeep from Cam Lo toward Con Thien had recently come to grief with a VC command-detonated road mine fabricated from a dud U.S. 750-pound aerial bomb. "All we found was part of his spare tire. But don't worry, if you run over something, that stuff on the floor will make sure you've got sand-blasted assholes." Reassurance.

The Quang Tri agents began driving to and from Cam Lo after receiving vague complaints of alleged "war atrocities." Specifics were not available. Early investigations revealed that certain SeaBees had apparently mutilated enemy dead killed by mines, then had taken photographs while posing with the corpses. The men were part of a small detachment operating a gravel pit for road building on the banks of the Cam Lo River immediately north of Route 9. This area, known as Leatherneck Square by marines, had been the scene of large, vicious battles with the North Vietnamese Army since 1966. It was within easy range of the DMZ and its artillery and had seen many battalion-sized incursions by the NVA. The gravel pit was located at the river, overlooked by sharply rising hills largely denuded of vegetation, and thus it was not an easy place to defend. Bunkers had been erected at key points, where the men took turns manning .50-caliber machine guns and small arms, while others excavated and processed gravel. Leatherneck Square was really indefensible against anything but a small-unit attack. As defense against artillery, the men were all billeted back at Cam Lo in large bunkers many feet underground. Interviews there implicated several men in the alleged mutilation but also revealed that rations and other supplies were being traded away to local Vietnamese for a variety of favors including sexual ones.

This was a matter that the command itself could have handled much better without NIS involvement. Ultimately we surrendered the case to them, as it involved difficult questions about the ethics of looking after homeless children in the fluidity of a war zone, in which nobody was available to feed them, even if their older sisters imparted favors to lonely sailors in return for the necessities of life.

In July 1969, when John Schlictman's tour of duty was nearing its end, SRA Don McCoy assigned me to operate NISSU Quang Tri. In my second year of service with NIS and with fewer than six months in Vietnam, I considered it a daunting prospect to be charged with the responsibility of a one-man post a long way from the advice and support of more experienced agents.

Before leaving Quang Tri, Schlictman had begun an investigative lead that originated at NISSU Hong Kong, a referral from the Royal Hong Kong Police who believed a senior Marine NCO was using Fleet Post Office facilities illegally. The gunnery sergeant's activities might also have had security implications, depending on his level of access to classified material, which was then unknown. Schlictman explained to me that liaison had been established with the division postal officer in Dong Ha. It would be necessary to visit the subject's command and take the investigation forward from there.

I carefully studied existing reports from Schlictman's first solo investigation at NISSU Quang Tri, which was based on criminal intelligence from Royal Hong Kong Police sources. The subject of the investigation had, while in Hong Kong on leave, caused people to believe he was shipping contraband using the facilities of the Fleet Post Office at the China Fleet Club. The sources implied he was using his military postal address in Vietnam to run an illegal commercial enterprise.

In Dong Ha, I interviewed the Marine postal officer. A watch had been kept for parcels addressed to the suspect, who was assigned to the Fourth Marines, then operating out of Vandegrift Combat Base. The postal officer was uncertain, however, as to how effective the watch had been; in fact, a parcel mailed from Hong Kong may have already passed forward in the mail system. It could be necessary to track and intercept the package as it was delivered.

In 1969 Vandegrift was the easternmost base of the Third Marine Division, established near a small crossroads close to Ca Lu; it supported ongoing combat operations against the North Vietnamese Army in rugged mountains near the Laotian border. Situated in a basin surrounded by mountains, it was the location for various battalion headquarters, artillery, and logistics. Only fourteen miles from Khe Sanh, then abandoned, its presence was designed to keep the NVA off-balance in northwest I Corps.

I caught a ride from Dong Ha aboard a Marine CH34D helicopter and flew westward over Route 9, the highway that once led from the South China Sea across Vietnam and Laos to Thailand at the Mekong River. The two Marine first lieutenant pilots, who had flown the route countless times, brightened up an otherwise uneventful trip by buzzing a Marine jeep at a level low enough to make the vehicle's canvas top billow out like a yacht spinnaker and to cause its driver momentary panic. The sergeant crew chief, manning his M60 machine gun at the doorway, smiled and shook his head: crazy pilots. With hapless jeep driver behind, the helicopter quickly gained altitude out of small-arms range, tracking above the road and the mountains that it skirted. To the north, flashes on the horizon indicated that a B52 air strike had impacted. Nearby mountains were pockmarked and scarred by four years of artillery impacts and aerial bombs.

At a lone outcropping crowned by a Marine observation post called the Rockpile, the course of the helo turned south, passing a battery of firing 175mm guns, beyond which was Vandegrift's valley location. Touching down on the eastern side, I jumped off to make way for a happy group of dirt-encrusted marines on their way rearward for leave or rotation home. I then began walking toward the antenna-festooned bunker containing the battalion command post. I was surrounded by a daunting cacophony—all the sounds of war made their assault, as nearby artillery bellowed, tanks and trucks rushed past, and distant helicopters clattered. At Vandegrift the war was very real.

At the subject's battalion CP, I briefed the XO. The subject had not returned but was expected at any time. A record check confirmed he had a low-level security clearance and was not handling sensitive classified material in his assignment at Vandegrift. A command-authorized search form was signed by the XO and the gunnery sergeant in charge of postal service assigned to assist in the search for contraband.

Battalion senior NCOs shared open-sided tents at the base; each man was assigned a cot and footlocker to hold personal effects. The gunnery sergeant, who also occupied the tent, identified the suspect's cot and personal effects, and the search was begun. What I noted immediately were large quantities of letters, all carefully bundled. Of more immediate concern was a large detonation nearby a few moments later, clearly not that of the adjacent 175mm gun battery. The gunnery sergeant, already moving toward one side of the tent, directed me to a buried culvert, which served as shelter from enemy rockets. Crowding in with others, we sat in cramped darkness as a series of NVA 122mm rockets slammed into Vandegrift. Friendly artillery began to fire, and after several minutes all emerged to return to their tasks. Before the search was complete, a further four attacks had been launched by the NVA, killing or wounding several marines. Reflecting on the circumstances that brought me there, I was prompted to think, "I hope this investigation really is important."

The search ultimately produced letters indicating that the subject was using the mail system to transmit and acquire pornographic material at a number of addresses in the Far East and Europe, perhaps as a business venture. He returned to his battalion later the same day but, as was his right under the Uniform Code of Military Justice, declined to discuss allegations against him. The battalion XO was again briefed about the results. Command would consider whether to charge the subject.

It was by then too late to fly out. I spent a sleepless night in the empty chaplain's tent one hundred yards away from the artillery battery, which fired harassment and interdiction missions through the night. Early the next morning I walked across the base to a small hill; Charlie Med, the forward Navy medical detachment, was housed inside the hill itself. There I found a bunker protected by ten feet of overhead earth, doctors and hospital corpsmen wearing shorts and sandals hurrying about their duties. Above, a row of quiet, bandaged walking wounded stood on the helipad at the head of the ladderway awaiting the next helicopter ride to the rear, all ignoring nearby body bags awaiting evacuation. Corpsmen told me an Army medevac Huey was expected within the hour. When it came I crowded on with the wounded, feeling unimportant in the events unfolding on all sides. This was my first trip to the everyday world of the combat marine, the first of many yet to come.

Suicide did occur in the stressful Vietnam environment. It was known that individuals compromised to commit espionage might kill themselves rather than face the stigma of their acts, and because of this historical connection between security compromise and suicide, NIS usually took an interest and investigated fully.

In late 1969 a marine stationed in a communication role at Dong Ha shot himself in the head with his issue M16 rifle. Witnesses said the episode occurred suddenly and without forewarning. The men who shared his hooch could offer no explanation for the death. The victim had regular access to classified material and to cryptographic equipment used for encoding and decoding messages but was not exposed to top-secret information. The officer in charge said the victim had taken his allocated R and R leave earlier in the year, in Australia, and on return had reported no contact with suspicious persons. This was significant because, at the time, a cadre of foreign enemy agents with suspected Soviet ties were befriending U.S. military personnel on leave in Sydney.

The victim's gear was thoroughly searched, and all collected correspondence was read for clues. He had the usual collection of Vietnam photographs taken with fellow marines at a weekend barbecue, letters from his family at home—and a bundle of perfumed envelopes from his fiancée. Therein lay the strongest explanation of the victim's decision to kill himself: the last perfumed letter had arrived the morning of his death aboard a two-and-a-half-ton mail truck emblazoned Dear John Express. It had been. The victim had picked up his rifle and shot himself after learning his relationship had been ended. Precautionary investigative leads were dispatched for confirmation by other NIS field elements in the United States, but nothing was ever developed to indicate the death had been anything other than a reaction to a Dear John letter.

It was a well-established tradition in Vietnam for a Dear John letter recipient to tell those with whom he served of his misfortune; friends would team together and write to the offending female congratulating her on her nomination to a select club of Dear John letter writers, in the hope of making their rejected colleague feel better and helping him cope with his rejection. This victim had told nobody of his plight.

There were no regular days off in the Vietnam routine, especially in northern I Corps. At Quang Tri, days began at 5:00 AM at the SeaBee camp and by 6:30 AM, trucks were rolling out to their work sites along Route 1. For the NIS agent needing to travel any distance from Quang Tri, early morning was the time to begin. Camp Evans, Hue, Phu Bai, and Camp Eagle were all more than an hour away by road. Navy detachments, SeaBee battalions, and marines were deployed in these areas. A request for assistance required a timely response. Because telephone and radio links were insecure, agents usually visited the command concerned in person. Weather was always an unpredictable factor. Vietnam regularly suffers at the hands of autumn typhoons, and 1969 was an especially severe season with road washouts and high winds that injured and killed military and civilian personnel alike. The NISSU Quang Tri office was damaged by flying debris and partially flooded.

During one particularly long-winded storm, I received a nonspecific request that I visit the SeaBee battalion deployed at Camp Evans, near Hue. Naval officers at the wardroom told me that water on the road was more than two feet deep in places near Quang Tri, certainly higher than it was safe to drive through in a jeep. Recently qualified by SeaBees as a heavy-vehicle driver, I asked for the loan of a three-axle, all-wheel-drive five-ton military dump truck. Given the truck's very high ground clearance, it seemed probable that the waters could be navigated. In camouflage utilities covered with a full rain suit, I started driving slowly south in the huge truck, battling driving rains and dodging Vietnamese civilians pushing bicycles and drowned motorcycles, the truck creating a bow wave even at slow speeds. Less than half the distance to Phu Bai, while crossing rice paddy fields, a small stream in full flood brought progress to a complete halt. The road was entirely washed away by the fast-moving waters. Pausing only momentarily to watch the passage of logs and other detritus, I reversed path and was safely back in Quang Tri by sundown.

Another week passed before the SeaBee command could be visited. Cordially welcomed by the battalion XO, I asked what the problem was and was told that a quantity of marijuana had been found in a garbage can on the main street of the cantonment. I had expected something far more serious, but I soon realized from speaking with the engineer officer that narcotics usage was virtually unheard of in the SeaBees. Battalion personnel were skilled tradesmen—builders, mechanics, equipment operators; a high percentage of them were second-class petty officers (E5 NCOs). They expected to work hard every day of their two eight-month deployments from the United States to Vietnam. Although there were recreational club facilities and some were known as "hard players," the executive officer knew of no "dopers" in his battalion and was seeking advice about countering a potential problem in its early stages.

I explained that many varieties of narcotics were available just outside the gate and pointed out that the garbage can might be a drop Vietnamese employed in the compound during the day as cleaners and sanitation workers used. Driving on to Da Nang to hand-carry my completed cases, I heard nothing further from this battalion. Unfortunately, the SeaBees were the exception, not the rule.

To avoid the long, potentially hazardous drive between Quang Tri and Da Nang, I cultivated a friendship with the U.S. Air Force Aerospace Recovery Squadron personnel who flew to Quang Tri every morning and used the airstrip as a dispatch point for extremely hazardous pilot rescue missions. Known in the aviation fraternity as the Jolly Green Giants, these men routinely drove their armored H3 Sikorski helicopters into the maelstrom that usually surrounded downed allied pilots. These missions often took them into North Vietnam and Laos to rescue aviators who might have been injured, who were frequently being pursued and attacked by an enemy intent on capturing American pilots and adding them to those already imprisoned at the old French jail called the Hanoi Hilton. Equipped for aerial refueling, the H3s flew into enemy-controlled areas of northern I Corps, Laos, and North Vietnam, where their highly trained crew were often winched down to paddies, jungle, or the ocean to rescue injured pilots. I held them all in high esteem: one senior NCO crewman once blithely stated that he had transferred to the unit from the Marine Corps because there was more action flying with the Jolly Greens!

Departures from Quang Tri to Da Nang Air Base were normally planned for late afternoon. I had only to grab my case files and walk from my office down the dusty main street and across Route 1 to the helipad. By this time, crewmembers were packing up air mattresses and other gear used to make their standby more tolerable and securing weapons and ammunition. Critical components in the H3s were protected by sheets of armor, making cargo and passenger weight considerations much more important than in a normal version of the helicopter. They expected to receive hits when hovering to rescue, surrounded by aggressive enemy troops.

Each flight was a little different from the previous ones. Pilots enjoyed low-level runs down the Thach Han River as the sun began to set. Occasionally the itinerary home included a swing past the hospital ship USS *Repose*, "to show the Navy nurses our refueling pod." Because rescued pilots were often rushed to the hospital ship, nurses were familiar with pilot antics, even the suggestive extension of the helicopter's refueling gear.

The coastline in the north tends to be mile after mile of unbroken white beach. It was beautiful, but not a wise place for low-level flight at dusk. Once over the waters of the South China Sea, elevation increased and all aboard were usually quiet, watching the dusk creep over the darkening mass of the inland Annamite Cordelera. Few disagreed that Vietnam had "someday" potential as a tourist venue. Rounding the shoulder of mountainous Hai Van Pass, often by then in darkness, the rest of the flight was a straight, descending run across Da Nang Harbor to the air base and, if my luck held out, a waiting ride to the NIS billet.

✧◆✧◆✧

Hue was on the route of any drive between Da Nang and Quang Tri. Route 1 passed the air base at Phu Bai and, about eight miles farther, entered the southern half of the city en route to the Perfume River, which bisects it. On the southern riverbanks, some of the heaviest damage had befallen Hue University, Thua Thien Provincial headquarters, and other buildings along Le Loi Street during the Tet Offensive of 1968. A year later the Vietnamese were fast rebuilding their beautiful city, even though passage across the river was via a pontoon bridge hastily installed to replace the adjacent dynamited span originally erected by French engineers at the turn of the century. On the opposite bank, the imposing mass of the Citadel's scarred walls rose, topped by a huge flag tower from which flew the red and gold colors of the Republic of Vietnam. Beyond was the Forbidden City and centuries of Vietnamese history. Route 1 and the Street Without Joy skirted the outer walls of the moated Citadel before turning due north, paralleling the rail line toward Quang Tri.

Hue was a Vietnamese city in the truest sense. Considered the cultural capital of Vietnam, its religious and educational leaders had steered many critical events in the country's tumultuous history. That tradition continued even during the current conflict. There were allied advisory units in Hue, including a SeaBee detachment, but they maintained a low profile. It was quite unusual to see U.S. military vehicles or personnel away from the main highway, and the remainder of the city was off-limits.

A majestic throwback, Hue was nevertheless surrounded by the reality of the war. The Perfume River formed an important arterial for war supplies. Navy and Army personnel manned a boat ramp on the south banks from which a constant stream of landing craft disgorged pallets of artillery shells and rations. Downstream, where the Perfume debouches into the South China Sea, Naval Support Activity Detachment, Thuan An, was situated on a sandy isthmus at the river mouth. A ferry had been established to carry vehicles across to the base. The surrounding countryside showed fresh evidence of conflict; every building and wall was pockmarked by bullet holes or by larger holes from larger-caliber projectiles.

In early 1970 Special Agent Fred Grim and I were dispatched to Thuan An to investigate an apparent homicide. Fred Grim had just transferred to NISRA Da Nang from Adak, Alaska. This was his first trip to the bush and his first exposure to a serious investigation under the unique conditions in Vietnam. Assessing the security situation at the time, I decided it would probably be safest to travel by sea, so we arranged to go aboard a patrol craft traveling northward up the coast from Da Nang. At dawn, the patrol boat skipper, standing to off the shore awaiting high tide, saw a Navy LCU.

We boarded the LCU in the dark for the final run into Thuan An. The boatswain's mate chief who skippered the craft realized Grim was a newbie, a newcomer to Vietnam, and regaled him with stories about floating mines and VC swimmer sappers known to frequent the Perfume River. As the morning light improved, the newbie's next surprise was the black stenciled lettering on the hundreds of boxes under foot in the hold: it was a shipment of 155mm high-explosive artillery ammunition destined for Army firebases inland.

Ashore, we contacted the naval command to begin the investigation. We were told that a Vietnamese female had been shot and killed in the early hours of a previous morning as she and her family were piloting their small boat nearby. Seen by roving Navy sentries in an outboard-powered Boston whaler, the Vietnamese had been taken under fire with the vessel's M60 machine gun. The victim had apparently been killed by a single through-and-through gunshot wound, and no effort had been made to hold the body for medical examination.

Believing the victim had been promptly buried, as was customary, we began inquiring about the availability of Vietnamese police and judicial authorities to assist with the investigation. Then we boarded a boat and went to search for the vessel the victim was alleged to have been shot in. It was found several hundred yards upstream from the naval installation, moored on the banks. Bullet holes consistent with those of an M60 were seen to have penetrated both gunwales. Finally, before any efforts were made to interview the U.S. Navy boat crew, we requested copies of the rules of engagement, which normally govern the conduct of military operations in a war zone. We found that these clearly set out a so-called no-go area for nonmilitary vessels after dark. Further investigation established that the unfortunate victim had been in a forbidden area during the predawn when visibility was very limited. Vietnamese witnesses confirmed that the rule was common knowledge among the fishing people, who knew a breach could have serious consequences. At the end of the day, it was determined that no criminal act had occurred and no further investigation was warranted. It was just another sad consequence of war, and unfortunately, not an uncommon one.

I managed three brief visits to Hue in 1969, always while transiting north or south. There was never much time, certainly not enough to soak up several centuries of history. In each instance, the experience of driving through the gates of the Citadel was much as if entering another time in history. There were uniformed men to be seen, but they were all Vietnamese. And Hue Vietnamese seemed quietly confident and almost insulated from much of what was happening outside the walls. This seemed an incongruity. There was a well-settled community within the Citadel, but not only had they been subjected to abduction and execution by communist forces that had overrun their homes just a year before, but U.S. Marine and ARVN forces had conducted a grim house-to-house assault to remove the enemy. The Hue people had an air of quiet self-assurance. Courtesy and good manners seemed the norm.

I always found the gates to the Citadel and the inner Purple City open and easily accessed. Vietnamese gave directions when required, although few people could be seen anywhere within the former emperor's living areas. On one occasion, an old Vietnamese caretaker removed the chain and lock from ornately carved doors of the emperor's throne room and showed Lt. jg. Mike Quinn and me the lacquered-columned reception area from which the king had presided from a raised dais. Despite damage from scores of stray small-arms projectiles, it retained its grandeur, embellished with ornate gold-leaf inscriptions overwritten on red lacquer.

Outside, grand steps and a bridge across frangipani-fringed reflecting pools led to the Noon gate and its massive central doors, for the exclusive use of the emperor. From the beautiful open pavilions atop the gate, Vietnam's last emperor, Bao Dai, had abdicated in 1945 and begun a life of exile in France. Beyond the pavilion gables fluttered the Vietnamese colors from atop the flag tower built on the ramparts of the outer wall. Called the King's Knight by Vietnamese, the flag standard stood more than one hundred feet above the Perfume River beyond. From it, Viet Cong had defiantly flown the NLF flag for more than three and a half weeks before their violent ejection in 1968. All that seemed far away. Despite reminders of recent violence, the Purple City was then a small cocoon insulated from the mainstream of war.

While working at Quang Tri City, I discovered the remains of a moated inner city, but years of war and neglect had robbed it of whatever claim to grandeur it had ever had. In Quang Tri, it was war as usual.

The onset of the autumn monsoons brought days of drizzle and low clouds, occasionally unpleasantly cool. This was a time of activity for the enemy, who was very aware that the weather the French called *cratchin* did not favor aviators. Air support missions, during which jet pilots used bombs, rockets, and machine guns to help allied units grappling with an enemy attack, were limited by weather. No pilot wanted to fly into a cloud-shrouded mountain, although very many attack pilots were willing to take grave risks to help infantry on the ground. Helicopters didn't fly as quickly as jet jockeys in the fast movers, but nor did they have as many navigation aids—and the mountains were equally unforgiving. For nonaviators, monsoon season was also a time of heightened awareness. Heavy rain was useful cover for enemy sappers trying to penetrate perimeter defenses and wreak havoc inside with thrown explosive charges and small-arms fire. Navy and Marine perimeter guards, who attended to normal duties during the day, were unusually alert; the instances of periodic fire from the bunkers increased.

SeaBees manned and maintained a sector of the Quang Tri Combat Base perimeter that extended along the banks of the Thach Han River and sometimes rose threateningly over the low beds of staked barbed wire and concertina emplaced before it to deter crawling sappers. Claymore mines were carefully pointed outward "toward the enemy" as the embossed inscription on their face instructed. In late 1969 there were no successful breaches of the Quang Tri perimeter but the enemy frequently used monsoon rains as a screen for night rocket attacks on the base. The NVA obviously felt safer with rain about. The counterbattery radar employed by base defenders to locate launches and alert those within was less effective when it rained. The chance that "Charles" would be accurately located and fired upon by artillery was smaller, as was the chance that a helicopter gunship could attack them in dark, rainy conditions.

Thus men who normally enjoyed a weather-tight roof over their heads and a warm bunk within the base endured many sleepless nights. Always fired late, the Soviet 122mm and 140mm rockets would arc indiscriminately to a point within, where they produced a dangerous explosion and shrapnel effect not unlike an artillery round. For the unprotected, a near hit was very likely to be fatal. Smart men therefore leapt from their beds donning body armor as they bolted for the nearest sandbagged bunker.

Special Agent Leo Gonzales and I experienced a number of these nocturnal interruptions, which proved more of an inconvenience than a mortal danger. There were casualties from the attacks, but no near misses for us. We squatted in rainwater in the dank confines of a bunker with the SeaBee officers who shared the hooch and waited for the all clear to come through on the field phone within. Two or three such interruptions in a night were not unusual.

Never one to dismiss the odds of being hurt or killed by a rocket attack, I had an unusual experience that boldly illustrated that the theater of war was a place where death, enemy-caused or accidental, was never very far away. I had met Army doctors billeted nearby during investigations at Graves Registration; they had graciously invited me to accompany them on an overnight trip to the "rear" hospital at Camp Evans. Evans, as I knew well, was really not much different than Quang Tri, save one important advantage: there were Army nurses at the hospital, and they were having a party for the doctors and the medevac (Dustoff) pilots who supported them. An Army Huey on standby at Quang Tri was due for routine service and rotation, and we expected a pleasant afternoon flight of perhaps forty minutes.

Once the four doctors and I loaded up in the Huey at the hospital helipad, it took off, climbing on a course south. Good-natured merriment abounded on the flight: none of us had had time off in some time, the pilots especially. All were thirsty, and looking forward to a good time. With the Annamite ranges rising just westward and the late afternoon sun reflecting off scores of rectangular paddy dykes below, we passengers were enjoying

Political demonstrations in the streets of Saigon in 1963–64.

Saigon Office
late 1964

Mort Tucker    Maynard Anderson    Sam Houston    Bob Kain    Lee Hayden

Agents assigned to the Saigon Naval Intelligence office in 1963.

Special Agent Paul Carr with the C47 destroyed
in a VC attack on Tan Son Nhut Air Base.

Da Nang SRA E. J. Fitzpatrick (left) interviews a Marine officer at a
remote combined action group outpost in Que Son Valley. The marine
was directing defensive repairs following a Viet Cong attack, 1970.

Agents often found themselves sharing aircraft with VC POWs,
or even escorting them.

Agents assigned to NISRA Saigon in 1965–66.

Special Agent Carl Merritt.

SRA Charlie Baldwin with the National Police.

The commander of III MAF, Maj. Gen. Lew Walt, USMC,
visits with Vietnamese children.

The White Elephant, COMNSA headquarters in Da Nang.

Special Agent L. A. Gonzales interviews a SeaBee witness
at a gunpit overlooking the Cam Lo River, 1969.

NISOV        APRIL 1967
Rear Row:    ENS D.L. CARR; LCDR W.H.J. MANTHORPE, JR.; W.H. FRY
Middle Row:  F.F. GIVENS; K.W. NICKEL; J.A. RENWICK; D.A. MCBRIDE; L.H. THANG
Front Row:   Q.V. NGAU; YN2 R.G. KRAUSE; YN1 J.M. SPRINGER; YN2 R.D. LANCING;
             YN1 A. LINGWAY

Special agents assigned to NISOV.

Street fighting in Saigon during the opening hours of the 1968 Tet Offensive. *Department of Defense*

Fire and damage caused to a Navy logistics facility by an ammo dump explosion on Tien Sa Peninsula.

Hooded Vietnamese POWs arrive at the Da Nang Air Base in 1967.
Photo taken by Special Agent Mike Nagle.

Special agents assigned to NISRA Da Nang in 1968.

DEC 1969 USNAVINVSERVO REP DANANG/USNAVINVSERVRA DANANG
FIRST ROW: S/A HUBBARD, YN1 MARTIN, S/A BOURKE, S/A SCHLICTMAN, S/A FOGHT
SECOND ROW: S/A BISCOMB, SN JACOBS, S/A ARNOLD
THIRD ROW: S/A SUNDSTROM, LT ZAPATKA, LT DONALDSON, MISS DIEU, MISS IAI, S/A MOODY,
S/A HEMPHILL
FOURTH ROW: YN2 DENNIS, S/A GONZALES, "PEANUTS", S/A WASHKO

Special agents assigned to NISRA Da Nang in 1969.

An aerial view of defenses erected by marines at Tu Cau Bridge in 1969.

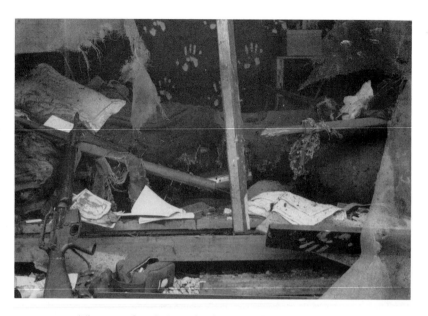

The cot of a victim of a fragging death on Hill 55.

A reenactment of the murder of Catherine Anne Warnes at the Camp Reasoner Club by survivors in Warnes's entourage.

The author with the ceremonial cannon outside the Noonday
Gate in Hue, 1969.

The raid of a
Vietnamese house in
Da Nang, in which a
Marine deserter and
alleged murderer was
believed to be sheltering.
*PH1 Rock, U.S. Navy.*

NISOV    NOVEMBER 1968
FIRST ROW:   YNG D. H. PAGE — YN3 T. E. FISHER — YN1 P. D. HALEY — YN2 R. L. REED
SECOND ROW:   R. E. LOGAN — Q. V. NGAU — T. T. DANH — R. J. TUGWELL — L. H. THANG — T. E. FERGUSON — A. D. NEWMAN
K. R. DOKTOR — N. B. DUY
THIRD ROW:   LT J. W. GAINOR — G. B. JOHNSON — LCDR W. A. ARMBRUSTER — R. G. MORRICE — N. D. NEIMS — J. P. PENDER
J. J. BAKER — LT J. L. LAW — LT L. B. COFFEE
FOURTH ROW:   YN1 C. E. CRISP — J. J. CALDWELL — L. E. FERRELL — D. L. WEBB — YN2 D. S. BODINE — YN2 R. W. PILAND
C. V. PAGE — YN1 W. A. SCHENKER

NISOV personnel in November 1968.

Special agents gathered in room 4 of the Five Oceans BOQ on the occasion
of Supervising Agent Alan Kersenbrock's relief by Richard McKenna.

COMUSMCV Gen. Creighton Abrams congratulates V. Adm. Elmo
Zumwalt at the COMNAVFORV departure ceremony aboard USS *Page
County*. Lt. Norman Idleberg is in a suit and dark glasses in the background.

VNNSB adviser Lt. Ron Lodziewski (center) and Lt. Cdr.
Tom Brooks (second from right) with VNNSB officers.

Room in the Le Lai BEQ after an M26 fragmentation grenade was throw into the far corner.

Lt. Cdr. Tom Brooks and Cdr. Donn Burrows at change of command ceremony.

Special Agent Clayton Spradley at Binh Thuy.

The arrest of an alleged currency violation suspect
at the Freedom Hill R-and-R Center.

NISRA SAIGON MAY 1972
Front row (L to R) Miss THU, S/A WOROCHOCK, Mr. DUY, S/A SEAL, Mr. THANG
Middle row (L to R) S/A HICKS, Mr. NGAU, S/A CAUBLE.
Back row (L to R) YN2 ROSS, YN3 SEDIVY, Lt. SIPE, Lt. KLAMPFER, CDR MOORE,
S/A HUBBARD, LT COUGHLIN, YN1 OTTNEY, YNC MOPPS, YN1 WATSON, S/A GIBLIN.

NISOV personnel in March 1972.

South Vietnamese arrive at Subic Bay, Philippines, after the fall
of Saigon in 1975.

the cool air blowing through the doorless chopper when all forward motion abruptly stopped. The Huey was in a hover for only a second or two when with a huge roar, an F4 Phantom laden with bombs screamed across the flight path. It was banking left, that wing pointed earthward, exposing at very close range the underside, bombs, and napalm tanks. It was so close that oil stains on the belly were clearly visible. Moments later, as all the chopper passengers stared in disbelief, the fighter unloaded its bombs from a low altitude, aiming at an enemy target on nearby ranges, then arced up into the skies above and was gone. With much-sobered passengers, all very aware of the consequences of modern warfare, the chopper continued on the remainder of an uneventful flight to Camp Evans.

After landing, the chopper pilot said he had reacted to a flash of sunlight off the fighter canopy, slowing as much as possible, just before seeing the fighter on its bombing run. He was certain the pilot had not seen the lone Dustoff thumping through the airspace.

Camp Evans was home to important elements of the U.S. Army's 101st Airborne Division. Spread out over low foothills west of Route 1, its metal airstrip was home to a large gaggle of olive drab Hueys and Cobras, all parked in protective sand-filled steel revetments designed as protection from enemy rocket and mortar attack. Helicopters were the workhorses of the 101st Airborne, then operating as paratroopers without parachutes. Helicopters had changed combat tactics irreversibly in Vietnam, allowing infantry to rapidly deploy to remote locations. As we walked from the Dustoff chopper toward the hospital, a group of recon soldiers practiced hot extraction exercises, dangling high in the air from individual ropes fixed to a Huey, life-saving tactics for a small group needing to get out of the jungle in a hurry.

At the hospital, a large maintenance tent erected on hardstand was being readied for the nurse's party. A pair of soldiers began by wheeling a jeep trailer into the tent, then filling it with ice and many cans of beer. A barbecue barrel was fired up, and with dusk fast approaching, the festivities began. Evans was a combat zone. The Navy had no nurses stationed ashore in northern I Corps, but the Army took a different approach. The few nurses wore the same battle dress as their male compatriots, and all showed signs of the fatigue that endless days in a forward hospital created. Amid hamburgers off the barbecue fire, many beers were consumed and a rosy bonhomie developed among partygoers. When the enemy rockets later began cascading onto the adjacent metal strip at Evans, no one rushed for cover. Exhausted, inebriated partiers sat and watched the fireworks nearby and eventually crawled off to find a spot for a few hours of sleep. The return flight to Quang Tri on the following morning was subdued, but without any of the alarming elements of the flight down.

In the midst of the insanity of Quang Tri Combat Base, there was a small oasis of peace and tranquility: a very old Buddhist monastery. When the SeaBees built their two camps on the west side of the airstrip and Route 1, the camps were carefully laid out to provide a buffer of space around the old site. An entry road was all there was to indicate what lay beyond; established trees and shrubs shielded the Vietnamese from the rush and roar of the American war effort on all sides of them.

The walk to the monastery from NISSU Quang Tri was short and an idyllic break. Monks were gracious hosts, seeming to appreciate the genuine interest of their visitors. A lotus pond, behind which stood a canopied statue of Buddha's mother, screened the entrance to the monastery proper. Said to have been build about 1820, the shrine and artifacts within were carefully maintained. Because of its position within the perimeter of the combat base, there could have been few Vietnamese visitors and fewer still Americans. The lotus pond and its ever-present butterflies were a pleasant relief from the press of war.

# 9

# POLITICS AND VIETNAM, 1970: DISSENT AND SABOTAGE

**The late 1960s were turbulent times in America.** It was inevitable that this unrest would spill over to Vietnam when men taken from the politically and socially unsettled United States were inducted or enlisted into the armed forces.

Race riots, beginning in the mid '60s, had set America alight, especially after the Reverend Martin Luther King was assassinated in Memphis in 1968. President Lyndon Johnson had refused the politically unpopular measure of calling up reserves to meet the growing requirement for troops in Southeast Asia. Instead, draft quotas were increased. To achieve quotas, standards for inductees were reduced. Perhaps the most infamous of programs designed to get the numbers, whatever the cost, was Secretary of Defense Robert McNamara's Project 100,000, which targeted uneducated young men who often did not meet the usual standards—frequently the disadvantaged living in America's ghettos. Along with some genuinely good recruits who served with pride and dignity, the Army in particular received a raft of delinquents and ne'er-do-wells.

The Marine Corps was not immune to the effects of McNamara's plan, however. The proud force had built a legacy of honor and tradition based largely on volunteers who wanted to be marines, who were dedicated to the mission. The draft had a definite impact on that tradition.

For a segment of poor American blacks plucked from the ghettos, Marine Corps discipline meted out by an NCO corps of predominately self-made non-blacks was a source of friction. In the later years of the war, some black Marine malcontents made it known that their aim was the disruption and destruction of the corps. Encouraged and sometimes supported by extremists in the United States, they made a mission of proselytizing other blacks, enforcing segregation by coercion and urging violent acts to achieve their aims.

Just as Ku Klux Klan members had earlier been carefully investigated and monitored, extreme black organizations like the Black Panthers were a concern of U.S. agencies. NIS participated in collection programs to assist in this monitoring and discovered that extremists in the United States were encouraging young men to select the Marine Corps for service as a means of acquiring weapons training and other military skills useful in an impending domestic revolution.

Information was gathered about a militant black organization in both the First Marines and Force Logistic Command (FLC), which called itself Maw Maw, presumably after the black insurgent group Mau Mau, active in the overthrow of the white British rule of Kenya in the 1950s. Maw Maw aims were nonspecific except to destroy the war machine at any opportunity and gain revenge for perceived misdeeds against "the brothers." Members wore a small plastic device removed from satchel charges (heavy demolitions explosives). Aggressive information collection allowed command to preempt some destructive Maw Maw activities then in planning. Preemption combined with transfers from Vietnam and administrative discharges served to defuse the worst of the tensions.

A consciousness of racial sensitivities extended clear to the desk of the commandant of marines. Commandant, Gen. Leonard Chapman, USMC, set out guidelines designed both to illustrate recognition of the issues and to instruct Marine Corps leaders that issues of equality and racial differences were to be managed in prescribed ways. Issues such as regulation haircuts, jewelry, diet, and the music in entertainment areas were found to be topics of frequent discussion in malcontented groups.

A future commandant of the U.S. Marines, then-Col. P. X. Kelly, commanded the First Marines during the Maw Maw inquiries. The most senior member of the command, he could well have been the most vilified by rebellious blacks. But he was not: "The man sees only green" was a universal comment by angry malcontents who were not shy about talking of plans for death and destruction in their blacks-only meetings in which "doing some beasts [white Marines]" was not an infrequent topic of discussion.

Their plans were, from time to time, taken from the planning and haranguing stage to actual events. An alleged plan to demolish an entire firebase by placing demolitions in artillery ammunition storage areas was neutralized by the abrupt break-up and transfer of members of groups about which intelligence had been developed. In other instances, radical group activities were learned of only after a terrible, violent act.

In February 1970 there were overt signs of racial tension at Force Logistic Command, Da Nang. Black marines had formed groups exclusive of whites and were holding regular meetings to discuss perceived grievances. When a three-girl Australian group calling themselves the Chiffons was scheduled to play at Andy's Pub, the maintenance battalion enlisted men's club at FLC, on the evening of February 5, several hundred marines crowded into an open patio area adjacent the club where a stage was situated for the performance. The area was fenced and much of it was paved with concrete to hold tables and chairs. As the performance progressed, black marines were warned to leave. When the Chiffons neared the end of their performance, an object was thrown over the fence from outside; a second object, an M26 fragmentation grenade, followed, exploding an instant later. The grenade had landed on sand adjacent to a concrete slab after first bouncing off the seven-foot perimeter fence. The devastating blast hurled hundreds of fragments—particles of wood and metal—into the packed audience. Sixty-two marines were injured (all but ten requiring hospitalization). Cpl. Ronald A. Pate, a decorated marine who had the misfortune to be standing next to the fence, was killed.

After realizing the unit was not under actual enemy attack, Marine authorities, backed by Marine Corps CID, carried out initial inquiries after the incident, only requesting assistance from NISRA Da Nang the following morning. SRA Don McCoy assigned the investigation to Special Agent Fred Grim. Grim left the office alone, drove through the city to a Route 1 crowded with humanity, and headed north in the direction of Hai Van Pass to reach Camp Brooks, at Red Beach. His first stop was the office of CID investigator Sgt. Joe Bean. Bean and his colleagues had developed information through the night that pointed the investigation toward black extremists. They had not yet developed firm leads, but the FLC's black extremist group seemed a good starting point.

As a priority, Grim requested that an immediate inventory of defensive ammunition and grenades be conducted. The agent soon discovered that someone had broken into a CONEX storage container and removed a quantity of M26 fragmentation grenades. Grim called McCoy for help; every available agent in Da Nang was rounded up and dispatched to FLC armed with crime scene equipment and fingerprinting supplies.

In the meantime, Grim had located and interviewed a young Hispanic marine who confirmed he had seen several black marines, whom he identified by name, enter the CONEX and remove grenades. The weapons, he said, were placed in a sandbag and buried nearby. At last, Grim had suspects. Arriving agents began putting pieces in the puzzle to determine whereabouts of suspects and witnesses before and after the incident.

A careful search resulted in the recovery of the stolen grenades, which were where the witness had said they would be found. With the stolen grenades entered into evidence, it became apparent that fingerprints might play a crucial role in the investigation. The grenades would be sent to the FBI laboratory in Washington, D.C., to permit highly qualified specialists to develop any evidence of human handling.

The dispatch of grenades from Vietnam to Washington, D.C., was in itself highly problematic. While FLC officers arranged a courier, Fred Grim approached the Marine explosive ordnance detachment (EOD) for assistance in rendering the explosives safe for the airborne journey to the States. "A gunnery sergeant turned up and said the detonator/firing assemblies could be unscrewed from the top of each grenade. This would make the grenades impossible to fire without a sympathetic detonation. I sat there nervously with the gunny, watching him unscrew firing assemblies from each of twelve grenades, carefully avoiding the round grenade body—which we hoped had finger or palm prints on them.

"That done, I decided we should take his finger and palm prints too, just to facilitate the process of elimination. To my dismay, the gunny's workingman fingers and palms were so hard and horny I was unable to get usable prints from them."

Meanwhile, a group of agents had set up shop in the maintenance battalion chow hall and were fingerprinting and palm printing scores of potential suspects. Assistant SRA Carl Sundstrom remembers, "At one time, we had everybody and his brother out there."

A happy Marine captain whose wife was resident of Washington, D.C., got orders to hand-carry the evidence to the FBI. That meant that to preserve the chain of evidence custody the grenades had to be under his exclusive control at all times. He was almost certain to be asked under oath during a future trial whether there had been any times when the grenades were not with him and thus were potentially available for tampering.

Said Sundstrom, "Although the courier's orders were carefully written and personnel along the way alerted, the air carriers went berserk when this guy turned up with a box of grenades."

To the credit of the young officer, the evidence was duly delivered to the FBI laboratory. Unfortunately, usable prints could not be developed on any of the grenades.

Grim and agent colleagues had meanwhile conducted interviews of key witnesses and potential suspects. In an effort to assemble the facts surrounding the killing—as well as inconsistencies in their telling—several marines were interviewed more than once in the interrogation room at NISRA Da Nang. A definite scenario was developing, but there were no confessions and key witnesses were giving little away. Setting the process back further, the witness who provided incriminating evidence about the grenade theft admitted without prompting to heavy, sustained narcotics abuse, thus diminishing his value as a credible witness.

The investigation had by then established that on the night of Pate's murder, a group of between twenty and thirty black marines assigned to the maintenance battalion had met on the basketball court. This had been a regular meeting place for the group, which used the court as a forum for grievances about issues such as haircut regulations and perceived mistreatment by NCOs and officers. One witness said that on the night of February

5, Lance Cpl. Joseph L. Jones had complained he was being framed after "pep pills" had been found in a surprise search of his gear. Jones allegedly had told the group he intended to kill white marines and advised all present to stay away from the USO show that night.

Jones and three other suspects—Cpl. Ronald E. Gales, Cpl. James B. Addison, and Lance Cpl. Andrew M. Harris Jr.—were arrested under charges of premeditated murder, conspiracy, and assault with intent to commit murder. Trial counsel for Corporal Gales sought immunity for his client for testimony against the other three marines. In a controversial move, command granted Gales immunity from prosecution, and he subsequently furnished a detailed statement in which he admitted breaking into the ammunition storage CONEX with Jones and Addison. He told agents he had accompanied Jones, Harris, and Addison to the enlisted club where Jones had entered the fenced, open entertainment area to warn blacks to leave. Soon after, he said, Harris lobbed a grenade over the fence; the grenade failed to explode because tape had not been removed from the striker lever. Gales then implicated Harris as the thrower of the second grenade, although some evidence indicated that Gales himself might have been responsible.

Harris, on February 5, was within days of transfer to the United States. He was arrested in California two days before his discharge date and returned to Vietnam to stand trial. Gales was sent to the brig in Iwakuni, Japan, for his own safety while awaiting the trial, and several other witnesses were transferred abruptly to Okinawa, out of range of immediate retribution.

The prosecution case was dependent almost entirely on testimony. Filtering through conflicting recollection and outright deception in the investigation was in itself a daunting task. Central to its success was polygraph operator Special Agent Tom Brannon. Patient, methodical Brannon was given carte blanche by his controllers in Washington to conduct interviews, interrogations, and polygraph operations. "This was the first time headquarters had not insisted on a case-by-case authority to conduct polygraph exams; they basically understood that I would need to use the box on short notice, and this was the case," Brannon said.

Brannon interviewed and confirmed the testimony of two witnesses on February 24, working in the tiny, windowless interrogation room at NISRA Da Nang, 20 Duy Tan Street. Both marines ran clean, that is, they were truthful in what they told the examiner. On February 26 Brannon conducted two more witness interviews and polygraph examinations. Significantly, the second witness after several hours of fruitless conversation, opened up— corroborating a number of important elements of the case.

"This guy was a decorated, squared away Marine NCO with a fine combat record. He just wasn't going to dime on other black marines. In the end, an appeal to his honor and loyalty to the corps convinced him to reconsider," Brannon recalls.

Da Nang agents assisted Brannon. Carl Sundstrom remembers long hours interviewing witnesses and reducing their statements to writing. "We worked our fingers to the bone, day and night. The longest statement I ever typed in my entire career was written during this investigation."

Lance Corporal Harris was the first of the trio to stand trial. Gales was called as a prosecution witness, identifying Harris in sworn testimony as the person who threw both grenades. Harris took the stand in his own defense in rebuttal, ably assisted by his counsel who undermined the credibility of Gales based on the witness's previous disciplinary record. The court chose not to convict Harris on the evidence presented, and he was found not guilty on all charges.

Addison's trial came next. Again, Gales was called as a key witness, providing essentially the same testimony as he had presented at Harris's trial. In rebuttal, Addison swore that he had run away from the coaccused at the club when he realized what was about to happen. The court chose to believe Addison in preference to Gales, and he was acquitted.

Twice rebuffed, the Marine Corps decided not to proceed with charges against Jones. He was administratively discharged on the grounds of alleged drug abuse.

A postscript—a bleak reminder of this sad event—came to Tom Brannon more than fifteen years after Jones walked free. A Marine major approached Special Agent Brannon, who was then conducting investigations at Naval Air Station, Lemoore. The major, a member of the JAG Corps, asked Brannon if he was the same agent who had investigated the killing of Corporal Pate. Brannon said that he was. The major thanked him, then explained that he had known and respected combat-decorated Pate and had visited his family in the United States after his own return as an enlisted man. He had attended law school on the GI Bill, his deceased friend never far from his thoughts. A subsequent request under the Freedom of Information Act identified Brannon to him. Tom Brannon recalls, "I was really touched that this guy sought me out to offer his thanks after all those years." The travesty of the trials that followed Pate's death has never faded from Brannon's memory, however.

Fragging incidents seemed to beget more fraggings: they could be very difficult to prove, and in the atmosphere of near-anarchy in some organizations, they spread like a disease.

Pvt. Ronald McDonald, USMC, may well have been a product of Defense Secretary Robert McNamara's social engineering plan to fill vacancies in the armed forces by lowering entry standards. McDonald was assigned to FLC, which had been built at Red Beach, near the site of the original marine landings in 1965. FLC sprawled over acres of white sand, situated back from the beach—the Annamite Mountains and Hai Van Pass towering behind.

Most of the buildings were of the SEA hut design, with smaller versions for living that were known universally as hooches. Dozens of hooches stood in rows, back from sandy streets. Many had sandbags or sand-filled barrels pushed up against the lower walls to act as protection against near-miss rockets or mortar rounds, but the hooches were still vulnerable to ground attack.

When Ronald McDonald decided to retaliate against an imagined affront from a career NCO, fragging was the technique he chose to use. Getting a grenade was problematic at FLC because offensive ordnance was carefully secured and controlled in the wake of previous incidents. He'd decided he was going to frag the gunnery sergeant but didn't know what he was going to use to do it. Finally, when he couldn't find a frag closer to home, he took the search out into the Vietnamese village beyond the FLC perimeter wire. There was very little not for sale in these settlements, which survived in large measure by dubious commerce with base occupants. McDonald went to a shanty built out of pressed beer cans, bought a drink, and asked the Vietnamese woman who sold it to him where he could buy a grenade. Because of language difficulties, she didn't understand him at first; but when she did, she thought the marine was *dinky-dau* (crazy). Still, recognizing a sales opportunity, she sent one of her kids off to search with a burst of Vietnamese invective; soon, McDonald's grenade arrived.

What the woman produced was a fragmentation grenade unlike anything McDonald had ever seen before: a British 36 grenade, known as a Mills Bomb. Bigger than U.S. designs, the British grenade was a cast-iron striated shell designed to break up into large, lethal chunks on detonation. A removable, threaded base plug allowed the weapon to be disassembled and cleaned in the field and was also the access point for installing the fuse/detonator assembly. The grenade contained a substantial explosive charge.

The source of a British grenade can only be conjectured. British forces entered Vietnam after the August 1945 surrender of occupying Japanese forces. Possibly the grenade had been left by them when the French returned to reclaim their Indochina empire. It was old ordnance, had probably been armed for many years—but it worked just as its British designers had intended.

In the cover of darkness, McDonald approached the gunny's hooch, opened the door, and rolled the grenade across the plywood deck toward the sleeping NCO. It detonated with a huge roar, sending chunks of cast iron in all directions. Fortunately, the intended victim made a habit of standing his helmet and flak jacket next to his bunk for easy access in the event of attack. The body armor absorbed shrapnel; both hooch occupants survived.

Special Agent Ed Hemphill of NISRA Da Nang controlled the investigation that was launched soon after the incident. Assistant SRA Carl Sundstrom assisted him in the preliminary stages.

Sundstrom recalls, "I remember the crime scene was a little different than other fraggings. There were fewer shrapnel strikes, and the holes were bigger. I particularly recall a neat round hole about the size of a fifty cent piece, penetrating the center bulkhead in the gunny's SEA hut." Likely, the threaded base plug common to the 36 grenade design had made the hole.

As was typical in these investigations, there was virtually no useful physical evidence to assist in building a case. Agents relied heavily on witness testimony, poring over statements and conflicting statements for clues. Through painstaking work and an excellent nose for clues, Hemphill identified McDonald as the perpetrator. However, he received little if any help from witnesses who, he believed, had knowledge that would confirm McDonald's guilt. Finally, assistance was requested of polygraph operator Tom Brannon, who once again flew into Vietnam from his Taiwan office.

Brannon and Hemphill, assisted by other Da Nang agents, methodically interviewed and reinterviewed witnesses. Then Brannon took over with his polygraph. The accused had little interest in speaking with agents, but witnesses ultimately gave up their knowledge, confirmed by polygraph.

McDonald was court-martialed and found guilty. In an extraordinary move, the court awarded the maximum sentence available under military law: eighty-eight years in a federal penitentiary. Brannon recalls, "They led this guy away in handcuffs, but he was still giving the black power salute."

Brannon and Grim teamed up one last time in June 1970 after a nonfatal fragging at a Marine aviation detachment perched on the crest of Monkey Mountain, overlooking Da Nang Harbor. An officer thought by his less-than-enthusiastic troops to be overzealous was targeted and warned by means of an exploding grenade. Clearly, this was intimidation and could not be tolerated.

SRA Ed Fitzpatrick teamed Grim up with Special Agent Walt Focht. Focht had been a second-class petty officer in the Navy before entering service with the Huntington Beach Police Department, where he achieved the rank of sergeant. He was a tenacious investigator, liked and respected by his peers.

Fitzpatrick, Grim, and Focht, called out late at night, navigated the narrow winding road to the top of Monkey Mountain and began asking questions. Not surprisingly, there was virtually no physical evidence to point them toward those responsible, but they soon identified malcontents who may have had a reason to throw the grenade. Witnesses cooperated up to a point; suspects, warned of their right to remain silent, gave up as little as they could. Grim and Focht were confident they had identified the perpetrator, who, despite a series of interrogations, continued to maintain his innocence.

Again, Brannon's services were requested—and the accused decided to talk to him; he admitted his guilt, which was later confirmed by polygraph on June 23, 1970. The next day the accused reconstructed the fragging for agents and a photographer.

Aviation has been a vital component of the U.S. Marine Corps since the 1920s. Successive commandants have embraced its importance. In Korea especially, Marine aviators earned respect and admiration for air strikes flown in support of the men on the ground, dropping explosives and napalm yards in front of friendly lines with uncanny accuracy. The Marine Corps had evolved the concept of close air support, and they were proud of it. Nobody did it better. Marine pilots deploying to Vietnam were well schooled and ready to carry on the tradition. They did so very successfully.

Unlike those in other services, Marine pilots are multidisciplined, and it was not unusual for a C130 Hercules pilot to later train and reach great proficiency piloting transport or attack helicopters. It was common scuttle-butt among grunts sandwiched in the rear of a C130 in a gut-wrenching banking turn to say, "Skipper's carrier-qualified," and receive a knowing nod in reply. Some Marine pilots flew four-engine cargo aircraft a lot like an F8 Crusader, with élan one might say.

Marines repair, maintain, and crew all their aircraft. This means enlisted men assigned to aviation are often highly trained and motivated. Marine aviation units did not, therefore, seem to receive as many visits from NIS as some others.

In 1971, with Vietnamization in full-swing and allied units being systematically withdrawn, it was common to hear men say, "I don't want to be the last guy killed in Vietnam." Morale was not what it had been. Neither was the quality of enlisted marines filling the lower ranks. Discipline is almost a cult in the Marine Corps, but cracks were beginning to show.

At Marble Mountain Air Facility, home to the Marine helicopter squadrons, two acts of sabotage within days of each other rattled commands and starkly illustrated internal problems. First, a retaining nut on the primary servo of a CH53 was removed. The maintenance NCO who discovered the condition as part of a preflight inspection described it as a completely fool-proof means of ensuring that the aircraft would spin out of control and crash at some point after take-off. Normally the nut was carefully torqued down and wired to prevent loosening. The wire had been removed.

NISRA Da Nang SRA Charles M. Bickley headed the investigation that followed. There was virtually no forensic evidence at the scene. Sentries and flight line personnel could recall no unusual activity. Bickley began inquiries aimed at discovering any clashes, conflicts, or motive for revenge and sent leads to other NIS components requesting interviews with personnel already rotated. Agents doggedly pursued every avenue of inquiry available and tried to develop new ones, but it was an uphill battle. A week later, shortly after the aircraft had been returned to service, it suddenly crashed into water south of Hue. There were no survivors and no witnesses to the crash. Crash site investigations into the cause of the tragedy were inconclusive. The event left a bitter taste in many mouths and more than a few wondering what was happening "to our Marine Corps."

Days later, in a Marble Mountain aircraft shelter, a crude bomb assemblage—using a taped M26 fragmentation grenade, a gasoline-filled coffee can, and a seventeen-pound high-explosive warhead—was discovered adjacent to a metal shipping container, itself packed full of explosives. The bomb was meant to fire when electrical tape wrapped around the striker lever loosened because of exposure to the gasoline in which the grenade was immersed. That explosion would initiate the rocket warhead placed immediately alongside. It was assumed that the seventeen pounds of high explosive would explode the contents of the rocket locker.

Agents arrived at the scene just before a Marine Corps EOD disposal unit. A Marine MP, the first to respond when the device was discovered, met them.

The concrete aircraft shelter was vacant except for the steel ordnance storage box, the explosive device and some stored equipment. The state of the fragmentation grenade was uncertain. A cursory inspection revealed that the tape securing the striker lever appeared to have loosened, causing the lever to extend outward against the edge of the can—but not enough to release the fuse-firing device. Deactivating the explosive clearly would be a job for EOD. Whatever forensic evidence possibly present was of secondary importance.

A salty Marine warrant officer, called "Gunner" in the corps, headed the two-man EOD team. This man, a veteran of at least two wars, took a very direct approach to the problem. Ordering all a safe distance away, he walked alone into the shelter, plunged his hand into the can of gasoline and firmly grasped the grenade, holding the striker lever against the grenade body. Walking out into the open, he was met by his sergeant assistant who forced a piece of wire into holes intended for the safety pin and then took it away. For EOD, it was a fairly routine incident, but it was illustrative of the daily danger in their lives and the professional calm with which they approached it. NIS agents, who had seen ample evidence of what explosives do to humans, were uniformly impressed.

The investigation, however, went nowhere. No worthwhile forensic evidence could be developed, and there were no witnesses other than the marine who made the discovery. Clearly, there were internal problems within the unit but no tangible leads that could identify suspects.

In the hills south of An Hoa and the Arizona territory was a mountaintop fire support base, FSB Ryder. From Ryder, marines had a clear view of the enemy from all sides, but it was the large An Hoa Basin to the north that underscored the base's strategic value. The North Vietnamese Army units moving to the Arizona, Go Noi Island, and favored rocket-launching sites closer to Da Nang passed through Ryder's artillery fan.

The Twelfth Marines and Marine engineers had turned the hilltop firebase into an impressive bastion. The perimeter, heavily wired and mined, was interspersed with strategically sited defensive bunkers with considerable overhead cover in the form of sand bags. Resupply was by regular helicopter lifts.

The cannon-cockers on Ryder were largely a proud bunch who knew they were doing a good job providing artillery support to fellow Marine infantrymen operating in the large valley below. They routinely sniped small enemy groups with their 105 and 155mm howitzers when unwise Northerners attempted to cross the valley. When laser-sighting gear arrived, NCOs claimed they were getting first-round kills on individual targets, without bracketing.

But there were a few troublemakers, chaffing at old-fashioned Marine authority imposed by senior NCOs who were concerned that a narcotics problem was developing. Nobody would sleep well on an isolated mountaintop surrounded by the enemy knowing some of the troops doing the guarding might be affected. Threats were made against NCOs and a frag was attached to the NCO latrine door. The NCO thought to be in greatest danger was moved to the rear and looked after by NIS. Special Agent Carl Skiff traveled to Ryder, where his inquiries implicated several marines in narcotics, predominantly marijuana, usage. As the investigation proceeded, more sinister evidence was uncovered: Malcontents intended to make a reprisal by detonating the central artillery magazines on the small mountaintop, ensuring the complete destruction of the entire installation. Satchel charges and explosives accessories had been assembled for the task and a date had been set.

This planned act, bizarre in the extreme, would certainly have resulted in the death of some or all of the conspirators. Command moved quickly to transfer suspects away from the base, and a disaster was averted.

In this atmosphere of uncertainty and turbulence, commands were exceptionally sensitive to overt expressions of discontent. The Marine Corps was not the only crucible of dissent: when a five-inch naval gun on a Navy destroyer, during underway replenishment by ammunition ship USS *Pyro*, command called NISRA Da Nang for urgent assistance.

USS *Blue*, a Fletcher-class destroyer, had been assigned to fire naval gun-fire support missions from its position off the coast of I Corps. Naval gun-fire was always in demand from units in trouble: renowned for accuracy, Navy ships on the gun line routinely fired their batteries at shore targets all night, following which the magazines would need refilling. The crew got little sleep. At night the batteries banged away with terrific explosions, and when daylight came, it was time to clean, service equipment, and get ready for the next mission—which might come at any time. The crew of a warship employed on the gun line endured both fatigue and stress.

Special Agent Lorne Hamilton was assigned the case. Lorne had an excellent knowledge of ship fire control systems through his own service at sea. He was flown by helicopter to the gun line, where he began inquiries aboard the two ships. He quickly determined facts central to the incident: *Pyro* had come alongside to pass ammunition to *Blue* for magazine replenishment. To access forward magazines, the five-inch turret had been turned to the side, muzzles depressed. The ammunition ship crew had begun rigging lines and other equipment for the operation when one of the guns, pointed directly at the supply ship, suddenly fired. There was no secondary explosion, nor had a projectile penetrated the supply ship. The gun appeared to have fired without a projectile. However, a *Pyro* crewman standing a few feet from the muzzle had been blown over, received burns, and seemed to be shell-shocked from his near-death experience. How, everyone wondered, could it have happened?

Hamilton, known for his methodical approach to investigation, interviewed the key players aboard the destroyer. He learned that a fire control petty officer had been showing a new crewmember the system; the petty officer admitted grasping the pistol grip used for manual firing and pulling the trigger to demonstrate for his new charge. The resulting explosion, he said, had been entirely unexpected; he had no explanation as to why one of the forward guns had come to be loaded.

Interviews of the turret crewmembers who loaded and serviced the gun were not initially productive. Hamilton, now suspicious, dug further, learning that the crewmembers had not always fully secured their gun turrets in anticipation of the next mission. In fact, the gun turrets had not been secured the night before the incident.

Destroyers are long, narrow vessels built for speed, not comfort. They buck and rear in large seas and are known to lean when making the sort of underway turns they're known for. Hamilton knew this. He patiently reconstructed events and then demonstrated that, when the destroyer was heeled over in a hard turn, a round left sitting on a loading tray could slip into the self-closing breach. This scenario was a potential recipe for disaster, but it was not sabotage.

# 10

# SAIGON AND CAM RANH, 1969 TO 1970

**Saigon was the gateway for all agents assigned** to Vietnam. Arrival at Tan Son Nhut Airport and the subsequent introduction to the city were unforgettable experiences for most.

By 1969 a large percentage of passengers to and from Vietnam were being flown in by contract carriers operating passenger jets. Travis Air Force Base, not far from San Francisco, California, remained a favored departure point for these aircraft, which were usually Boeing 707s or DC8s configured to carry as many passengers as possible. Meals were spartan and service not commercial grade, but the stewardesses were considerate of the lot of the young men then heading to their uncertain destinies. Stops at Hickham Air Force Base, Hawaii, and Clark Air Force Base in the Philippines allowed the lucky ones not traveling the full distance to the war zone to disembark.

Normally, sixteen hours or so after the California coast faded away, passengers stared downward at a barren, red coastline when an announcement was made that the aircraft was then coming over Vietnam. Pilots maintained altitude until quite close to Saigon, then began a rather uncivilian steep approach to the strip. Few passengers said anything when the wheels touched the tarmac and a cheerful stewardess welcomed all to Vietnam.

Even men familiar with Far Eastern tropic climes were taken aback when the passenger door opened and the humid mantle that covered Tan Son Nhut wafted in, smothering the last vestiges of Western hygiene. A cocktail of burned jet fuel, excrement, rotting vegetables, and humanity, the smell was unforgettable. Some new arrivals compared the exit from the aircraft to a passage from one world to another. Entering customs hall in the old airport terminal reinforced the impression. Faded Air France posters printed in the '50s announced destinations like Angkor Wat and Paris, while Vietnamese officials scurried around under slowly turning ceiling fans.

Immigration formalities completed, tired new arrivals looking forward to finally finishing their journey next faced the Vietnamese telephone system for the first time. The system was a series of overlapping exchanges operated by Vietnamese women. A caller needed to know what exchange the number was a part of before a connection could be made. Naval Investigative Service Office, Vietnam, was located in the southern, Chinese quarter called Cholon: the Tiger Telephone Exchange serviced Cholon. Callers, once they had been connected to the Tiger Exchange, needed to tell the operator they wanted Tiger 3967. Even a friendly Air Force security policeman might have trouble getting through to the Tiger switchboard, but eventually a voice on the other end told the new guy to sit tight and wait. Somebody was on the way.

Beyond the airport gates, Saigon festered. Grossly overtaxed by the war's refugees and opportunists, few of the city's basic amenities such as water, electricity, or sewerage were fully functional. Those that were could not be considered dependable. An agent's first exposure to Saigon would be the drive from Tan Son Nhut through areas of the Gia Dinh District, hastily thrown up in the false boom of the war. Traffic was chaotic because there were no rules of the road other than "largest has right-of-way." The battered Navy sedan shared the street with pedicab drivers (called cyclo in Vietnam), farmers pushing carts loaded with produce, buses, pretty Vietnamese girls on Honda 50 motorcycles, and military vehicles spewing clouds of diesel fumes. Along street verges and sidewalks, the commercial panoply was everywhere: repairers of tubes and tires were set up beside cigarettes and bread loaf vendors. People were everywhere. Fecal matter stood in the gutters. Every now and then, a bare backside was thrust over the curb to deposit more of the same. It was not, perhaps, such a bad thing that prudence dictated that car windows be rolled up when Westerners drove through the streets. Open windows might attract a grenade, and if not, certainly some well-fed flies.

Cholon, scene of grim street battles and considerable damage during the Tet Offensive the year before, was well mended a year later. Successive generations of Vietnamese had become adroit at plastering bullet and shrapnel chips in masonry walls. Street verges, once broad sidewalks, were cluttered with humanity—but many graceful tamarind trees remained, casting afternoon shadows over narrow storefronts and the dwellings above them. Where no building front faced the street, high walls topped with glass or barbed wire did.

NISOV and the NISRA field office were situated behind such a wall. This one surrounded an entire city block, enclosing the premises of the Army Post Exchange, a military post office, and the Chase Manhattan Bank. The old home that housed NISOV had been built on a corner, behind the seven-foot wall, which in more peaceful times must have provided its owners with a quiet refuge from the city beyond. A permanent sentry in a guard post adjacent the steel entry gate monitored the street, guarded Navy vehicles, and controlled entry. Clutching a well-worn M1 Garand, his smiling face greeted every new arrival, who was by then seriously wondering what the next 365 days would bring.

Inside the gate a covered walkway lead to the front entrance. Large mango trees provided shade. Immediately inside the door was a small waiting area, decorated by a collage of photographs of staff and agents assigned. Clerical staff was immediately beyond, with the CO's office to the immediate left. Here Navy yeoman accepted orders and arranged for onward flights to up-country if required. The XO and the adviser to Vietnamese counterparts were quartered in a former bedroom, along with the supervising agent and the NISRA senior resident agent with his assistant. Agent offices were in former servant quarters immediately at the rear. The agents, arriving hot and dirty at the end of the day, typically welcomed new arrivals and got them settled with a bunk for the night. Late in the afternoon, the migration from the office would begin, preceded by the sound of security containers being slammed shut and combination dials spinning. In small groups, agents would leave the office compound to cross the street, dodging motorcycles and cyclos to reach the opposite corner where semipermanent street vendors were established outside a walled eatery called Fuji's Restaurant. Many believed that Fuji had been a holdover from the Japanese occupation of Indochina, but this was unconfirmed. Some yards north, a second street had to be crossed and disused railway tracks and Vietnamese market stalls negotiated before the Five Oceans BOQ came into sight.

Army BOQ managers assigned three men to each two-cubicle room. Agents assigned to Saigon had passed room assignments on to successors for years. Room 4, on the ground floor, was the epicenter of NISOV social life. Its bar, with a refrigerator and a few chairs and coffee tables, was the after-work gathering spot for agents, assigned naval officers, and often the supervising agent. A "mystery man" had been assigned the bunk behind the bar, meaning a bed could always be found for transit personnel. Newbies often spent their first night in this bunk, in the most popular room in the BOQ. If they were lucky, they were treated to a meal on the rooftop and perhaps a few drinks afterward before lapsing into exhausted sleep; hardcore revelers might linger until late.

Room 4 not only had a well-equipped bar, it also had a very large rat resident in the primitive shower drain. Shower water, definitely nonpotable, was not carried away from the tiled shower by a central floor drain; rather, it collected and drained out one side through a gap about the size of a common brick. On occasion, room 4's rat became alarmed when water poured through his home. He was known to make a rapid foray into the shower, run several quick circuits, sometimes over the feet of the showerer, before exiting again into his lair. Newbies especially found the experience disconcerting: there were knowing looks when room 4 drinkers heard a yell from the shower area, all part of the initiation process.

For both new arrivals to the Saigon office and agents in transit to Da Nang, breakfast at the Five Oceans was an eye-opener. As was the case in most buildings of its vintage, the roof area of the old hotel had been intended first as a service area. When the Army took over its management, the roof became a logical location for dining facilities. Bar facilities were available, a small stage could be erected for entertainment, and barbecues were popular. When the weather cooperated, an evening on the rooftop could be very pleasant. A cool, freshening breeze carried away some of the dust and fumes of the day, and the whole visual array of Saigon could be seen in the distance.

Breakfast, however, was devoid of charm. The tropical sun rises early, as did the patrons and merchants of the market that convened daily, immediately adjacent to the BOQ. Breakfast was served in a timber-framed, fly-screened SEA hut erected on the roof. It served as a shelter from rain and to a lesser extent from errant insects, but all the odors of nearby rotting produce, fish, garbage, and waste could and did waft through.

The term "Vietnamization" has appeared fleetingly in earlier chapters. It deserves further explanation at this point because by 1970 it was much more than a catch phrase: it had become the policy that changed everybody's lives in the Republic of South Vietnam.

President Johnson, before his March 1968 decision not to run for reelection, had several strategic options for pursuing the war. The president had not been a vigorous prosecutor of the basic military stratagem of punishing the enemy until meaningful negotiation occurred. The Tet Offensive, undoubtedly a military victory for the United States and its allies, had been perceived in the United States as a stalemate at best. Bowing to growing domestic pressure and dissent about the war, President Johnson decided upon a strategy that would increasingly turn over responsibility for the prosecution of the war to ill-prepared South Vietnamese forces. Perhaps not surprisingly, the president did not consult America's Vietnamese allies before initiating his plan. In reality Johnson's strategy was at heart a means of extricating the United States from the war, whatever the cost.

Newly elected President Richard M. Nixon waited until the middle of 1969 to embrace Vietnamization. This time a policy crafted by Secretary of Defense Melvin Laird set the ball rolling. By the end of the year, the United States would withdraw some of its troops and South Vietnamese would assume certain military roles. The Vietnamese did not, ironically, see it as a cut-and-run strategy by the Americans but as an accelerated equipping and training program.

The war was a long way from over in 1970, but by then it was being fought in different ways. The increased accent on pacification and joint operations with South Vietnamese rendered more of the country at least relatively safe. Killing occurred every day but large-scale military movement had decreased from previous years. This was, in many ways, a reflection of more than a decade of hard work and investment in South Vietnam by the U.S. government and people.

In 1970, as I neared the end of my first year in Vietnam, I decided to extend my tour. Most of 1969 had been spent in far-north I Corps. My new assignment was another one-man satellite unit at Cam Ranh Bay. While not exactly a backwater, Cam Ranh was known as relatively pleasant duty both because there had heretofore been very little enemy activity on the Cam Ranh Peninsula and because naval elements were relatively law-abiding.

Cam Ranh is a magnificent natural harbor, situated in what was then II Corps about midway up the coast between Da Nang and Saigon. The U.S. Navy had visited during World War II and French armed forces had made use of the anchorage for many years, so it seemed logical that the United States would choose to transform the sandy isthmus and bay into a huge logistic facility. Aided by civilian contractors, a massive air facility was completed, fuel storage tanks were built, and substantial ammunition and logistic storage parks were constructed. Topography rendered much of the base, especially the Navy at the southern end, relatively immune to enemy rocket attack.

In 1970 U.S. Navy elements at Cam Ranh were divided between aviation elements located at the air base and personnel in support of patrol vessels and communication farther down the peninsula on the water's edge.

I had seen Cam Ranh earlier, during a weekend away from Da Nang in late 1969. A school friend was officer in charge of an Army military intelligence detachment set amid sand dunes with sweeping views of the South China Sea. My weekend away had been quiet, a very pleasant change from the more hostile atmosphere farther north. The base was really a city made up of hundreds of SEA huts set in individual cantonments and was noticeably devoid of Vietnamese civilians. Only one fishing village fell within the base area, and it had been entirely fenced off with military police assigned to ensure U.S. personnel were excluded.

When I arrived in Cam Ranh to take over the NISSU in March 1970, I was looking forward to having my own office again. The office, which was furnished with little more than a desk, chairs, and a security container, was located at the Navy base in among spaces previously used by U.S. Navy patrol craft, fast (PCF or swift boat), support personnel. The Vietnamese were taking over the swifts, and it was anticipated that the VNN would soon have the entire office building. As a result, a move became essential: I could not comply with security regulations governing storage of classified material if my safe stayed in space controlled by non-U.S. personnel. Fortunately, the U.S. Coast Guard detachment had a single room available in a small office built overlooking the beach. I quickly arranged to have office accoutrements moved across the sand to the new building and soon grew to appreciate my

Coast Guard hosts. In time, with other moves afoot in the Vietnamization program, the Naval Intelligence liaison officer (NILO) also shared the building.

I was one of the lucky ones. With a magnificent view of the sweeping white-sand beach and azure waters of the South China Sea less than twenty yards away, my workspace could hardly have been improved upon. Sleeping quarters were nearby. A simple private cubicle, screened and louvered, provided just enough room for a cot, table, and fan. Previous owners had built shelves from ammunition boxes to hold several dozen paperback novels. My predecessors too had learned that reading was one of the safer after-hours pastimes in Vietnam.

As more Vietnamese were moved onto the base, a proportion of the U.S. Navy sailors became unsettled. Shower and toilet blocks had to be designated for different nationalities. Peasant Vietnamese had an unpleasant habit of standing on toilet seats, squatting, and spraying excrement in places other than the bowl. Fixtures were broken. Security of personal effects, always an issue, became more of a problem. Theft was likely to be blamed on Vietnamese, and in many instances this was justified.

Settled into my new routine, I began learning the ins and outs of how Cam Ranh worked. The naval base was under command of a U.S. Navy commander, a helpful dynamic leader unfortunately burdened with an aging reserve executive officer who had a talent for putting both feet in his mouth. A short distance northward on the beach was the Naval Communication Station, a large facility of considerable importance. Some miles away at the massive concrete airstrip, Naval Air Facility (NAF), Cam Ranh, occupied the western edge of the taxiway, sharing its hangars with a detachment of Army P2V Neptune aircraft supporting an Army Security Agency unit. Here, the senior naval officer in II Corps, a naval aviator captain, hung his hat. Here also was the II Corps Navy legal office, a key point of contact for me.

It was soon plain that changes were afoot. Young enlisted men were not privy to the guidelines that then directed the conduct of the war, but they were particularly attuned to changes brought about by Vietnamization. When an infantry unit was withdrawn, those who did not see it read about it in the next day's edition of *Stars and Stripes* newspaper or heard via Armed Forces Radio. Envy wasn't what unsettled people; it was the realization that the United States was pulling out of Vietnam. There was nothing glorious about the prospect of being killed or wounded when all anybody, especially people at home, could think about was bugging out. Very many men began to think about little other than the day they were due for rotation out of country.

In the first month or two, my life as Cam Ranh's naval intelligence agent became almost routine. Lead cases came to me from my SRA in Saigon. Trusting neither the post office nor sailors at the communication station who might be tempted to read my message traffic, I began routinely catching the Navy's Friday C117 flight to Saigon, hand-carrying my file folders. I was back at Cam Ranh again on Monday. I began to know many more members of command and to learn more about what was happening at the grassroots level. Concerned about the menace of drug abuse then sweeping Vietnam, commands asked me to conduct drug awareness programs, mostly for senior NCOs. The troops seemed quite knowledgeable about narcotics then in circulation, but I soon learned that many chiefs could not recognize the distinctive odor of burning cannabis. I burned old marijuana seized as evidence on a Bunsen burner, passed around opium, and showed them illustrations of heroin.

At about this time, SRA Bernie Taylor gave me a classified case that was unlike any I had thus far encountered. A "confidential informant of known reliability" (i.e., another agency in the intelligence community) had intercepted a letter mailed from NAF Cam Ranh addressed to a Soviet governmental division in the USSR. The mailer was a Navy officer with whom I was acquainted, who had expressed an interest in traveling to the Soviet Union. I first carried out discreet checks to determine the officer's current access level to classified material. Over several informal contacts, using my personal interest in international travel as a catalyst, I learned from the subject that he hoped one day to ride the Trans-Siberian Railway and had even written for information and a brochure. This provided at least an explanation for the probably innocent indiscretion. The Navy had a very real and legitimate concern about any member contacting by any means a hostile, enemy power, the Soviet Union in particular. Mine was, I'm sure, only a facet of a much fuller investigation.

I began to notice that more of my time was being devoted to narcotics investigations. A new Navy padre had reported aboard. Straight as an arrow, the chaplain would look men who asked for advice about their narcotics problems in the eye and tell them they had a duty to report it. I soon had sailors turning up at the office, many signing confessions implicating others. Barracks searches and interrogations followed. Concerned commands normally took the most expedient option of ridding themselves of these people— none of whom were model sailors—either using military justice or the administrative discharge process. Admin discharges were on "other-than-honorable" terms. Selfishly, I was glad to see them go because I was billeted among a growing group of recalcitrants and was very aware of my vulnerability to an attack by frag grenade.

Despite the distraction caused by "the dopers," life at NISSU Cam Ranh was reasonably pleasant. The officers' club, adjacent my office, had good company and a huge verandah. Occasionally, Army veterinarians (called dog mechanics in Vietnam) would gather up several Air Force nurses from the large evacuation hospital at the air base and take them down to the beach. There was considerable competition for the attentions of any American in Vietnam, perhaps even more in the hothouse atmosphere of the Cam Ranh enclave.

About August 1970 Cam Ranh suddenly became less immune to the war. Rockets fell on and near the naval air facility. Bunkers were quickly repaired, extra barbed wire was erected, and patrols increased. The aerial attacks were followed by sapper attacks led by North Vietnamese Army regulars. Aircraft were always a favorite sapper target. On one occasion during my tenure, they breached some of the perimeter. Several sappers were killed in the attack and one was captured. I met him the next day when he arrived at the portion of my office I shared with the NILO. He was wearing a sandbag over his head and was escorted by a young Vietnamese Navy officer whom I believed to be a member of the Vietnamese Naval Security Bloc. Small, dark, and wiry, the North Vietnamese soldier looked remarkably fit for having survived the privations of a march down the Ho Chi Minh Trail and living in rugged, mountainous terrain inland from Cam Ranh. The interrogation was very much a Vietnamese affair. The sapper was secured to an office chair, blindfolded, facing his interrogator. Never raising his voice, the young officer kept firing a string of questions at the captive, periodically prompting a response with a sharp smack on the bare inner thigh with a ruler. Later, a field telephone was produced and electric shock used. I did not stay. I learned later that valuable information had been obtained, and the wiry young soldier was then on his way to a POW compound on Phu Quoc Island "for the duration."

By mid 1970 the Navy facility staff at Cam Ranh was beginning to act more like a group of naval advisers, which in some ways was what many roles had become. Vietnamese officers and soldiers needed a good deal of tuition and follow-up advice before they could be expected to effectively operate the fleet of patrol vessels given to them by the United States. Those swift boats and gunboats were necessary to halt the flow of contraband being transported by sea from North Vietnam. The U.S. Navy, with Coast Guard assistance, had set up an effective blockade of the coast; now it was time for Vietnamese to take the reins.

Navy SEALs—the U.S. Navy's unconventional Special Forces personnel—had been active in the Vietnam War from the very earliest time. Their Vietnamese counterparts were called the LDNN, an abbreviation that translates roughly to soldiers who fight under the sea. LDNN units had played an important role in early covert operations in North Vietnam. It was logical that a SEAL detachment should play a pivotal role in training new LDNN recruits, and Cam Ranh was an ideal location for this purpose.

The training camp was a rough conglomerate of hooches and scrounged material located immediately outside the Navy perimeter. SEALS were ostensibly an element of a Vietnamese command; this suited their purposes well. They were expected to observe normal military rules and courtesies while aboard the base but were largely free to act independently and travel where they wished. The SEAL detachment commander, Lt. Richard Kuhn,

USN, was a powerfully built officer with a penchant for unconventional approaches to the daily challenges of command. He was ably assisted by petty officers led by Churchill, a salty master chief hospital corpsman who had begun his combat career on August 7, 1942, with the invasion of Guadalcanal. Churchill wore among his many decorations the Purple Heart Medal with five clusters: "four of the six wounds were in the head," he was heard to say. With more than two decades experience in treating combat injuries and a range of maladies, troops preferred his basic approach to medicine—in part because it did not involve a medical record entry. The standard treatment for chancroid involved immersion of the infected member in an open beer can filled with a potent, colorful solution of silver nitrate. Results were guaranteed.

The central hooch, used for meetings and planning, also had a bar built into the central partition. That plywood wall was adorned with a variety of trophies including captured NLF flags, a portrait of Ho Chi Minh captured in a cross-border raid, photographs of various personalities (including those undergoing Doc Churchill's renowned chancroid treatment), and a number of badly torn skivvy shorts. "Skivvy checks" are a long-standing SEAL tradition. SEALS do not wear underwear, and unwritten law dictates that skivvies are not to be worn. Visitors to SEAL premises might be subject to a skivvy check and offending garments removed forthwith, normally by reaching behind the waistline of the outer garment to grasp the undergarment and tear it off.

All of Lieutenant Kuhn's men had served multiple tours in Vietnam under the most intense combat conditions. They were unconventional, just as their often-secret missions were. I enjoyed their company, watched with interest as they polished each group of Vietnamese recruits, and observed with awe the brutal punishment of the recruit's final test. During "hell week," the nights were broken by squads of chanting LDNN aspirants, running down sandy streets carrying rubber boats over their heads, each no-doubt wondering if they had what it takes to survive a nonstop week with virtually no rest.

In 1970 a Navy presence remained at the port of Qui Nhon, some miles north of Cam Ranh. Qui Nhon had been a particularly important base in earlier days of the war when most supplies for the war in the Central Highlands were funneled across its docks. The Army maintained important logistic facilities to support military initiatives in the highlands and northern coastal areas of II Corps. Its harbor protected by a seaward island of considerable elevation, Qui Nhon was well protected but congested both by military and merchant shipping. This, combined with scores of Vietnamese coastal and fishing junks, made it easy to understand why much shipping in support of the war went elsewhere.

The Navy detachment was situated on the island, facing the protected harbor and city of Qui Nhon. An LCM regularly traveled between the city and the base and was the source of logistic supply.

One of my trips to Qui Nhon was made in response to a command request for assistance after irregularities were suspected in the small fleet post office. Fleet post offices supplied most of the services then associated with civilian postal service, including mail order purchase and insured parcel service. Mail service was additionally a very morale-sensitive issue since mail call was normally the only link service personnel had with the outside world during their yearlong tours of duty. The telephone link from Qui Nhon was not a good one, meaning details of the problem were not clear, but I agreed to travel the following day.

Agents wishing to avail themselves of the comprehensive air transport system operated by the U.S. Air Force required patience and a set of orders. We carried a sheaf of mimeographed orders that authorized us to travel wherever and whenever we deemed it necessary. As long as the Air Force had two copies of these and agents checked in at least two hours early, a sling seat would be reserved on a regularly scheduled C130 that flew north and south daily, with intermediate stops. I avoided Air Force flights whenever possible because of the two-hour check-in policy and delays. For flights between Cam Ranh and Qui Nhon, however, I had few other options. Arriving mid-afternoon, I was met by a Navy jeep and treated to an afternoon LCM trip through the busy harbor.

That evening, I interviewed several witnesses about their suspicions regarding the post office. Indications were that the postal clerk was simply stealing items of value from the mail system. Everybody in Vietnam at one time or another used the mail-order catalog service provided by the huge PX operated in Japan, which offered everything from stereo amplifiers to Mikimoto pearls. Ordered items were often delivered by mail to Vietnam within a week or ten days, or they might be dispatched to a U.S. address if the purchaser desired. Customs declarations were prominently displayed on all orders; this meant the mail clerk knew what most parcels contained.

I decided to test the clerk's honesty by making up a parcel with distinctively marked contents and provided it to one of the victims to mail. Soon after he dropped off the package, the post office and its clerk were searched. Clear evidence of theft turned up, and the subject was interrogated and confessed to a number of offenses. Mail and items stolen from it were recovered, and eventually much of it found its way to the rightful owners. Command put in an urgent request for a new mail clerk. I took the LCM trip back across Qui Nhon Harbor to catch a southbound flight back to Cam Ranh.

The once-quiet Cam Ranh office was never anything but busy during my tenure. Late in 1970 I was transferred to Saigon after turning the operation over to Special Agent Anderson T. Lambert. Lambert's caseload skyrocketed soon after his takeover. A deteriorating situation at the southern end prompted him to relocate the office to the naval air facility. There, soon after the move, a 122mm Soviet rocket plowed through the roof of the officers' club moments after he had left it to return to his office. There were numerous casualties. Andy Lambert was seriously shaken by the episode, and it haunted him the rest of his life.

# 11

# SAIGON, 1969 TO 1970: POW RESCUE, *EAGLE* MUTINY

**In mid-1969 NISOV came under the inspired leadership** of commanding officer Lt. Cdr. Thomas A. Brooks, USN. At that time, Tom Brooks already showed the hard-charging brilliance that characterized his ultimate rise to directorship of Naval Intelligence. He quickly learned the ropes in Saigon, set his goals, and started making things happen. Junior officers soon learned to make a note when the CO made a request or gave an order—because Tom Brooks never forgot.

Troop levels had reached their peak; more than five hundred thousand Americans were assigned to commands in the Republic of Vietnam. U.S. Navy forces were also at a record level. NISOV special agent staffing reached its high water mark of twenty-one. These men were distributed among the two resident agencies and four one-man satellite units then in operation. In contrast, the Army had, literally, hundreds of criminal investigators and military intelligence agents assigned in Vietnam; Air Force OSI was also very well represented.

Commander Brooks has said the quality of the all-volunteer agent force permitted his command to do far more with fewer resources, but he acknowledges five times the number of special agents could have been usefully employed in Vietnam. "The special agents were uniformly outstanding. All were volunteers. They were dedicated, hard-working professionals, and we had great admiration for them. The two men who were my supervising agents—Don Schunk and Allan J. Kersenbrock—were two of the finest men I have ever worked with. When I returned to the United States, I told the then-director of Naval Intelligence, R.Adm. Rex Rectanus, that I wished the naval intelligence officer community at large possessed the level of professionalism and dedication I found in the NIS special agent corps."

The reality of a twenty-one-man agent force was simply that NIS agents could not take every request for assistance that came their way. In the field, it was prudent for agents on the scene to examine carefully the fine ground between war-induced incidents and those involving overt criminal acts before agreeing to investigate. NIS accepted no requests for nonfelonious criminal investigations, but by 1969 the sheer volume of serious criminal cases dictated that virtually all available agents were so involved. Despite its earlier history of successful counterintelligence operations, agent resources became devoted predominantly to criminal investigation.

In Da Nang, Tom Brooks exploited his successful relationship with Vietnamese Navy intelligence officers by designing and implementing a program to recruit civilian informants employed within U.S. Navy installations. Co-coordinated with the U.S. Army's 525 Military Intelligence Group, the mission objective was to utilize informants to identify Viet Cong sympathizers or other internal problems. The initiative was expanded to recruit and run agents in areas near Navy and Marine Corps facilities in I Corps to report movement of VC in the area. These collection efforts produced information about graft, theft, and intimidation rather than identifying enemy within.

Naval counterintelligence requirements were satisfied in a variety of ways. U.S. Army counterintelligence personnel were distributed throughout South Vietnam and they shared information. So did well-established CIA resources. The Vietnamese Navy Security Bloc, to which a full-time adviser from NISOV was assigned, also provided information on a regular basis—and it was more than willing to assist when needed.

The VNNSB was needed in the case of the VC's capture of naval intelligence officer Lt. Cdr. Jack Graf, USN. As one would expect of a career intelligence officer, prior to his assignment to South Vietnam, Graf had been exposed to very sensitive, compartmentalized information. His capture, the only such loss by the Navy in the Vietnam War, was viewed with alarm by senior naval intelligence officers. They wanted Jack Graf back as soon as possible.

Graf's Vietnam assignment had been fourth coastal zone intelligence officer. His area of responsibility encompassed most of the Mekong Delta area—the most densely populated region in the country—including riverine areas in which Viet Cong forces remained a potent force. It was over such an area, the coastal mudflats of Kien Hoa Province, where the tributaries of the Mekong flow into the South China Sea, that Graf was lost. He had been flying in a U.S. Army Mohawk on an intelligence collection mission when the aircraft was taken under fire by enemy forces. Both Graf and the pilot survived the crash and were captured by Viet Cong troops.

COMNAVFORV senior intelligence officer Capt. Robert Pyle, USN, requested urgent assistance from the U.S. Army's Joint Personnel Recovery Center (JPRC). He asked Tom Brooks if he would travel to Honolulu, find Mrs. Graf, and assure her that everything possible was being done to find her husband. Brooks found a seat on an Air Force C141 returning to Hawaii and flew into Hickham Air Force Base a few days before Thanksgiving 1969. His first stop was the Commander in Chief Pacific Fleet (CINCPACFLT)

Chaplain's Office for the name of the casualty assistance coordination officer (CACO), a Marine lieutenant colonel who was not there at the time. Brooks took Graf's address and drove over to the house, but Graf's wife no longer lived there and neighbors were unable to provide her new address. Walking through the neighborhood looking for somebody who might know, he came across an older man sitting on his porch who provided the new address from his daughter. Armed with this, Brooks called on Mrs. Graf.

The Grafs had no children. Mrs. Graf and her very big German shepherd dog lived alone in a nice new housing development, where they had moved immediately before Graf deployed. Mrs. Graf had no relatives on the island, knew very few people, and was obviously a lonely and worried lady. Incredibly, although she had been notified about her husband having been shot down some weeks before, nobody had been to see her. Brooks recalls, "I mentioned the CACO's name, but the name meant nothing to her. I assured her of our efforts to recover Jack, left her my name and address, and set out to find that CACO.

"I found him at his CINCPACFLT desk and angrily accosted him demanding to know why he had not done his duty with regard to Mrs. Graf. He turned beet red and was about to dress me down for talking disrespectfully to a senior officer when I suggested that we go see the chief of staff if he had a problem but if not, then answer my question."

The Marine officer immediately turned defensive, saying he had tried to see Mrs. Graf, but she had moved and he had been unable find her. Brooks provided the address and telephone number, and some further, unsolicited words of advice. The next day he called Mrs. Graf. She said the CACO had been to see her that previous afternoon and had been pleasant and apologetic; she characterized him as a nice and helpful man. "I didn't tell her any of the story, but expressed my pleasure and wished her well."

Tom Brooks had no Thanksgiving in 1969; as luck would have it, he skipped the holiday when he crossed the International Date Line going back to Saigon.

Back in Vietnam, the Graf rescue effort was not going well. It soon emerged that no U.S. elements had intelligence capabilities in the area and the closest South Vietnamese presence was fifty miles distant from the crash site. Moreover, it was becoming evident that the Army staff at JPRC was capable neither of imaginative operational planning nor of prompt reaction to the crisis. It fell to Tom Brooks and his Vietnamese counterparts at VNNSB to make an all-out effort to force a rescue of Graf before it was too late.

Of primary importance in the early planning stages of the operation was dependable intelligence about the situation at and around the crash site: What enemy units were present, where were they, and what stories were in circulation about captured Americans? Commanders Nguyen Nhu Vy and Nguyen Do Hai of VNNSB set about locating a dependable Vietnamese with knowledge and connections in this lonely, hostile area of the delta. They found a VNN junior-grade lieutenant with relatives in the area who volunteered to assist.

This brave Vietnamese officer set off alone aboard a Honda 50 motorcycle into Indian country dressed as a civilian, with full knowledge of the consequences should one of the many Viet Cong sympathizers in the area identify him. He covered a good deal of country in his efforts to acquire information. Ultimately, his relatives provided the first tangible intelligence about the crash and its victims. In return, they expected Americans to evacuate them by helicopter and resettle the family at a location well away from VC influence.

Armed with this intelligence, U.S. Army officers at JPRC proved a model of bureaucratic inertia. Alternative operational plans were drawn up and debated as valuable time dribbled away. Their final plan envisaged floating 155mm howitzers down the river on barges and using Laotian Montagnards to conduct the rescue attempt in the swamps of Kien Hoa. To put all of this rather astonishing plan together would take "several weeks." Clearly Jack Graf was not going to get any meaningful help from that quarter.

Finally the Navy took the matter into its own hands. Tom Brooks visited the province chiefs senior (American) adviser, a retired U.S. Army lieutenant colonel, in Ben Tre (Kien Hoa City). The senior adviser immediately volunteered to help and tried to make a team of U.S. SEAL advisers and their South Vietnamese SEAL counterparts available for the operation, but this plan met with JPRC resistance and it was concluded that he could only use assets that belonged to him and over which U.S. headquarters in Saigon had no say.

Thus Lieutenant Commander Brooks and VNNSB adviser Lt. Ron Lodziewski were given two squads of Vietnamese Regional Forces militia, known as RFPFs (or ruff-puffs), and four or five Kit Carson scouts, who were Viet Cong deserters now working for the ARVN. They piled into two very overloaded Hueys and set out for the tip of Kien Hoa Peninsula, where the Kit Carson scouts interrogated villagers and were able to learn that "a white man" (Graf) and a black man (the Mohawk pilot) had been taken by the VC down the river by boat some twelve hours before. The team climbed back into the helos and tried to reconnoiter the river on the way back, but the jungle canopy was so dense that a boat could easily hide at the sound of approaching helicopters.

Tom Brooks remembers the Graf episode as a crushing disappointment, "On December 11, 1969, I was sitting in Ben Tre with my adviser to the VNNSB, Lt. Ron Lodziewski, waiting for a ride back to Saigon after our operation had failed to locate Graf and the Army pilot. It was already obvious that American incompetence was central to the failure. But I will never forget that brave Vietnamese lieutenant junior-grade who got nothing more for his efforts than a rather emotional thank you from me. It was enough for him."

Returning to Saigon, after the abortive rescue attempt, Brooks and Lieutenant Lodziewski debriefed Captain Pyle. Brooks was careful not to reveal too many details, but he nonetheless found out the two been much too closely involved in the operation and had actually gone out into Indian country with the RFPFs. Brooks remembers, "This got me a sound chewing out for my second offense at traveling places where I was not allowed to go because of my clearances. The first one was for driving by jeep from Quang Tri to Da Nang down Bernard Fall's famous Street Without Joy, which was very interesting and totally uneventful, but very much against the rules and, in retrospect, not too smart."

A number of months later, when most of the Kien Hoa Peninsula had been pacified, a U.S. Army helo pilot observed a black man waving his shirt from a clearing and landed to investigate. The man was the pilot of the Mohawk who had escaped his captors. He confirmed that the NISOV team had, in fact, missed them by only twelve hours and also related that Jack Graf had been killed attempting to escape. A subsequent interrogation of a VC defector revealed that Graf's body had been buried in a bridge embankment but that spring flooding had later washed away the bridge and embankment. Jack Graf thus received the burial at sea he would have desired in the nearby, downstream waters of the South China Sea.

Brooks relates, "I have often thought about her and wondered how Mrs. Graf made out. I can still feel sorrow for her. More importantly, I can still feel anger for that CACO. Brave Vietnamese risked their lives to try to rescue a man they had never even met, and the CACO couldn't take the trouble to track down Mrs. Graf's new address."

Historically, a cornerstone of the NIS mission has been to protect sensitive information that, if compromised, could result in serious damage to U.S. interests and personnel. Procedures for safe custody of classified material were drummed into every person exposed to it. Particularly in a war zone, it was expected that all material classified for official use only through to top secret would be carefully maintained under lock and key in a designated secure area. Thus reports NISOV received from an informant that a Vietnamese street vendor was selling bakery goods wrapped in official Navy documents that were believed classified caused considerable concern. The informant said that a Vietnamese employee of COMNAVFORV who had access to the burn bags used to store discarded classified documents before destruction was selling the documents to the street vendor.

Soon christened the Cookie Lady by those working the case, a female

Vietnamese street vendor was identified potentially as a low-ranking element in an enemy espionage operation. NISOV's Vietnamese case officer was sent to a Saigon street corner not far from the premises occupied by COMNAVFORV, where the Cookie Lady was known to operate. He engaged the entrepreneurial Saigon citizen in conversation, then bought three cookies from her. The Cookie Lady obligingly wrapped each in a sheet of message paper; all were official U.S. Navy documents classified confidential.

Investigation quickly disclosed that neither the Cookie Lady nor the enterprising Navy employee who had supplied the "used paper" could read English. Nor did further inquiries give rise to suspicions that either had connections with enemy personnel or sympathizers. Some glaring deficiencies in security procedures at COMNAVFORV were quickly addressed.

NISOV maintained an interest in activities in and around Saigon's waterfronts, as it had from the earliest days of operation. Under Tom Brooks, a network of informants was activated to target Viet Cong activity in the vital maritime commercial hub, with executive officer Lt. Norman Idleberg, USN, serving as the case officer. Because vast quantities of war supplies moved across the docks, it was important to know whether the VC had influence among longshoremen, deck hands, local boatmen, and merchants. The network, which used civilian informants of various nationalities, produced interesting results—though perhaps not what was expected: commercial opportunities in the dockside underworld community were so attractive that the enemy had been unable to establish a toehold. Chinese and Vietnamese criminal societies and families carefully guarded their interests at the Port of Saigon. Consequently, they were aware of most activity in the area, and they were willing to cooperate and share their information as long as the status quo was maintained with their business activities. NISOV did not ignore reports of criminal activity at the docks entirely; it was also necessary to pragmatically consider the best interests of the Navy.

As Maynard Anderson had discovered four years earlier, the presence of so many Americans in South Vietnam spawned new opportunities for criminal enterprise. A staggering volume of materiel—not limited to weapons of war—was required to sustain more than five hundred thousand military personnel and the vast system that supported them. U.S. personnel had access to military commissary and post exchange facilities that were in some ways superior to hometown supermarkets and department stores. South Vietnam was an economic backwater, a country of agrarian peasants unaccustomed to merchandise Americans took for granted as daily necessities. Naturally, when this material was offered for sale to Americans in stores Vietnamese could not access, opportunities were created for illegal activity. Whereas, in the years before, entire shipping containers had been stolen en route to U.S. supply stores, in 1970 the increased volume of material and numbers of troops with legal access to stores created opportunity on a massive scale for more subtle black marketing. GIs were not supposed to buy supplies at the PX for Vietnamese friends, and they were certainly forbidden from reselling merchandise. Profit margins for this type of activity were attractive, and potential gains—particularly in the minds of Vietnamese entrepreneurs—were staggering. Underworld elements in Saigon quickly learned there were easier ways to get U.S. merchandise than taking chances with overt criminal activities such as robbery and theft. They turned to the growing community of U.S. deserters and fringe-dwelling civilian technical representatives and support contractors, most of whom enjoyed legal access to at least some of the military supply system.

Saigon supported by far the largest deserter community in South Vietnam. A very large city growing more overpopulated daily, it offered hundreds of places where a deserter could hide from authorities. While runaway Americans had money of their own, they could maintain a certain amount of independence from criminal elements of the Vietnamese community. Bar owners and the Vietnamese women who managed them kept a sharp lookout for men without much money or deserters with a serious drug habit. Recruited, these men represented an immediate line of access to the U.S. supply system. Vietnamese criminals ran cribs of deserters, furnishing them with forged and stolen identification, which facilitated access to stores. Particularly if they had to fund a drug habit, these men could be counted on to return with the merchandise they'd been sent to purchase.

South Vietnam's fragile domestic economy precluded conversion of the local currency (the Vietnamese Dong, known to all as the piaster) to foreign exchange, which might be traded internationally. Viet Cong elements had from the outset devised schemes to acquire U.S. currency as the means to purchase internationally the materiel required for its war against noncommunists. Domestic demand for U.S. dollars (known in-country as green) was so strong that U.S. authorities withdrew all U.S. currency from circulation and introduced military payment certificates (MPC) as a substitute. In theory, MPC was valid only for transactions within South Vietnam, and Vietnamese civilians were not supposed to possess it. In reality, MPC was freely exchanged in bars and tailor shops for piasters. This prompted authorities, on several occasions, to secretly change MPC types overnight by locking up Americans in their compounds to limit contacts with Vietnamese holding old MPC. The old MPC issue was rendered valueless unless a Vietnamese could find a way to get it into the compound to a compliant American who would exchange it. Few were successful.

Unless MPC could be converted into saleable merchandise such as tobacco, liquor, or stereo components, it was of little value to the Vietnamese criminal element. What was most wanted was MPC safely converted into U.S. dollars and deposited in a Hong Kong bank that asked few questions. They needed a negotiable instrument. The U.S. postal money order suited their purpose perfectly. Once again, deserters armed with false or stolen identification could legally purchase money orders at their unit post office. Once this ruse became known and widespread, MACV went to considerable expense installing a massive IBM computer to track money order purchasers by name, date of purchase, and amount of money involved. NIS and similar organizations regularly received multipaged computer printouts indicating illegal currency manipulation had occurred. In Saigon, these often led agents to the deserter community.

NISOV's mission dictated that careful scrutiny of deserters be maintained, especially if there were indications the man might defect to the enemy. Lieutenant Idleberg recalls being involved in a mission to recover one such serviceman, "I became involved because of my role as point of contact with the Vietnamese Navy Security Bloc. We may have received information from VNNSB that initiated the plan to extract him from his hideaway near Dalat, in the Central Highlands. I flew aboard a U.S. military aircraft to Dalat dressed in civilian clothes with a team of Vietnamese, and after dark we moved in close to the hut where this guy was supposed to be. We hid behind an earthen berm, then charged in together and apprehended the American and his Vietnamese consort. She was released; he was returned to the naval brig on Plantation Road in Saigon. I recall that he made good an escape before we could talk to him again. This he somehow did without any clothing, and it was reported he ran stark naked down Plantation Road before losing himself in one of the myriad back streets. He was eventually recaptured."

Although NIS was always on the lookout for potential defectors, Norm Idleberg believes few deserters ever contemplated defection, "Most of those guys were either scared, disenchanted with their lot in the war, found the girl of their dreams—finally found someone of the opposite sex who paid attention to them—or they were disgruntled."

There were never sufficient resources in any allied organization to seriously attack the deserter problem. Nor was there the political will to undertake an operation that would have pitted American MPs against American soldiers and probably would have resulted in casualties on both sides. Some deserters were very well organized, armed, and shielded by sympathetic Vietnamese. Importantly, NISOV never discovered indications that the VC were using the document-forging capabilities of the underworld to further their aims. Our belief was the criminal elements were not interested in such an arrangement because little commercial advantage could be derived from it.

❖◆❖◆❖

Jurisdictional issues exacerbated NISOV's problems dealing with illegal activities in the U.S. civilian community. During the early years of the Vietnam War, courts had held that civilian employees of the U.S. government were not subject to the military legal framework afforded by the UCMJ. The Vietnamese National Police was seldom genuinely interested in alleged offenses by U.S. civilians, unless the offenses had extortion potential or its help was specifically requested by a U.S. agency.

The U.S. military initiative in the Republic of Vietnam was highly dependent on civilian contractors not only for construction of critical infrastructure such as bridges, roads, and airfields but also for specialist projects such as aircraft maintenance and reconditioning. President Johnson had earlier encouraged several prominent American contractors, lead by companies from his native Texas, to assemble the world's largest construction consortium, RMK-BRJ. The consortium employed hundreds of U.S. citizens with specialty construction skills to tackle huge projects such as the massive military facility at Cam Ranh Bay. The civilian contractors formed a separate stratum in the mélange that made up the U.S. presence in Vietnam. Attracted by generous salaries, tax breaks from their government, and the spirit of adventure, they lived on the Vietnamese economy, surviving by their wits in sometimes-insecure areas, their only protection often the goodwill of neighbors. Many stayed for several years, and most had Vietnamese mistresses or wives. A kindly appraiser might have labeled them "pioneering stock."

RMK employed many thousand Vietnamese and expatriate Korean personnel, as well as Americans. Other U.S. construction and maintenance identities included Pacific Architects and Engineers (PA&E). Also in-country were many technical representatives representing aircraft companies, communication manufacturers, and helicopter maintenance companies.

Few but direct-hire U.S. civilian employees enjoyed full access to PX, ancillary banking, and military post office facilities, but a majority had at least partial privileges. And anyone who needed something badly enough could find service personnel to buy it. This resulted in strange anomalies in the PX supply system as it tried to compensate for the strong domestic demand for basics like laundry detergent. Purchase of PX items such as sanitary napkins (when they were available) might instantly brand the purchaser as a black marketer at worst or as a skivvy honcho at best, a skivvy honcho being someone renowned for prowess with the local ladies.

On the other end of the value spectrum, the latest and best in Japanese refrigerators, stereo systems, radios, fans, and jewelry were much sought after in the Vietnamese civilian economy. All were stocked in the larger post exchanges, and if an item was not actually in stock, it could quickly be ordered from the main Pacific exchange warehouse in Japan. Where there is demand, there exists financial opportunity, and many in the civilian community abused the PX system for personal gain by making purchases to sell at inflated rates to Vietnamese clientele.

One such man had been the subject of prolonged investigation in Saigon and Japan. A former U.S. Navy enlisted man from the Deep South, with aircraft maintenance expertise, the civilian employee of a U.S. company had missed very few opportunities to turn a dollar in the hotbed of Saigon's underworld. He was linked to a major narcotics importation scheme after NIS agents intercepted multiple kilo bundles of opium, and he was alleged to have been involved in a scheme to steal platinum from critical helicopter components during maintenance inspections. He was also linked to illegal trade in gold and had been arrested and imprisoned by Vietnamese authorities for complicity in car theft and fencing schemes. There was compelling evidence also that he had been involved in various illegal currency manipulation scams.

Other than encouraging Vietnamese authorities to act, NIS agents had little recourse against the man—and he knew it. But Special Agents Don Webb and Mike Jones were patient men. They accumulated scores of reports on the suspect's activities, and a small Vietnamese police group with a name that translated roughly to Treasury Fraud Repression Unit elicited interest. Funding for the organization was founded predominantly on the assets it was able to seize. This, then, provided potential legal means for arrest and remand of the subject.

By the time the Treasury Fraud Repression Unit agreed to help with the case, Webb and Jones had pieced together details of the suspect's latest scam. He had traveled to Japan, purchased vast quantities of stereo equipment and other high-value items, then made use of the military postal system to have them delivered to him for sale in Vietnam, without the inconvenience of dealings with Vietnamese Customs officials. Checks presented to the exchanges as payment had all been written against an account opened at the Saigon branch of Chase Manhattan Bank. The account had been established using identification stolen from another serviceman months earlier; and as the minimum $50 was the only amount ever deposited, all checks written had been dishonored. NISO Japan agents confirmed in considerable detail aspects of the purchases, banking, and postal transfer and forwarded these to NISSU Vung Tau resident agent Ben Johnson.

Johnson remembers, "I received a lead from Japan requesting I check the military post office for parcels mailed by the suspect from the Yokosuka Navy Exchange. At the post office, I found two parcels, one of which contained about five pounds of pachinko balls such as the Japanese use in gaming machines. As instructed, these were seized and returned to Saigon as evidence. While I was there, I checked with my contacts at Vietnamese National Police and was able to locate the house in Saigon where the suspect was living."

When, some time later, further evidence surfaced, Special Agents Webb, Jones, and Johnson went back to the house in middle-class Saigon in the early hours of the morning in an attempt to locate their quarry. Jones recalls, "There were no guards in the neighborhood; however, the homes were protected with heavy metal gates and barred windows, and frequently the residents had dogs freely wandering about the premises. On this particular morning Webb and I were driving an International Scout and we were adequately armed. I had my NIS issue .357 Magnum and a small caliber backup in my waistband. Webb was wearing his model 19 in his John Wayne holster. We arrived at the residence and began banging on the metal gate. Shortly a Vietnamese female, who appeared to be a maid, approached. Upon seeing that we were armed and displaying Vietnam Military Security Service cards she decided to allow us entrance. Once inside the two-story house we observed the suspect, fully clothed, asleep on a couch in the living room area. We woke him up and properly identified ourselves. Still being very unsure of our legal jurisdiction, we assertively invited him to accompany us to the Cholon Office. During the course of this conversation we suddenly noticed he had a Russian K54 automatic in his waistband. With each of us having a grip on our model 19s we asked him to slowly remove the automatic. He responded, dropped the magazine, and pulled back the action showing that there was no chambered round. After the tension eased, he agreed to accompany us."

The suspect was interviewed in depth at the NISRA Saigon office. Well aware he was out of the legal grasp of the agents, he made partial admissions about his illegal activities. He was afterward released but agreed to keep regular appointments with Jones, and in the course of several months actually provided the agent with useful intelligence about black market activities in Saigon.

The agents were certain they had proved the man had been involved in important violations of U.S. federal law. But at that time no established legal mechanism could bring the man to trial, nor did a legal precedent exist for trying him under U.S. law for offences committed in Vietnam and elsewhere outside U.S. boundaries.

Representations were made to the U.S. attorney in Honolulu to determine whether federal prosecutors would consider a groundbreaking prosecution. There followed exchanges of messages between Hawaii and Saigon, requesting the particulars of the investigation. Finally, word was received that the accused would be tried under U.S. law if he could be delivered to U.S. marshals on American soil.

Anticipating this development, agents had carefully orchestrated with Vietnamese police the arrest and detention of the accused, on a range of offenses pertaining to violations of immigration law. He was remanded to the notorious Chi Hoa Prison in Saigon as the wheels of South Vietnamese justice ground ahead, albeit very slowly.

When news was received of the U.S. attorney's decision, secret negotiations were begun with Vietnamese authorities to secure their cooperation in the plan to return the man to U.S. courts. Ultimately, they agreed to formally deport and deliver him to our place of choice. In the meantime, the NISOV CO and supervising agent were seeking assistance from the U.S. Air Force. They needed a cargo aircraft returning to Hawaii without personnel aboard. After assurances that an agent assuming responsibility for the prisoner would accompany the accused at all times, the Air Force command at Tan Son Nhut Air Base agreed. Arrangements for the process were begun.

Military Airlift Command officers soon contacted NISOV to advise a certain C141 Starlifter had been scheduled to fly into Tan Son Nhut, unload, and return the next day to Hickham Air Force Base, Hawaii, with Kadena Air Force Base, Okinawa, as a midway fuelling point. In Hawaii, NIS Pacific special agents liaised with U.S. marshals, providing them with aircraft arrival times.

For reasons of security and to keep the accused in the dark as to his impending travels, Vietnamese police and prison authorities were the last to be told of the plan. Webb and Jones had contacts at Chi Hoa Prison who monitored the prisoner's activities. Those sources said it was apparent the man had no idea of what was in store for him. No longer with disposable income, he was living on bananas and complaining to anybody who would listen.

On the day the flight was scheduled, NIS agents drove out on the flight line at Tan Son Nhut, where the C141 was in final stages of preflight preparation. The flight was under the command of Air Force Colonel Curley; his copilot was a young first lieutenant. The crew chief was a senior NCO, then checking stowage aboard the aircraft. SRA Fred Givens and Special Agent Art Newman stood by, anticipating the arrival of Vietnamese police with the prisoner. As prisoner escort, I was attired in a new, never-worn linen tropical suit. It looked smart but was not comfortable in the growing heat and humidity of a Saigon morning.

On time, two green and white jeeps loaded with National Police drove up alongside the parked aircraft. In the rear of the second was the prisoner, handcuffed and manacled. His captors helped him to his feet, out of the open-air jeep, and onto the tarmac. Clutching the front waistline of his beltless trousers, he was obviously taken aback by what was happening. Givens and Newman, ignoring his whining protestations, hustled him up the lowered aircraft stairway and into a readied sling seat, where the crew chief fastened a seat belt for him.

Colonel Curley lost no time getting under way. I said good-bye to the other agents, who wished me well on my trip back to "the world." The crew chief closed and bolted the hatch, and a few minutes later we were taxiing and taking off in a steep climb, eastbound.

Every Air Force crew chief I have ever met has been a consummate professional whose first worry is the airworthiness of his aircraft and, consequently, any potential threat to its well-being. The master sergeant on Colonel Curley's flight was clearly such a man, and he was uncomfortable about my charge. After his no-nonsense installation in the seat by Newman and Givens, the prisoner decided to test me. First, he ignored safety instructions about his seat belt; then, after the aircraft had reached cruising altitude, he announced he was going to get up and move around. I ordered him to remain seated and moved to refasten his seat belt, but the prisoner resisted, lashing out with his manacled legs and arms. I pushed him back and refastened the belt with the assistance of the crew chief. Moments later, he made another attempt. I turned to the crew chief again for assistance. After an impromptu conference in which the crew expressed concerns about the welfare of the aircraft and crew, we removed the still-resisting prisoner from the relative comfort of his sling seat and secured his handcuffs and manacles to the deck. Things became much quieter after that, and the pilot expressed his gratitude for the action taken.

At Kadena, Okinawa, we landed to take on fuel and were met by two very large air police who took the prisoner in charge while we attended to business on the ground. Soon, we were on our way once again.

Even seasoned air travelers seldom have the opportunity to observe the splendor of the Pacific Ocean that pilots see from the flight deck. Flying eastward through the night at very high elevation, we were treated to a sunrise of such magnificence as to be almost surreal: glorious colors filtered over and through a fluffy bed of white clouds far below.

We arrived at Hickham Air Force Base, Honolulu, soon after dawn on a Sunday morning. Two U.S. marshals were alongside soon after the engines were shut down and moments later had taken my prisoner away.

Monday morning's edition of the *Honolulu Tribune* devoted several columns of space to a story about a man allegedly kidnapped by federal authorities. I was not mentioned by name.

Some months later, the man was tried and convicted in federal court. The conviction was upheld on appeal, and a valued court precedent, which spelled the end of automatic immunity for U.S. civilians who commit offenses against their country in offshore locations, was established.

Similarly vexatious legal issues surfaced in March 1970 when civilian crew aboard a vessel chartered by the U.S. government chose to seize her as an act of political demonstration against the Vietnam War. SS *Columbia Eagle* was en route to Thailand with a cargo of napalm and bombs when mutineers took control of the ship and forced most of the crew into lifeboats, casting them adrift in the South China Sea. The mutineers then set sail for Cambodia, believing delivery of the vessel to a neutral port an effective means of voicing their condemnation of the war to the international community. On the night of March 14, 1970, a passing freighter—the SS *Rappahannock*, also en route to Thailand with a load of munitions for the U.S. Air Force— saw flares fired by the castaways and hove-to to investigate. The *Columbia Eagle* crewmembers had been adrift for seven hours, having left their master and several other crucial officers and crewmembers aboard at the instruction of two armed mutineers.

The senior officer, who boarded *Rappahannock* on the instruction of the master, Captain Lignos, under gunpoint, identified himself as *Columbia Eagle*'s second mate, Robert W. Stevenson. He told Lignos there had been an abandon-ship alarm the day previously at about 1:30 PM; the men had realized the alarm was not a routine drill and had quickly proceeded to their boat stations, where they asked the mate on watch whether the alarm was genuine. Herbert Gunn, standing on the wing of the ship bridge, told them that there was a bomb scare and that they should man the lifeboats. Responding to Gunn's instructions, Stevenson shepherded all but fifteen crewmembers into the boats and awaited instructions to cast off. Gunn, he related, had withdrawn into the wheelhouse, apparently consulted with unidentifiable persons inside, and then returned to the bridge wing, where he yelled orders to Stevenson, telling him to cast off immediately and pointing to the north, saying that the nearest land was about a hundred miles in that direction. The boats took to the water and pulled some distance away. Nearly an hour had passed when a plume of smoke from the *Eagle* stack signaled she was getting under way. Soon the men were bobbing alone in the open waters of the Gulf of Thailand.

The castaways were made at home aboard *Rappahannock* and delivered to nearby Sattahip, Thailand. Once safely ashore, they were moved to a Thai hotel, where they waited several weeks while events surrounding the mutiny unfolded.

Meanwhile, responding to requests from senior naval authorities, NISOV commanding officer Lt. Cdr. Tom Brooks dispatched to Thailand special agent Don Webb, a well-respected agent who served two tours in Vietnam, accompanied by executive officer Lt. Norm Idleberg, USN. They were instructed to interview available *Columbia Eagle* crewmembers. After meetings at the U.S. embassy in Bangkok with U.S. advisers and a U.S. Coast Guard investigative team headed by a Lieutenant Commander Spiker, Webb and Idleberg traveled to the port town of Sattahip and began their interviews, fully expecting that *Eagle* would soon be released and that the remaining crewmembers would be available for interview.

Norm Idleberg dispatched regular reports from the embassy to his headquarters in Saigon. Ultimately, he and Webb completed their interviews and had to wait to access the remaining crewmembers. By late March, Norm Idleberg was getting anxious. "I was scheduled for R and R to see my wife in Hawaii and as the date for that travel neared, I expressed my concerns to Tom Brooks."

Brooks ordered Idleberg and Webb both back to Saigon, where Lieutenant Idleberg soon after boarded his R-and-R flight and Webb returned to normal duties, awaiting news of *Columbia Eagle* movements.

The mutineers had managed to navigate *Columbia Eagle* to Kompong Som, Cambodia's main seaport. The ship's master, Capt. Donald Swann, at gunpoint, charted and set a circuitous course, probably in hopes U.S. Coast Guard patrol vessels operating in the Gulf of Thailand would intercept the vessel. At Kompong Som, *Columbia Eagle* was anchored some distance from the port, owing to its dangerous cargo of bombs and napalm. The mutineers—Fireman Clyde McKay and Bedroom Steward Alvin Glatkowski— and the ship's master Swann were soon taken ashore and flown to the Cambodian capitol, Phnom Penh. There McKay and Glatkowski declared themselves political revolutionaries and were granted asylum of the then-government, headed by Prince Sihanouk. They "gave" *Columbia Eagle* and her cargo to the Cambodian government, renounced their U.S. citizenship, and soon were extolling revolutionary messages to Phnom Penh's overseas press corps.

Two days later the Sihanouk government, which had tried to steer a nonaligned course between North Vietnam, its communist backers, and the U.S.–South Vietnamese coalition, was overthrown by a pro-U.S. political faction headed by Gen. Lon Nol. The mutineers were incarcerated, the new government uncertain what to do with them. Some three weeks after the mutiny, Captain Swann was returned to his ship. After an inspection by Cambodian naval authorities and a contingent of foreign journalists, he was permitted to sail *Columbia Eagle* from Cambodian waters. U.S. Coast Guard Lieutenant Commander Spiker, dispatched to conduct preliminary investigations of the incident, boarded the ship as she departed Cambodia and sailed directly to Sattahip, Thailand.

With its castaways repatriated from Thailand, *Columbia Eagle* set sail for the giant U.S. Navy base at Subic Bay, Philippines, where its munitions cargo was to be offloaded. U.S. Coast Guard cutter *Chase* accompanied her. In the weeks after the rebellion and seizure of *Columbia Eagle*, the U.S. media had reported many facets of the story, including profiles of the alleged mutineers.

Idleberg and Webb, then in Saigon, utilizing typical NISOV ingenuity, rushed to join *Columbia Eagle* as she steamed across the Gulf of Thailand. They boarded an unscheduled Air America flight to An Thoi, a Vietnamese village on Phu Quoc Island in the Gulf of Cambodia. From there, they flew in an Army helicopter to a U.S. Coast Guard cutter on patrol. On April 8, 1970, the U.S. Army helicopter landed them aboard *Chase* in the Gulf of Thailand, from which they later transferred by boat to *Columbia Eagle*.

Webb and Idleberg approached *Eagle* as she lay in open water. The old ship's sides were festooned with crudely painted white peace symbols. Uncertain what they faced aboard, the men clambered up a swinging Jacob's ladder and were greeted by Coast Guard investigator Lieutenant Commander Spiker. They soon found the reunited ship crewmembers to be unsettled and distrustful of each other. The NISOV team joined with Coast Guard personnel to begin an investigation designed to determine the facts surrounding the rebellion as well as whether any of the conspirators remained aboard. Additionally, Idleberg, NISOV's counterintelligence officer, was keen to learn what he could about affiliations the rebels might have had with subversive U.S. and foreign organizations. There were unconfirmed allegations that the pair had been supported in some manner by U.S. antiwar elements, including Students for a Democratic Society (SDS). SDS was allegedly involved in violent attacks against targets in the United States.

Working in the captain's stateroom by day, investigators systematically interviewed crewmembers to profile the role each person had played in the mutiny. In the four days it took to traverse seas to the Philippines, no direct complicity was discovered between crewmembers and mutineers McKay and Glatowski. Several crewmembers, however, admitted narcotics use.

Glatkowski surrendered to authorities at the American Embassy, Phnom Penh, in December 1970. McKay and a U.S. Army deserter escaped from custody that year and found their way to communist Khmer Rouge positions in the Cambodian countryside. They have not been seen or heard of since and are believed to have been murdered by those they sought to join and support.

Several years later Lieutenant Commander Idleberg, then assigned to attaché duty at the U.S. Embassy, Rome, was called to testify in a government court case convened in Seattle, Washington. *Columbia Eagle*'s owners were suing the U.S. government, which had not paid for the ill-fated voyage on grounds the cargo was never delivered. Special Agent Don Webb was also ordered to testify. Ultimately, the government won the case.

# 12

# SAIGON, 1970 TO 1971: FRAGGINGS, HEROIN ARRIVES

**By 1970 Saigon was familiar turf for me.** I had a permanent bunk in room 5 at the Five Oceans BOQ, next door to our gathering spot and watering hole. Special Agent Bernie Taylor was SRA, my immediate superior. NISOV was under the leadership of commanding officer Lt. Cdr. Thomas A. Brooks, USN, and Supervising Agent Allan J. Kersenbrock.

Al Kersenbrock had begun his career in his native Hawaii, where he had served in the Honolulu Police Department. An extremely capable investigator, his powers of alternative thinking helped resolve a number of cases with previously uncertain outcomes. He was, besides mentor and adviser, a good friend to me. Eschewing the predictable Army fare on the BOQ roof, we often ventured across the street to Fuji's Restaurant or down to the corner where a Chinese Vietnamese family ran a well-patronized soup kitchen. There, Asian men in white singlets sat in groups around worn round wooden tables of indeterminate vintage, clutching bowls of steaming *pho* and rapidly shoveling the mixture into their mouths with chopsticks. Though our technique with the chopsticks was not nearly so polished, we enjoyed the noodles, beef, and coriander every bit as much as the locals. Certainly, we did not know whom we were sharing lunch with. And it is possible that others thought we were becoming complacent about the enemy threat. But we were always armed, and we used common sense to pick our table. Eating at the soup kitchen was for us simply a risk worth taking.

Opium trafficking had always been a problem for us. Cholon was well known for its opium dens; liquid opium in small quantities was always available in the city's underworld market. NISOV had made several important quantity seizures, one of which is memorable because the seized opium blocks, stored in the converted closet that served as an evidence locker, melted during one especially warm month. The office janitor, Mr. Ngo, was quick to clean the tarry substance from the locker floor. Taking it outside to add to a smoke, he grinned at us, assumed a body builder's stance and said, "All-same tiger!" He knew very well what smoked opium did.

Heroin came to Saigon very suddenly, surprising us all. NISOV's premises were incorporated into a compound housing the Cholon PX, the Chase Bank, and an Army post office. It was thus a gathering place for military shoppers. Heroin vendors immediately began stationing themselves out under the trees at the compound gate, where they could easily accost likely purchasers and show their wares. Women sold souvenirs, drinks, and pornographic photographs in a roaring trade, which lasted as long as the exchange stayed open. As military police and the Vietnamese National Police became aware of the trade, more vendors entrusted heroin vials for keeping to young, agile kids, who were far more likely to make a successful getaway from the police. Special Agent Clayton Spradley, standing in a check-out line behind a young soldier at the Cholon PX, was unnerved to see a vial of heroin fall out of the soldier's breast pocket as he reached for cash to pay for his purchases. The container had been opened and was kept ready for use, just as his cash was.

We assumed the heroin probably came from a single source because it always seemed to be sold in the same small plastic phials, but intelligence as to its point of manufacture was a closely guarded secret and one I was never privy to. Once heroin hit the street, overdose deaths occurred. The material was 97 percent pure, and users typically inhaled it into their nostrils, getting a huge hit. Those who overdosed died abruptly, often after heavy hemorrhaging from nasal passages.

Heroin this pure also had the potential to earn exporters large dividends if it could be safely transported to the United States. Before long military police were even assigned to the mortuary in an effort to halt narcotics shipments in the remains of men killed and processed through the facility.

Overdose deaths increased the frequency of our trips to the Army-operated Saigon mortuary. Special Agent John Morgan and I arrived there one morning to inspect the body of a sailor who had died while on liberty in Can Tho. It was a quiet day. None of the dozen or so preparation tables that lined the walls were in use by any of the civilian morticians on the Army staff. A cheerful young black Army NCO greeted us; after we explained our business, he rolled out a gurney with a zipped body bag on it and then left the room. I unzipped the bag to expose the deceased, a robust black male of about twenty-two. His heavily muscled arms were crossed over his chest, and I had some difficulty unbending them to inspect for needle marks. My inspection was inconclusive, but I knew the pathology report would tell more when it came through. I zipped up the bag, washed my hands in a nearby sink, and moved to leave with Morgan. In another area, an MP was looking into the open thoracic cavity of a soldier recently run over by a forklift on

Newport Docks. "Enough of this shit," Morgan said as I thanked our helper, and we walked out into fresh air.

Soon after our trip to the mortuary, another sailor billeted at the bachelor enlisted quarters (BEQ) along Plantation Road, on the way to Tan Son Nhut Airport, was discovered dead on his bunk. Morgan and I went to the scene to carry out a detailed search as a part of an investigation designed to verify the cause of death. The body had been removed, but little else appeared to have been disturbed. The victim's pillow was indented from use and was saturated with blood. A magazine, bloody and crumpled, rested on top of the pillow. Heroin powder was scattered over the sheet, and an open phial lay nearby. Curious, Morgan stooped to see what the victim had apparently been reading when he decided to snort near-pure heroin. Snorting, he turned to me and said, "It's some hippy magazine which sings the praises of discovering your inner self with drugs." Turning back, he said, "Blow your mind, baby!" I stood on the bed with my Navy Leica and took an unforgettable photo with all the key elements clearly evident: heroin, the magazine article's exhortation, and the blood of a silly young man who wasn't getting a second chance. The photo found its way into drug education lectures, but few of us thought it made much of a difference.

In another incident, while returning to the office from the nearby PX, Morgan arrested a soldier assigned to the Army post office as he was buying heroin from a street vendor. The soldier's coworkers witnessed the incident and became belligerent. In normal circumstances, the coworkers' reaction would not have worried John Morgan in the least, but the Cholon Army Post Office handled all the NISO mail, every day. And it was hard to get Morgan out on the street until after morning mail call, when he waited expectantly for a sweet-smelling envelope from his love far away. After the arrest, the postal workers received some harsh words if Morgan's daily letter wasn't there. Mail was a very serious part of his life in Vietnam—as it was for most of us.

In many ways, working out of the Saigon office was quite different from the experience of working the north. Most days, Saigon agents wore civilian clothes to work. Civvies were hardly a cover for anybody who knew what to look for; every agent carried a credential case in his breast pocket, held in place by the distinctive money clip that all Vietnam agents wore as a badge of honor. Side arms were often worn outside of shirts, depending on individual preference and circumstances.

Investigations in Saigon tended to center around areas where Navy personnel passed en route to field elements. Transit facilities and barracks were located along Plantation Road, a less-than-salubrious area characterized by a high density of bars and massage parlors. A pall of dust, diesel smoke, and rotting garbage hung over Plantation Road—except when welcome showers cleared the atmosphere and transformed road verges to mud. Aside from having fewer opportunities to meet Vietnamese women (on a strictly commercial basis), sailors were in better surroundings at many of the more distant forward duty stations.

Logistic support bases (LSBs) had been developed in key river locations for the benefit of the riverine navy, called the Brown Water Navy. At these bases, maintenance functions were carried out on the many small craft that allowed the U.S. and Vietnamese navies to prosecute the war in the densely populated Mekong Delta. There were fast alloy-hulled PCFs, armored Monitors bristling with heavy weapons, fiberglass-hulled riverine patrol jet boats (PBRs), and many others. All required skilled maintenance staff and drydock facilities. Nearest to Saigon was the important Nha Be Logistic Support Base, which was less than an hour from Cholon by road. The drive to the base was normally an easy one through the center of Saigon, where a bridge near the Majestic Hotel led to Nha Be's gates.

Nha Be supported patrol forces that kept the river to the port of Saigon open. It was also a useful jumping-off spot for operations into the nearby Rung Sat Special Zone. Infamous as a hideout for Viet Cong for many years, Nha Be was a labyrinth of dense mangrove swamp and extremely difficult to patrol.

The base itself was a series of timber-framed barracks, workshops, and warehouses largely surrounded by water. As was typical, the town had grown up outside the gates, coming as close to the base as the authorities would allow. Commercial enterprises of all descriptions—mechanics, coffin-makers, grocers, bars, and fishermen's huts—could be found there. When in Nha Be, the SEAL team frequented an establishment known simply as the Green Door. Their postoperation scenes there were legendary; everybody stayed clear.

With the advent of Vietnamization came the accelerated handover of Navy assets and materiel to the VNN. As I had observed at Cam Ranh, the handover program also provided temptation and opportunity to Vietnamese with criminal propensities. Incidents of burglary and ingenious theft increased. We had a low resolution rate for these events, although when VNNSB could spare a man to assist with interrogations, the odds of finding the perpetrator jumped dramatically. Vietnamese recalcitrants did not respond well when interviewed by men who treated the thiefs like the hardcore enemy insurgents they were used to extracting information from.

Large-scale loss in Navy thefts was not a regular event, but we did uncover a scam operated by a fuel-hauling contractor who had built false baffles in the trailer tank. The baffles retained fuel when the tank was emptied into the Navy's fuel farm. Thus, the U.S. Navy was unwittingly supplying fuel for a large proportion of Saigon's private vehicles.

One morning in late 1970 I drove to Nha Be with a lead case, intending to interview a sailor assigned to a ship I believed was anchored there in the river. Once I'd parked my vehicle within the base perimeter, I checked the river and could see no ship. Below, a cheerful boatswain mate was sweeping up aboard his LCM, a ramped landing craft. I asked him if he knew where the ship was. "Sure," he said. "Six miles or so downriver she's anchored." He was delivering mail and a few other supplies and said he'd be glad to have me along. He expected two more passengers, and perhaps half an hour later we got under way.

This was my first up-close look at the Soi Rap River. I'd flown over the broad, muddy tract several times but enjoyed this opportunity to view the array of Vietnamese river life up close. The sailors transiting to their ship found places in the vehicle well to sack out; I stood with the boatswain and his rail-mounted M60 as we burbled downstream, passing sampans and fishermen hauling in their nets. Several miles downstream the river split. Dead ahead on a spit of land overlooking the junction stood the ramparts of an old French fort. I commented as I inspected the fortress with field glasses that the only thing that appeared to be missing was a detachment of Foreign Legion. The boatswain, noting my interest, said he would stop on the way back from the ship. A detachment of Regional Force militia was there, he said.

Minutes later we rounded a bend to see two Navy logistic ships anchored in the river. The coxswain swung his boat in a wide arc and pulled alongside the vessel I was visiting. I clambered up a swaying Jacob's ladder, holding my file folder in my teeth. The XO greeted me, introduced me to the master at arms, and arranged a private office for my interview. Soon after, the master at arms, a burly boatswain mate chief, delivered my witness. He was lucid and cooperative; I had what I needed in less than an hour. After lunch in the wardroom, I waited while materiel was loaded on the LCM for delivery at Nha Be. We got under way perhaps an hour later and headed upstream for the stop at the French fortress.

French military engineers had built a substantial reinforced-concrete jetty and a small railway to deliver supplies to the fort. Several Vietnamese fishing on the jetty jumped to their feet when they noticed the LCM heading toward them. Picking up their M16 rifles and other gear, the militia personnel waved and stood by to take lines. We were soon alongside. Although they did not speak English and we did not speak Vietnamese, we gave them rations and indicated our interest in a visit. They seemed happy to have us and began helping us onto the crumbling wharf. I carried a fine compact camera, a Rollei 35, with me on all my travels in Vietnam, and I wanted an opportunity to record this site, which I believed had witnessed many important events in the contemporary history of Indochina.

The Vietnamese led, following a well-worn track in the bed of the now nonexistent narrow-gauge rail line. To one side, a narrow steel cylindrical observation tower, which must have been a claustrophobic post for the soldier assigned to it, had been toppled by high explosives, perhaps an aerial bomb. About seven hundred yards from the jetty were the gates to the fort. An inscription in French and a date from the late nineteenth century were embossed on the keystone. I climbed the staircases above the monsoon-flooded courtyard to inspect the massive eight-inch guns that had once protected Saigon from seaborne invasion by France's enemies. Later, I learned that the fort had been used not only by the French but also by the Japanese during the occupation of French Indochina in World War II, by Viet Minh in the first Indochina War, and even briefly by Viet Cong forces. I mused that the tiny militia detachment would be unable to do much more than call for help by radio if they were attacked. My pictures taken, we thanked our Vietnamese hosts, returned to the LCM, and started toward Nha Be.

Soon after our departure, possibly noticing my concern that mid-afternoon had already passed, the coxswain swung the boat into a side channel, explaining it was a shortcut. I said nothing but watched the increasingly narrow mangrove inlet for signs of human activity. I knew what was in the Rung Sat Special Zone and was not keen to surprise the enemy from an LCM carrying one machine gun. Several minutes later, as diplomatically as possible, I pointed out that the channel showed no signs it would widen and suggested perhaps we had taken the wrong turn from the river. In good humor, the coxswain slowed and then began to reverse until a turnaround was possible. I was nervous, knowing the noise of the boat diesels would have resonated all over the flat country and hoping nonfriendlies weren't at that moment racing along a track to the mangrove banks to ambush us. As it happened, they did not. But, as happened at several, easily remembered points during my Vietnam tour, I felt I had taken a silly, unnecessary risk, which could well have exposed me to a nonglorious death—the kind nobody wants their family to hear about. The photographs turned out well, however.

The French officially pulled out of Vietnam after the defeat at Dien Bien Phu in 1954. Though the colonial government had gone, various commercial arrangements remained to tie France to Vietnam. By 1970 few overt signs of the French or French business remained, except in places like the huge Michelin rubber plantations. I was not privy to intelligence about French activity in South Vietnam, but it seemed apparent that the Europeans were pursuing activities very much in their own interests. I had heard rumors about cash protection payments to the Viet Cong by plantations anxious to save their trees for the day when rubber production could be started anew. It followed that it was often not in the French's best interests to cooperate with U.S. forces or their allies.

One day on the flight line at Tan Son Nhut near the Air America terminal, I was looking at a hangar whose door was partially open. Curious, I had a good look inside until my presence was noted and a surly man of European appearance pulled the sliding door closed. Inside was parked a twin-engine Beechcraft of recent vintage, festooned with antennae. It was a French plane, obviously configured for an electronic intelligence/intercept role. Who was there to spy on in South Vietnam other than the Americans and their allies? I was uncomfortable at the thought that French intelligence might be benefiting the enemy as part of a French initiative to protect their investments in South Vietnam, but of course I could not prove this in any event.

My suspicions were again raised in 1971 when a NIS technical countermeasures team visited Saigon from Honolulu. With them came several mysterious metal boxes containing equipment used to sweep areas for evidence of enemy intrusion—gear that was classified and needed special custodial arrangements in Saigon.

The team came to sweep premises used by the commander of Naval Forces Vietnam at his headquarters. Both the intelligence division and the admiral's own office and conference areas required periodic scrutiny. The technicians, both special agents, began their work the next morning. All proceeded without incident. As I had by then been in Vietnam for more than two years, one agent asked me what I knew about COMNAVFORV's neighbors. I told him that the French diplomatic mission maintained consular premises opposite and diagonally from the main entrance to the naval headquarters. Further, I commented that the admiral's office had large, old-fashioned windows, which were within view of the French buildings. I was not privy to the world of the techs; I had no need to know this type of information, so good security practice dictated that the details be kept from me. But I had been briefed about Soviet initiatives to gather information within the U.S. embassy in Moscow, which involved powerful external radiation and listening devices. There was, I surmised, little reason to doubt that the French would give much to learn what was being said in Adm. Robert Salzer's office, and I assumed it was quite possible they had access to the state-of-the-art technology necessary to carry out the threat. I do not know whether any evidence of intrusion was discovered in the resweep, but I believe countermeasures were suggested.

I don't believe I was alone in my disgust at the threat posed by French self-interest, despite a general awareness of the role information gathering played in the national interests. Allies on the surface could become otherwise if an opportunity arose. Given the amount of wealth the United States invested in France's efforts to counter communism in Indochina, I remained unimpressed. My elders told me this was simply youthful idealism.

Saigon had its share of mayhem, but it was not of the scale that the I Corps agents in Da Nang had been conditioned to. Fraggings had not become a problem in Saigon, perhaps because commands had taken measures to limit ready access to offensive ordnance. There were shootings and serious assaults, but no fraggings until late 1970. One evening after work several of us had gathered in room 4 for a few beers when a call came through for the duty agent; that was me. I took the call and was told a frag had just been thrown into a small room occupied by two enlisted Navy advisers at a downtown BEQ. Both men were seriously injured and were being rushed to Third Field Hospital for treatment. I requested that U.S. Army military police establish a cordon around the BEQ and that all personnel be confined to their rooms; then I rushed across the street to the office, where I hastily assembled crime scene equipment. All available agents turned out to help.

We got to the crime scene about forty minutes after the explosion. The Le Lai BEQ was situated in central Saigon, a typical drab former Vietnamese hotel of indeterminate age. Surrounded by security wire, barricades against vehicle attack, and security bunkers, the MPs had had no difficulty in shutting access to and from the premises as we had requested. Agents spoke to the MPs who had first responded, then began interviewing witnesses—but none had actually seen the act committed. After the initial round of interviews, the agents began checking stories and digging deeper to learn who the victims had been seen with that evening. I walked upstairs to begin processing the crime scene.

On the seventh-floor landing, I saw a pool table that had been used as an emergency treatment area to stabilize the victims before they were rushed to hospital. Several items of clothing were recovered; all bore evidence of shrapnel injury.

The room was a narrow rectangle, typical of budget Vietnamese hotels, with a toilet at the rear. The two victims, whose beds had been on opposite walls, shared it. The entry door opened onto an open balcony seven floors above ground level. Windows, taped to reduce the effect of flying glass in the event of enemy attack, had been shattered by overpressure created by the explosion in the room, and the wooden entry door bore marks of numerous shrapnel strikes from the grenade. Against the rear partition wall, a fan-shaped powder stain and numerous fragmentation strikes identified the seat of the explosion. I surmised that the grenade had been thrown into the room and had rolled against the wall before detonating.

An M26 fragmentation grenade produces a fearsome explosion in the open; in a confined space in a brick and concrete structure vented only by an open casement window, the blast must have been incredible. Considering thousands of minute fragments moving at several thousand feet per second, I had always considered the fifteen-meter kill radius estimate conservative. That the victims had not been killed outright seemed nothing short of miraculous. The room contents had been reduced to fragmented pieces littering the floor. Everything seemed to have holes in it. Carefully searching and photographing the room, we found no evidence to link the victims with an offender.

By this time, other interviews had disclosed information about what had happened in the room before the incident. We learned the two victims had been drinking with an outsider, beginning that afternoon. Drinking had continued in the victims' room and had been accompanied by some noise, but no witness would say an argument had taken place. One interviewee suggested the unknown third man did not seem to be an engine-room rating, as the victims were. Special Agent Clayton Spradley issued orders to search teams to begin looking for the suspect, the victims' drinking partner from the day before.

The day following the fragging, the suspect came to the NISOV office in Cholon. He had been told we were looking for the man who had been drinking with the two victims. Clayton Spradley and I interrogated the suspect. A first-class petty officer in the SeaBees, he was interviewed in NISOV office spaces, after waiving his right to remain silent. He admitted he had been with the victims when it became apparent we had confirmed these facts with witnesses. Becoming uncomfortable, he nevertheless did not terminate the interview, and we continued to go over details of his story.

Spradley and I were an effective interrogation team. We had several successful confessions behind us and had developed a close rapport and ability to read each other. Spradley was a quiet Floridian, a few years older than me, with a soft voice and pleasant manner. Some may have thought, to their ultimate detriment, that he might be duped; he, however, had a voluminous memory for minute facts and could call these up effortlessly when the time was right. I worked as an opposite to keep the interview flowing.

After two hours the suspect was very aware that a comprehensive investigation into his activities on the evening of the fragging had been carried out. His alibis had been systematically disproven. Spradley and I were already at the stage of illustrating the inconsistencies in the alibi that, ultimately, a court-martial would hear. "Why don't you just tell us and get all of this behind you," Spradley finally said. After a long pause, the suspect nodded his head and said, "OK. I threw it." He then related how he had started drinking with the two victims late in the afternoon after coming in from the field. He was ready to relax after the "bush-time" and had joined them in a friendly spirit. The victims were engine-room petty officers, while the suspect was a SeaBee, a part of the Civil Engineer Corps. There was some gentle banter about SeaBees in comparison to fleet sailors. They had been drinking for several hours before the victims suggested all go to their room to continue the party there.

The suspect said that once in their room, the victims' moods had turned surly with drunkenness. The banter had become vicious, culminating in the victims' assaulting and ejecting the suspect from their room after he had accidentally disturbed cards in a poker game. Angry and bleeding after the beating, he had gone to the room where his field gear was stowed, removed a fragmentation grenade, and returned to the room where he heard the victims talking and laughing about what had happened. He pulled the pin and threw the grenade through the open window, retreating as rapidly as possible.

We reduced the suspect's accounts to a statement, which he signed. By this time, he and Spradley were talking about hunting and fishing experiences.

Both victims eventually made full recoveries, but they'd paid a high price for their assault. Spradley vividly recalls watching medical personnel at the Army Third Field Hospital extracting dozens of grenade shards from their bodies. When the time came for the suspect's court-martial, his excellent service record and character references were of little help: he was awarded a dishonorable discharge with forfeiture of all pay and allowances, and he was returned to the United States. He arrived at home with no pay and a felony conviction. I've often wondered how he fared.

Spradley and I inherited another fragging, this time at Logistic Support Base Ben Luc. At first the incident was reported as the possible result of enemy attack; personnel had been injured in their quarters by shrapnel penetrating the plywood hooches. But there were inconsistencies in this report. Supervising Agent Al Kersenbrock, not convinced by the preliminary investigation, ordered Spradley and me back to Ben Luc to do more digging.

Ben Luc is a village situated on one of the many river tributaries over which the road from Saigon to the Mekong Delta traverses. Near the north side of the bridge, the U.S. Navy built the base to support the monitors and patrol craft of the Brown Water Navy, which the navy used to fight the enemy on the inland waterways. A hardstand area on the riverbank facilitated the haul-outs necessary to repair battle damage and perform the intense maintenance required to keep sophisticated machinery operable in harsh tropic climes. There were docking facilities, a headquarters building, SEA huts for the troops, and new concrete masonry houses, recently erected for Vietnamese Navy personnel and families. Vietnamization was an active proposition at Ben Luc; many vessels had by this time been turned over to the VNN, who were taking a larger role in riverine patrol and offensive operations. Vietnamese families were settling into the modest dwellings recently completed by SeaBees, and there was considerable command focus on how well assimilation and handover were working.

Thus, both COMNAVFORV and VNN headquarters were concerned when the "attacks" occurred. NISOV turned to its VNN counterparts,

VNNSB, to see what information had been developed through their sources. VNNSB personnel were similarly unconvinced that the explosions were a result of enemy action.

Clay Spradley and I drove south out of Cholon early one morning and, after battling unusually heavy Vietnamese traffic, pulled into Ben Luc an hour or so later. At the headquarters building, we received a sketch of the incidents and were escorted down to inspect where the latest of four explosions had occurred. We noted the predictable fan-shaped spread of grenade shrapnel on plywood siding of a SEA hut. There seemed to be little doubt that a U.S.-made grenade was responsible; however, this fact did not by any means implicate an American. Vietnamese allies used our ordnance, as did the Viet Cong when they could, and the delta is a heavily populated region. We concluded the grenade could have come from anywhere.

We next conducted several grenade-throwing trials in an effort to isolate areas from which the frags could have been thrown. The extreme height of the perimeter fence ruled out manual throwing from outside the wire.

We carefully reviewed the duty rosters to determine who was on duty and where they were at the time of the incidents. Off-duty status was confirmed, too; sailors were asked where they were and what they were doing when the grenades exploded. A VNNSB officer carried out discreet inquiries on the Vietnamese side of the base to determine whether VNN witnesses might be able to assist. We had no witnesses who could point us to the offender.

There was no evidence of friction between U.S. and Vietnamese personnel. Spradley and I both thought the VNNSB investigator would easily turn up this sort of information, if it existed. We started concentrating more on U.S. Navy personnel. We checked to see whether command problems might have sparked retribution or incidents involving any of the persons nearest the blasts, which could be related. There were none.

We went back to the results of our grenade-throwing trials and looked afresh at the perimeter. Elevated watchtowers overlooked the wire at several key points. We wondered why the sentries had not been more help in our investigation to date and reexamined the names of those on duty. One sailor had been on duty on both of the nights when the "attacks" had occurred. Although he had been voluble and helpful when initially spoken to in the early hours of the investigation, we began to wonder if he was telling us everything he knew. We looked closer.

The young sailor had recently transferred from the United States. He had volunteered, leaving a wife and new baby in California while he began a year of duty in Vietnam. He seemed a cheerful character, but we nevertheless wondered what made him tick under the surface.

We discussed the case all the way back to Saigon that afternoon, and in the office we talked to Supervising Agent Kersenbrock about both our findings and feelings about the investigation. A great lateral thinker, Kersenbrock felt quite certain we had isolated the Ben Luc fragger. He urged us to interrogate the suspect. Spradley and I agreed an interrogation was necessary; we were not quite so certain the time was right, however. We wondered and silently worried about what we would have to go on if our suspect exercised his right to remain silent—as many do when confronted by a federal agent searching for facts.

The next morning we were back in our gray Navy Dodge pickup heading south to Ben Luc. We would do the interrogation. We'd go into it trying to learn as much as we could about the suspect before broaching questions about his movements on the two nights in question.

At Ben Luc, we arranged to use a private office, and the suspect arrived soon after. Warned in accordance with article 31 of the Uniform Code of Military Justice, he cheerfully waived his right to silence and signed a waiver. He was, he said, glad to assist us with our investigation and was soon explaining why he had volunteered for Vietnam. Being in a combat zone was for him—we soon learned—a rite of initiation into manhood. He was proud to stand watch over the sleeping inhabitants of the base at night.

Spradley and I both had a feeling about this man and his story. We let him know that we genuinely respected his desire to serve and told him we were volunteers, too. "You must have seen them coming through the wire that night?" I said. Surprised, he hesitated before answering. "We know you were just trying to do your job," Spradley quickly followed up. The subject visibly reacted to this but said nothing. Spradley changed the subject, and as I had provided most of the pressure during the interview, I got up and left the office for perhaps ten minutes. When I returned, the suspect and Spradley were showing each other wrinkled family photos from their wallets. I said nothing, staying in the background as they talked. Eventually, the conversation lagged and I looked at Spradley. He said again, using the suspect's name, that he knew he had done his best to defend the base. Nobody had died, but we needed to understand exactly what had happened.

The suspect hedged. I urged him to take an honorable option; he would be respected for that. "Just tell us what happened," I said. "You saw them coming through the wire, didn't you?" Spradley added in an effort to push the suspect toward coming clean. "You threw the grenades?" I said. Staring into his lap, he paused then nodded his head in affirmation. "I threw them," he said.

The interview ended on a low key. We shook hands and wished the man well; then we walked over the headquarters where we explained to the man's CO what had been said. "He's your man," I said. Later, on the road north, we talked about him. "If there is such a thing as a John Wayne syndrome, this man could have it," Spradley said.

As it happened, an Army psychiatrist in Saigon agreed the man was likely experiencing delusions when the phantom attacks occurred. He was hospitalized and later returned to the United States. COMNAVFORV, VNN chief of naval operations, and even CINCPACFLT gave kudos to NISOV. Al Kersenbrock rewarded us with something a little more tangible—a chance to travel to Thailand to pursue leads on a large-scale larceny investigation.

For agents assigned to Vietnam, opportunities to work in Thailand were eagerly sought after. Thailand was a very important bridgehead in the fight against communist North Vietnam, and although there was probably not enough work for NIS to justify a full-time presence in Bangkok, enough work accumulated that a trip each month was necessary. Agents from both Da Nang and Saigon shared the Thailand caseload. For Clayton Spradley and me, this was an "extra." For any agent in the Vietnam war zone, Thailand's relative safety, modern hotels, and restaurants were something to look forward to.

We were given an investigation that had originated with the officer in charge of construction (OICC), Thailand. The senior SeaBee believed a certain Thai national had stolen many thousands of dollars in construction materials by diverting or selling them. Other agents had conducted preliminary inquiries; it fell to us to do several interviews and hopefully wrap the case up.

With buoyant spirits, Clayton Spradley and I boarded a regular Navy Scatback flight—a C117 on a beer run to Bangkok—and two hours later we were walking across the steaming tarmac at the military side of Don Muang Air Base in Bangkok. Dressed in civvies, we decided to check into our hotel, then visit OICC Thailand that afternoon.

Thailand's senior SeaBee greeted us courteously in his high-rise Bangkok office, then briefed us about his suspicions and concerns. He told us the suspect was a Thai national employee assigned to the Vientiane, Laos, detachment. Examination of documents associated with the granting of service contracts to civilian contractors in Laos had created a strong suspicion that the suspect was rigging the process for kickback payments. Witnesses and records were all to be found in Vientiane. The captain suggested it might be most effective to pursue the investigation in Laos, and we had to agree with the logic of his argument. I telephoned Al Kersenbrock to tell him of our intention to travel to Laos. He seemed less than enchanted with the plan but assented. Next, we visited the American embassy to explain our mission to the security officer. Everything seemed to be in order as we boarded the overnight train to north Nong Khai. Fortified with several cold quarts of Sing Ha beer, we sat back in our Pullman bunks to watch the Thai countryside go by until it became dark.

The next morning a SeaBee lieutenant dispatched from Vientiane to assist us with the investigation met us at the train station. Nong Khai was the end of the rail line north; beyond was the sweeping expanse of the mighty

Mekong River and the towering mountains of Laos. What neither of us knew was the extent of the bitter, very secret war being waged in Laos against North Vietnamese by the CIA and its hill tribe allies. We would soon receive some none too subtle hints.

At the Thai border post, we learned that our travel documents were not in order because we had entered the country on a U.S. military transport. Thus, the ferryboat to dockside Vientiane was not an available option for us. Our SeaBee assistant was plainly anxious to get across the river to complete the investigation. "Don't worry about it," he told us. "We go back and forth across the river in private boats all the time." Spradley and I looked at each other, knowing full well we had probably already violated Thai law but not wanting to go back empty-handed, and agreed to go. A few minutes later we three big Americans were in a small motorized sampan with only inches of freeboard, sailing across the Mekong. I was relieved when we got to the other side and taken with the quiet beauty of Vientiane as our host drove us to the office. Laos was truly a step back in time: young saffron-clad Buddhist monks, heads shaven, walked in line for their rice ration, as did herds of ducks. Cars were few. Buildings were a fascinating mixture of French colonial architecture and the sweeping gables of traditional Lao structures.

At the OICC office we were able to quickly identify what records were required and who was needed for interview. We would, we decided, continue the inquiry after checking into our nearby hotel. There the phone call from the security officer at the American Embassy, Vientiane, found us. The officer told me that although the ambassador was as yet unaware of our unauthorized presence, if we did not depart from Laos, he soon would be. I could do nothing but assure the ambassador's security officer that we would be leaving soon. But we weren't in that big a hurry. After coming all that way, it seemed foolish not to carry the investigation as far as possible, even if the spooks didn't want us around. We did what we could, arranged for records and witnesses to be shipped to Bangkok, then made our way back across the expanses of the muddy Mekong to Thailand. Staying well away from Thai officials, we boarded the next train to Bangkok. Several days later, the case was complete, allowing OICC Thailand to do some badly needed housekeeping.

On our return to Bangkok, I immediately telephoned Al Kersenbrock in Saigon to tell him of our brush with American Embassy, Vientiane. At the end of the call, I thought the matter would remain in a holding pattern until our supervisor knew a little better what repercussions he could expect. Clayton Spradley and I genuinely thought the sense of initiative that previously had earned accolades might this time get us some unpleasant form of discipline.

Two weeks later, back in Saigon, we asked Al Kersenbrock if we were in the clear. We were, and we put the worry of our major diplomatic gaffe behind us.

To support riverine forces, the U.S. Navy deployed two aviation attack squadrons to the Mekong Delta. These were VAL-4, a fixed wing squadron flying OV10 Broncos, and HAL-4 (Helicopter Attack Squadron Four), called the Sea Wolves. The chopper gunship squadron used aging UH1B Hueys configured as gunships. These carried side-mounted rocket pods and flex M60 machine guns.

Sea Wolf helicopters were often stationed away from the squadron base at Binh Thuy, near Can Tho. The Navy reasoned that a nearby gunship could save lives in the sort of heavy contacts riverine forces frequently encountered on the rivers and canals where they fought the Viet Cong. Sea Wolf gunships were stationed aboard barracks ships, which had landing pads constructed on their upper decks. The gunships were also sent to forward bases when there was an operational need.

Thus it was that a pair of Sea Wolf gunships had been stationed at LSB Ben Luc and flew missions upriver in the area known as the Parrot's Beak on the Cambodian border. Flying in tandem at several thousand feet, the choppers were returning from a mission one evening. It was a routine flight until the lieutenant commander piloting the lead aircraft reported one-to-one vibration from the overhead main rotor and said he was reducing revolutions. The following aircraft acknowledged and reduced speed to stay in formation. There was some more discussion about the problem by radio, when suddenly, without warning, the entire rotor assembly and transmission broke away from the lead helicopter, leaving the cabin and its occupants to tumble downward to the mud of the Plain of Reeds. The followers watched in horror as fellow squadron members fell to their deaths. They could do absolutely nothing to help.

The next day a Navy recovery team went to the site to recover bodies and critical pieces of the crashed aircraft for the investigation that would follow. The rotor assembly and portions of the main rotor were pulled from the mud and returned to squadron headquarters at Binh Thuy where experts would pore over the broken machinery looking for clues as to the cause of this catastrophic failure.

After thorough cleaning, the work began. Examiners looked for inconsistencies in the badly mangled machinery. Considering the pilot's final broadcast about experiencing vibration each time the main rotor turned, the examiners began looking at main rotor remains. On the end of one of the two blades, machining marks were discerned on an internal component. These, they reasoned, should not have been there. Had sabotage been committed by someone sawing into the leading edge of the blade, thus weakening it and causing a catastrophic in-flight failure? Experts concluded the imbalance caused by one rotor suddenly losing part of its length and becoming unbalanced would be more than sufficient to cause the transmission and both blades to separate from the aircraft.

NIS has a mandate to investigate all acts of sabotage. The command was quick to ask for assistance after the rotor blade examination raised suspicions. There were also concerns that other aircraft might also have been affected and might be flying in a dangerous condition.

Special Agent Bill Worochock, then the Binh Thuy resident agent, came to Saigon and joined me for preliminary investigations at Ben Luc, where the fateful mission had originated. Worochock and I didn't get much chance to see each other. Binh Thuy was a busy office, with Worochock having responsibility on his own for the entire southern delta region. He flew to Saigon periodically to deliver cases and consult with the SRA, but this was far from a regular occurrence. We used the driving time to Ben Luc to discuss what we knew about the incident. At that point, I was still uncertain why aviation experts thought sabotage might have occurred. How, I asked, could somebody climb up on a parked Huey and make a hacksaw cut through the leading edge of a main rotor without being seen? And, assuming such a thing was possible, would not a normal preflight examination have shown up even a small cut? Perhaps it was possible to make a cut and fill it? Compounding my curiosity, Worochok told me the alloy rotor surface metal showed signs of tearing, rather than a clean cut. To cut the rotor, it would have been necessary to cut through the outer skin to reach internal components. Scientific examination would be necessary to verify whether this had occurred.

At Ben Luc, we pulled into the compound, told headquarters we were there, and walked over to the helo pad, where a Sea Wolf Huey sat, apparently in stand-by status. No crew was present. Worochock and I walked around the helo pad, considering the likelihood that a night intruder could successfully evade sentries and others to hacksaw components of a parked helicopter. We considered it possible but unlikely; it remained a possibility we could not yet dismiss.

As we finished inspecting the area, the chopper crew chief arrived to begin a preflight check. We watched carefully to see what he did and how he did it—especially when he ran his bare hand along the leading edge of the main rotor blades. When we engaged him in conversation, he explained that gunship maintenance people were especially careful of critical mechanical components because the aircraft came under fire regularly. He assured us that all crewmembers were equally as fastidious as he had been. "They're careful if they want to stay alive," he told us. The next question was obvious: "What kind of a crew chief had the man been who had gone down?" "One of the best," we were told.

It was one of those typical mornings in the delta: hot and getting hotter, with soaring humidity levels. The crew chief had unzipped his flight suit and pulled it off his shoulders, sweat running off his torso. After our brief interview with the chief, the pilot and copilot walked toward us, around the blast revetment. As all three—the two officers and enlisted crew chief—had witnessed the incident, we quickly interviewed them. The day of the crash they had been on a support mission, and as those usually came when somebody was under attack, there was an air of urgency as the flight inspection went ahead and the rocket ordnance and machine guns were checked and rechecked. In essence, all confirmed the flight had been routine, neither aircraft had been under fire during the mission, and all had assumed the vibration problem was a mechanical problem—though certainly not one of major magnitude. All were young men, and each had his own way coping with the loss of very close friends and comrades. Theirs was a very dangerous profession and this was not the first time they had lost wingmen, but that didn't make it any easier. None had any idea how or why the incident had occurred, each seeming to attribute it to fate and bad luck.

A few minutes after the interview, with turbine screaming, the Huey lifted off amid the heat waves of the metal matting and climbed out over the river en route to another rescue mission. We stood and watched the chopper as it flew away from us and out of sight. After a pause, Worochock said, "If this was sabotage, I don't see any way it could have been carried out here in Vietnam." We would have to wait for the results of the scientific investigation of the rotor before knowing which way to take the investigation next.

The FBI crime laboratory assisted by examining the mystery cut in the leading edge of the recovered rotor blade. Their findings some weeks later were definitive: the end of the leading edge had been cut at the point where the blade failed, but the metal covering over the leading edge—which must be a single, unified piece of metal to retain strength and integrity—had not been cut. The FBI concluded that the U.S. aviation maintenance company that had reconditioned the blades had used two pieces of material in the leading edge.

As hardened as we had become to the vagaries of war, Worochock and I were both shocked at the implications of the examination. Somebody had clearly put profit ahead of the lives and safety of helicopter crewmembers, possibly assuming the odds were not high that they would ever be implicated. Instead of waiting for a full-length leading edge, they had used a leftover and a scrap to achieve the length required, and then covered it as usual with metal skin. Five Navy men had paid for this greed with their lives.

There could be no happy ending to this story. The investigation was referred to the FBI, along with our investigation that showed who the blade reconditioning contractor was and when the work had been done. None of us were asked to testify, but we later learned that a successful prosecution against the contractor had been made in federal court.

Cdr. Donn T. Burrows, USN, replaced Tom Brooks as CO NISOV in 1970. Well-liked, Burrows kept up the momentum of a number of programs he inherited in the takeover.

COMNAVFORV was situated in Saigon, not far from the CO's villa. NISOV's CO wore a second hat as an intelligence officer of COMNAVFORV's intelligence section, N-2. Thus NISOV had a ready conduit for intelligence and investigative support.

N-2 was commanded by a captain, USN, with an intelligence designator—in other words, a career intelligence officer. Being N-2 could be a particularly thankless job if command initiatives were not running favorably or if the admiral was a taskmaster. N-2 was the man expected to know the answers, sometimes even when required information had yet to be acquired. He depended on a network of NILOs posted in key areas whose duties essentially involved acting as information sponges from all available local resources and then referring the gathered information to Saigon for assessment and evaluation. N-2 relied on these junior officers; if one of them let him down, he could be very vulnerable at the admiral's infamous working breakfasts, which occurred promptly at 6:00 AM daily.

Commanders Brooks and Burrows, with Supervising Agents Schunk and Kersenbrock, often called in to brief the N-2 before the breakfast meetings. The routine provided some interesting insight into the operation of the command—and doubtless occasionally caused them to reflect on their good fortune, being quartered well away from the pressure cooker of the command headquarters.

V.Adm. Elmo Zumwalt, USN, had built Naval Forces, Vietnam, into a substantial fighting force over several years of dedicated service. In 1969 he transferred to Washington, D.C., was promoted, and was replaced by V.Adm. Jerome H. King, USN. King, a dynamic leader and a great friend of NISOV, was a tough, ruthless taskmaster who was known to give his staff early morning indigestion at the dreaded breakfast meetings. Al Kersenbrock, many years later, recounted the sight of glassy-eyed Navy captains staring at their office walls after facing their commander's caustic criticism at one of Jerry King's breakfasts.

These were interesting times in the N-2 shop. Ever the opportunists, the intel officers in the shop were always looking for ways to further the allied cause against the Viet Cong and North Vietnamese. One such opportunity came in the form of a near-dead carrier pigeon, which landed, exhausted, on the deck of a patrolling U.S. Navy vessel assigned to coastal surveillance duties under Operation Market Time. Crewmembers rescued the bird, fed and cared for it, and considered making it a pet before Asian characters and numerals were discovered to be tattooed inside its wing. Realizing they might have stumbled upon something important, they turned the bird over to shore-based intelligence staff, which conveyed it to Saigon and the compound of COMNAVFORV. Intelligence staff quickly realized the bird was a trained carrier pigeon of the North Vietnamese Army.

While N-2 was considering his options, the pigeon was assigned to a young sailor from the Deep South, a pigeon fancier with an aptitude for birds. Quarters for the bird were found in an attic area of one of the compound buildings, all of which were fine examples of French colonial architecture and thus replete with spacious attic areas. N-2 staff and a curious Al Kersenbrock, who watched the pigeon's rehabilitation with interest, visited the pigeon loft regularly.

Ultimately, a plan was hatched in which the bird would be released with a radio homing device attached to its back. This, staff reasoned, created a reasonable probability the bird would home in on an important enemy staff installation somewhere deep in the jungle of II Corps. The pigeon trainer began affixing small parcels to the bird on his in-house training flights to build up its stamina for the mission. The radio homing device was fairly large, perhaps half the size of a deck of playing cards, and thus no small cargo for a pigeon. However, over several months the bird increased its fitness to a point that allowed the N-2 to put finishing touches on the operational plan and start thinking seriously about the pigeon's release.

The pigeon had come down at a point off II Corps; Cam Ranh Bay was the nearest naval facility. The bird was released in the same general area in hopes that it would quickly find its bearings and continue with the interrupted initial flight. Fixed-wing and rotary-wing aircraft with observers and appropriate radio tracking equipment were organized to chase the pigeon, the planners thinking the bird's flight home would be quickly followed by a huge aerial attack on some elusive enemy complex.

There was thus considerable excitement and anticipation in the confines of N-2 office spaces in Saigon when the Vietnamese pigeon was finally released many miles to the north and sent rapidly winging inland with a homing transmitter on its back. Assigned aircraft rushed to keep up with the bird's flight, but they could not; he was soon out of range, and no amount of searching could find the bird with a beeper on its back. The operation was a washout. The speedy bird was never found, nor was the elusive NVA headquarters—which must have been rapidly relocated if the radio-carrying bird made it home.

An incident in early 1971, which early reports suggested was simply another enemy attack on shipping, led NIS agents to discover important information about communist Chinese off-shore intelligence operations.

Registered in Somalia, captained by a Dutch national and crewed by mainland Chinese seamen, SS *Yellow Dragon* came under attack while sailing up the Mekong River. Destined for the Cambodian capitol, the ship came under heavy attack from both shore and water, at a point close to the international boundary between South Vietnam and Cambodia. It was generally assumed that Viet Cong forces had carried out the attack.

Panic-stricken, the Chinese crew abandoned ship and took to the river in a lifeboat. River currents swept the crew downstream, where the leaking boat lodged on a mud bank and crewmembers were able to make their way ashore. The captain, knowing that he had a responsibility to the crewmembers but that he could do little to save the vessel without their assistance, then decided also to leave *Yellow Dragon*. He gathered up his sailors, who were without even the most basic identification papers, and led them to a nearby township. Vietnamese Navy personnel had assisted with the evacuation, but they had charged the castaways in U.S. currency for the service.

The ship's abandonment triggered an orgy of looting by Vietnamese Navy personnel, who enjoyed unfettered access to the *Yellow Dragon* for about three days. They began by stealing the cargo and the crew's personal effects; then they started on paneling, fittings, and even major engine components. Meanwhile, the ship's master had reached Saigon, where he alleged his vessel had been subject to acts of piracy by the South Vietnamese, implying complicity by U.S. personnel. Though it was known that the captain was married to a Shanghai woman and maintained a residence in communist China, COMNAVFORV was predictably disturbed to hear allegations against his Vietnamese allies at a particularly sensitive period in the Vietnamization process. NISOV was asked to investigate the incident and furnish a report to the admiral as a matter of urgency.

Special Agent Clayton Spradley was assigned the case and began his investigation by contacting the VNNSB to determine what facts it knew of the incident. Spradley was surprised to receive "friendly" advice from VNNSB that his investigation might prove fatal, a warning that provided direction to later establish VNNSB complicity in events following the attack.

Spradley and interpreter Sergeant Trieu flew by Navy helicopter to a logistic support base, and from there they traveled by boat to the sunken *Yellow Dragon*. The vessel had been systematically plundered—not, it was said, unlike a cow caught in piranha-infested waters. Paneling had been removed from the master's cabin, major components had been stripped from the ship propulsion system, and virtually all cargo taken from the hold.

Spradley and Trieu established that the weapons used against *Yellow Dragon* were all of U.S. manufacture, and they were soon satisfied the attack had been launched by the South Vietnamese Navy. The case was therefore one of considerable sensitivity given that the Vietnamese allies were shouldering more responsibility for the conduct of the war. Incidents underscoring differences between allies, or indeed, examples of lawlessness by allied forces were not helpful to the Vietnamization process, particularly if word reached the journalist corps on their bar stools in Saigon.

Discreet investigation in riverside towns confirmed Spradley's suspicions. Before leaving Saigon, he had been supplied with several hundred dollars worth of local currency to be used for the purchase of information from local citizenry. With the information he thus purchased he identified a number of Vietnamese naval officers as the sources of much of the loot then on display in local markets, including bolts of uniform cloth, watches, imported perishables, and fruit destined for Phnom Penh. Watches, stereo equipment, and cameras had been packed into barrels with false baffles, over which apples and similar produce were packed to act as concealment. Spradley bought several watches, then he and Sergeant Trieu engaged the services of two young men with motorcycles to return them downriver to the Navy logistic support base.

"We hired these two cowboys with Vespas to take us down the trail which skirted along the bank of the Mekong. In many places, the jungle grew right up to the edge, and the trail was never very wide. I remember the local people, undoubtedly surprised to see a large American on a motor scooter, coming out to wave and say, 'OK, GI' as I passed. As soon as we had gone by, all vanished into the foliage. I found it disquieting and couldn't help but wonder if the enemy had been told I was out there."

Spradley and Trieu arrived safely at the base, caught a helicopter ride back to Saigon, and were briefing Al Kersenbrock soon after.

In the meantime, despite many obstacles, the Dutch captain found his way to Saigon with his crew. He was immediately embroiled with South Vietnamese officials in a nightmare of bureaucratic red tape. Worse, the Hong Kong merchants sponsoring the voyage abandoned him because he had left his ship. None had permission to enter the Republic of Vietnam, so no permission could be granted for their departure. They had no money and the Chinese crew was without even basic identification papers; they had been left on *Yellow Dragon* in their haste to leave her.

Aware of the captain's travails, Al Kersenbrock befriended him and offered the hospitality of the villa at 98 Phan Dinh Phuong: the Dutchman accepted with gratitude. In the days that followed the captain visited the Dutch and British diplomatic missions in Saigon and ultimately arranged for the crew to fly out to Hong Kong. He granted Special Agent Kersenbrock access to his Chinese communist crew; valuable intelligence was thus acquired and forwarded to eager analysts at N-2.

As the commanding officer was then absent, Kersenbrock and the master had a number of evenings together at the villa, characterized by animated conversation about the relative merits of Chinese communism versus Western capitalism. The Dutchman, a resident of Shanghai with a Chinese wife, considered communism an unstoppable social force that would ultimately overwhelm all opposition to it. But his political orientation was influenced much more by opportunism and circumstance than by conviction. He preferred a mainland Chinese crew because these came complete with a Red Book–carrying proselytizer who provided the sort of discipline most other nationalities lacked. He had learned his trade first through navigating the waters of the Dutch East Indies. Commercial circumstance and Indonesian independence had moved him northward.

That a friendship had developed was made evident at a restaurant shortly before the captain's departure. A reporter, chasing a vague rumor of piracy on the Mekong, approached their table, asking the captain if he was the Dutchman whose ship had been attacked. The captain denied not only his identity but also any knowledge of the incident. Al Kersenbrock was much relieved; a story in the international press about the Vietnamese Navy's participation in acts of piracy might have had wide-ranging political consequences.

The final gesture of goodwill came as the captain prepared for his flight from South Vietnam: he left the ship's log and important correspondence in Kersenbrock's custody with instructions they be mailed to him in Hong Kong in certain knowledge every binding would be carefully disassembled and each word pored over by intelligence analysts. It was his way, Kersenbrock said, of expressing his thanks.

N-2 had a Chinese expert on staff. He knew the trading consortium underwriting the voyage was a notorious communist Chinese front, which had been involved in nefarious intelligence acquisition activity. *Yellow Dragon*'s papers and crew interviews helped add important new information to Naval Intelligence files. A week later the files were forwarded to Hong Kong with no indication they had been examined in any way.

# 13

## THE DELTA EXPERIENCE, 1968 TO 1971

**By far the greatest amount of U.S. Navy men** and materiel was concentrated in the area south of Saigon—in the region known as the Mekong Delta. This made perfect sense: the rich alluvial plains that produced most of the nation's rice were home to South Vietnam's densest population concentration. The mighty Mekong bisects in Cambodia, and these branches split again in the delta, becoming four substantial rivers that finally spill into the South China Sea. Those rivers, their tributaries, and scores of canals have provided the region with maritime communication links for centuries. The Communist National Liberation Movement had strong links to riverside communities to the south, particularly My Tho. Thus, a strong naval presence in the waters of the delta was necessary to swing military advantage to the allies.

The U.S. Navy chose to create key command structures at Binh Thuy, immediately adjacent to the important delta city of Can Tho. A construction program for improving roads and bridges was begun and temporary buildings were erected in a self-contained base just back from the Mekong's southernmost tributary, the Ba Sac River.

Logically, as increased concentrations of naval personnel created more work for NISOV, a full-time agent presence became necessary, and so NISSU Binh Thuy was born. It was a one-man post manned by one special agent, normally on a six-month rotation.

Special Agent Bob Tugwell established the office in early 1968 and was relieved late that year by John Triplett. Triplett had begun his tour in Vietnam with an assignment to NISRA Da Nang. A well-liked and respected agent with considerable field experience, Triplett was a logical choice for the post. His predecessor had completed nearly two years of service in Vietnam.

NISSU Binh Thuy was a demanding assignment. The unwritten boundaries of the post covered the entire southern area of Vietnam. Saigon agents normally covered commands only as far south as My Tho and Dong Tam, as these were typically accessible by road—tactical considerations of course permitting. The Binh Thuy agent had to quickly master the geography of his area together with the locations for key command elements; he also had to quickly learn the labyrinthine transportation system so he could respond to requests for investigative assistance in good time. Helicopters provided a majority of rides around IV Corps Tactical Zone—the Delta, to those who worked it.

Special Agent Don Masden replaced Triplett as NISOV's delta agent. Masden had the advantage of an excellent grounding in criminal investigation. Formerly a state trooper of the Kentucky State Police, he was appointed to special agent, ONI, in December 1956 at Norfolk, Virginia.

"Our financial situation meant I had to leave my wife, two sons, and a daughter behind in Frankfort to take up the appointment." Masden remained at Norfolk until 1958, when he was returned to the U.S. Naval Ordnance Plant, Louisville, Kentucky. Responsible for sixty Kentucky counties, he traveled extensively for ONI until 1966, when a position opened up at the Camp Lejeune, North Carolina, office.

Camp Lejeune, for much of the Vietnam conflict, was a crucible of racial tension and crime. The office was certainly the busiest criminal investigation shop on the East Coast. Masden went to work for SRA Matt Hudgeons, later replaced by Al Kersenbrock—who established his own place in NISOV lore.

In January 1969 Don Masden requested a transfer to Vietnam. "Like others in the organization, I thought this was an appropriate move for a career special agent." The Masden family moved back to Louisville, and on June 19 Masden boarded his plane at Travis Air Force Base for the flight to Saigon.

"I was met at Tan Son Nhut by Special Agent Jeff Baker and taken to the office in Cholon for processing. Saigon was a pretty big shock to the system."

Masden was quickly phased into the NISRA Saigon team, under SRA Royce Logan. He learned the unique aspects of working in Vietnam, most particularly some of the challenges to one's personal safety. Assigned to investigate narcotics violations at the Navy's riverine base at Dong Tam, Masden accompanied Special Agent Ben Johnson on the forty-mile drive southwest of Saigon. Aircraft were at times simply not available, and this was one of those times when driving was necessary to accomplish the mission. Johnson and Masden left Saigon in a Navy Ford Bronco and were in Dong Tam by late morning.

Masden's investigation was complete that afternoon, but by then it was far too late to return to Saigon. The two agents were assigned quarters in a SEA hut for the night. At 3:00 AM, awakened by insects and the sounds of a strange environment, Masden got up, intending to take a short walk. Stepping outside as quietly as possible to avoid awakening the sleeping Johnson, he had taken only a few steps when he heard a large explosion aboard one of the anchored crane barges nearby. A VC mortar round had scored a direct hit, and others were following. Wasting no time, a startled Don Masden made for the nearest bunker. Ben Johnson had made it there before him.

The next day, while Ben Johnson ran more leads, Masden elected to return to Saigon by air. Two young Army warrant officer pilots flying a LO-ACH helicopter offered him a seat in the small craft, and they were soon winging at treetop level across the verdant jungle. Several minutes out of Dong Tam, he learned they intended to put a strike in on a suspected Viet Cong base camp. Soon after this revelation, he was hanging on tight as the pilots made strafing runs over the camp. Don Masden learned after that to ask questions in advance about flight plans in Vietnam.

In August 1969, appointed as new Binh Thuy agent, Masden packed up his gear at the Five Oceans BOQ, drove to Tan Son Nhut, and found a ride south aboard an Army Huey. It was his first trip to the delta, and he had responsibility for a very large patch of unfamiliar terrain. Landing at Can Tho, he was greeted by the pungent odor of a delta town: "There was raw sewage running down the street in Can Tho, and I said to myself how glad I was to have all those inoculations up to date."

A passing Navy truck on its way to Binh Thuy stopped to pick him up. After a short drive, the driver deposited Masden inside the Navy base. He found a bustling complex in the grips of change and expansion. The parent command, Naval Support Activity, Binh Thuy, was maintaining a substantial fleet of U.S. Navy patrol craft throughout the delta and training South Vietnamese sailors to assume these duties—as well as building facilities for the Vietnamese Navy at key strategic locations in the region.

Earlier in the year the U.S. Navy had established a combat aviation capability at Binh Thuy to support its delta forces made up of the squadrons HAL-4 and VAL-4. The aviators and their Fleet Air Support Unit backup increased the base population by about twelve hundred men. Binh Thuy had a twenty-one-hundred-foot runway to accommodate its aircraft. The two squadrons added a formidable air attack/support capability to the Navy's delta arsenal.

The main force of the Binh Thuy base had always been River Patrol Boat Flotilla Five, the Navy's PBR force of about 180 vessels. Charged with interdiction of enemy men and materiel on the myriad waterways of the delta, the Brown Water Navy sailors found the jet boats well suited for their mission. The fiberglass-hulled boats could travel at speeds of as much as twenty-five knots; each was armed with three .50-caliber machine guns and an assortment of lesser small arms, and many had radar. River Flotilla Five officers found office space for Don Masden in their administration building, and he was assigned a room at the base BOQ. He didn't have long to wait for his first investigation: the shooting death of an enlisted man who had been a passenger of a U.S. Navy truck.

"The victim had been seated in the center of the cab. The round was fired through the rear of the cab where it struck him in the back. He died almost immediately."

Masden's investigation established that the fatal shot came from an unholstered .45-caliber issue pistol in the charge of one of the Navy men riding in the rear of the truck. It was an accidental discharge. Nevertheless, to formally conclude the investigation, a postmortem examination would be necessary. Don Masden flew to Saigon and the Army mortuary for this purpose.

"I had attended autopsies at Camp Lejeune; these are never pleasant. But my recollections are most vivid of other bodies at the mortuary, mostly maimed victims of modern warfare."

Shortly after the conclusion of the accidental discharge case, while on a routine visit to headquarters in Saigon, Don Masden received a call for help from the Navy detachment at An Long, upriver from Binh Thuy: a PBR had been sabotaged, a crewmember injured.

"I was in Cholon at the time, so caught the first available aircraft down to Can Tho, where the injured coxswain had been hospitalized. When I interviewed him, he told me there had been an explosion aboard his PBR, apparently originating in a one-gallon salad-oil container. He said he had been on a routine mission at the time."

Pressed for details as to what he had seen in the moments before the explosion, the man told Masden he thought he had seen, fleetingly, an object drop from overhead just seconds before. A Vietnamese sailor had been seated overhead acting as lookout at the time. The coxswain also commented that he was not on the best of terms with this sailor because he had refused him permission to take leave.

Doctors said the coxswain's injuries to legs and feet were consistent with those caused by fragmentation.

Needing to inspect the scene of the explosion, Masden turned to the aviators for transportation. It was one of the rare occasions when they couldn't help; however, the explosive ordnance disposal officer in charge, CWO3 John Lomburg, said he would use his Boston Whaler to take him upriver. Masden and Lomburg made a fast trip in the outboard-powered boat to An Long, where they inspected the vessel thought to have been sabotaged. Then Masden interviewed the suspect Vietnamese sailor, with the assistance of an interpreter. "The Vietnamese sailor was cooperative, but he denied any responsibility for the explosion."

Masden turned to other crewmembers for their recollections and background information about the PBR mission. He learned that two of the vessels had been assigned, an older Mark I PBR and a much newer Mark II. The newer boat was more powerful and had a better top speed.

"One of the crewmen told me that the victim, the coxswain of the Mark II, had been driving around the slower boat in circles. This had caused wash to splash onto the Mark I, specifically on the twin .50 machine guns in the forward mount. The gunners mate whose guns were getting wet became angry with the coxswain when he refused to stop circling—and he threw a grenade at the offending boat by way of remonstration. This was clearly not sabotage, either by friendly or enemy persons; it was a serious assault."

In February 1970 Don Masden took R-and-R leave to Honolulu, where he met his wife. While in Hawaii, he also saw his former SRA from Camp Lejeune, Al Kersenbrock, who was then on his way to relieve Don Schunk as supervising agent in Vietnam. "I was amused to find Al on his way to Vietnam because he had told me at Camp Lejeune he couldn't understand why I was taking an assignment at NISOV in preference."

Kersenbrock had seen his duty in Vietnam too. He asked Masden where he was then assigned and how long he had been there. "I told him how long I'd been in the delta, and he promised me a transfer back to Saigon as soon as it was feasible." Don Masden was returned to NISRA Saigon in April 1970 to work for SRA Bernie Taylor.

Adding to the challenges posed by a one-man posting to the active delta area, fate often dictated that agents assigned were newly arrived. As Don Masden had before him, Special Agent Clayton Spradley took over Binh Thuy fresh from the United States. Similarly, Spradley was relieved after six months on his own by Rudolph Dees, another Floridian.

Spradley recalls his takeover of the post had an element of shock: the delta was a new, very foreign environment, overtly hostile, and the agent's workload could quickly reach unmanageable status without careful judgment as to what was worthy of investigation. An early lesson for Clay Spradley came just days after he moved into office space shared with the officer in charge (OIC) of the SEAL Team. The base commander came to him with a complaint that his personal jeep had been stolen.

In any other environment a complaint of this type would have been investigated as felony larceny. Spradley dutifully accepted the case and filed the paperwork formally initiating the investigation. This, in effect, meant all levels of the NIS chain of command right up to Washington knew the case was pending and would be monitoring its progress.

Spradley quickly learned he had entered an environment where jeep stealing was endemic. Records checks told him that the Navy had no jeeps at all entered on their inventory, even though a number of the vehicles, all painted Navy colors with Navy numbers stenciled on them, were present on the base. When, eventually, the commander's jeep was located some time later, it was seen to be painted Air Force colors. As the paint was carefully removed, Navy paint came up—and when finally the paint job investigations were complete, it could be seen that the vehicle had at one time been the property of all three services. Spradley speculated privately that the base commander had probably seen him coming—a gullible newcomer who might just take the bait. He accepted no other cases of alleged jeep stealing.

Prime Navy contractors RMK-BRJ were active in the delta, building roads and bridges. In the unique environment of a war zone, the construction conglomerate had arrangements in place that allowed claims to be made against the government for losses in material and equipment. NISOV had never had sufficient resources to fully investigate RMK's claims against the Navy, but when paperwork was processed to claim for a loss of ten six-by-six five-ton trucks, Supervising Agent Allan Kersenbrock asked Spradley to investigate. Spradley disclosed a pattern of behavior whereby persons assuming responsibility for inventoried equipment assigned to RMK routinely reported it stolen or destroyed. The trucks in question had not been stolen; they were found at a new, distant construction project in full working order and still wearing the RMK-BRJ livery. Soon after the discovery, the contractors reported the theft of an asphalt mixing plant worth several hundred thousand dollars from off the flat barge being used to transport the machinery. That too had been relocated. "I often wondered how much gear the Navy paid for twice," Spradley said.

Death was never very far away in the delta. Agents were often astonished at the futility—and often, the stupidity—which surrounded much of the killing they were involved with. A case in point involved two longtime buddies assigned to the NAD at the Gulf of Cambodia seaport of Rach Gia. Both NCOs, they had located an off-base room to share for liberty time in the town. Coincidentally, the building was also home to a number of prostitutes and other local business people. It was not located in the best part of Rach Gia, but it was equipped with a refrigerator and phonograph, and it served its purpose well.

One afternoon the two friends were drinking beer, playing cards, and listening to records in their off-base room. They had had a long day and consumed many drinks. The smaller of the two, unsteady on his feet, lurched into the phonograph, damaging it and the record then being played. Enraged, his friend arose, announcing his intention to "Kick your ass." "Like hell you will" was the reply as the smaller made good his escape. Pursued, he grabbed his issue sidearm and shot his buddy four times. The last shot was fired into the victim's head at close range.

The investigation was straightforward. Spradley flew to Rach Gia. Witnesses were located and cooperated fully. The suspect was formally interviewed and readily confessed to his crime. The murder weapon was found and recovered.

"What I remember most vividly was my visit to the small Navy com-pound in Rach Gia, where the deceased's remains were. A group of sailors were enjoying some rare time off with a barbecue and a few beers. Perhaps ten feet from the group was the body bag with the victim in it. I was anxious to see if a bullet could be recovered from it because previous experiences with the Army mortuary with physical evidence had not been good. I opened up the bag, swatted away the flies, and probed two wounds with my govern-ment-issue ballpoint pen until I found a projectile lodged immediately under the skin and was able to remove it for evidence. Those sailors, through it all, were unconcerned about what I was doing. It was almost as if that sort of thing was pretty routine. This was just another example of the crazy ways we had to operate in Vietnam."

Perhaps the most distant and remote Navy detachment was located far down at the tip of the Ca Mau Peninsula, the southernmost tip of South Vietnam. This was flat mangrove swamp, intersected by the occasional river. The U Minh Forest to the northwest had been under enemy control for many years. It was truly Indian country.

To establish a logistic support bridgehead, the Navy moored several flat barges in the river. Upon these were erected sandbag-protected SEA huts. Dubbed Sea Float, this was a favored jumping-off place for SEAL opera-tions. It was also, then, a place wise men avoided if possible. Stories circu-lated in Navy rear echelon circles about ambitious officers who arranged a visit to Sea Float for a trip up around the first bend of the river, where enemy fire was guaranteed—as was a career-enhancing Combat Action Ribbon.

Clay Spradley's last exposure to Sea Float was memorable not because of the investigation that took him there but because of the journey he took once his business was complete. After wrapping up his inquiries, Spradley prudently began asking what transport out was available, as being in almost any other venue was preferable. An LST was anchored off the coast, and as helicopters could readily land on its long deck, it seemed a good bet for a ride back to Binh Thuy. Sea Float sailors were happy to take him out to the ship in a motor launch, and once there he settled back to await a passing helicopter.

After a short wait, a small group of SEALS came alongside in one of the fast flat-bottom boats they used for raiding. Dirty and covered in green camouflage face cream, they had two VC prisoners, whom they had snatched during an overnight operation. SEALS were extremely adept at finding and abducting enemy prisoners, who were a rich source of intelligence about the other side's movements and intentions. Because he shared an office with their OIC back in Binh Thuy, Spradley knew all the men, and they greeted each other. They told him a helicopter mission was rostered to take the prisoners to the rear for interrogation, but the pickup would be made from the detachment's small outpost upstream. Knowing he might be stuck on the LST, Spradley elected to join the men for what seemed to be a surefire ride.

Their business at the ship complete, the SEALs, with their bound, blindfolded prisoners and Spradley as passengers, sped over to the coast, then worked their way up a nearby river to their base camp. Entering the river, the open, fresh air was replaced by the fetid, closed atmosphere of a mangrove swamp. The tide was going out, exposing the scores of roots in dense black mud, which supported the forest. Lowering water levels also dictated the boat be taken slowly upstream, and several times it was necessary to get out and drag it over obstacles. Several small firefights could be heard in the distance, adding to Spradley's disquiet. Eventually, they arrived at the team's camp in the forest—an unpretentious rest area that did nothing to make the agent feel any more secure in the war zone environment.

Upon hearing the comforting whump-whump of a Huey approaching in the distance, Spradley felt a good deal of relief. He might be in the company of the world's toughest Special Forces operatives, but he knew there were far better places to be than sitting under a tree in the U Minh Forest. He thanked his hosts, boarded the helicopter with the two VC prisoners, and was soon winging away over the swamp. The flight took him as far as Ca Mau. The following morning an Army helicopter came through and dropped him off back at Binh Thuy.

Like every agent who consistently worked in the field, Clayton Spradley wondered what people on the outside—his fellow agents outside of the war zone—would think if they knew what he had gone through to complete this lead request. Investigative leads had to be done, it was that simple; but there was so often a strange twist in the Vietnam environment.

"The tour in Vietnam was just absolutely amazing. The investigations were so intense; the friendships we made there are just everlasting—'til the day we die," he says.

When his six-month assignment at Binh Thuy was ending in mid-1971, Spradley was looking forward to getting back to the relative comforts of Saigon. He would have been glad to fly out on the same day Rudy Dees arrived to take over, but Dees protested that he needed to learn more about the job and its area of coverage. Knowing it was the right thing to do, Spradley agreed to stay on. There was, he told Dees, a long-lingering case involving a stolen portable swimming pool that could be pursued. He had heard rumors it had been seen at a small detachment situated up on the Cambodian border, so they might go up and have a look together. Rudy Dees gratefully agreed that this was a good plan.

The day over, the two agents retired to the Binh Thuy Officers' Club for some drinks. The club was the most likely place to find helicopter pilots who could tell them what missions were being flown the next day. As they were enjoying their drinks, an Army medevac pilot named Pretcher approached them in the club. Also from Florida, he told Spradley he was rostered to fly a Dustoff mission early the next morning; he was confident he could take both men to Chau Doc if they could be out on the flight line by 7:00 AM.

Pretcher left, but plenty of other good company kept the agents in the club until it closed. Not ready to call it a night, Spradley suggested it might be a good time to introduce Rudy Dees to the bright lights of nearby Can Tho. Three hours after the 8:00 PM curfew, they left Navy Binh Thuy in their jeep heading for the city.

They were disappointed to find Can Tho closed also, with nobody apparently interested in having a party. They could do nothing else but head back to the base. There was the occasional kerosene hurricane lamp alight in Vietnamese houses set back from the road, but because of the curfew, they encountered no road traffic except for the occasional Army patrol. When a dog ran across the road, Dees swerved and lost control, and the pair skidded into an adjoining canal. The jeep more than half immersed, they soberly considered their predicament as awakened Vietnamese began to gather to see what had caused the commotion. Soon, an Army MP patrol came by, followed by a motor pool wrecker. The jeep was quickly pulled out of the water, somehow restarted, and the two agents were sent on their way none the worse for wear. The dog survived, too.

Dees and Spradley were not out on the flight line for Pretcher's early morning mission. They were late, ragged, and hung over but determined to run down the report about the stolen swimming pool. Sheltering back from the revetments that protected aircraft adjacent the flight line, they were approached by an Army warrant officer pilot. "Hey," he said, "Did you hear Pretcher crashed? They're bringing the bird in now." In the distance, the bulky outline of an Army CH47 Chinook could be seen on the horizon, carrying a load slung on cable beneath it. Soon it was apparent that load was a crumpled Huey, the same helicopter they would have been aboard that morning but for their evening activities. And the story does not end there.

Clayton Spradley was convinced he would have died in Pretcher's helicopter. That was bad enough, but the thought that he might have been killed chasing a vague lead about a stolen swimming pool rankled him too. Some years after the war, Spradley boarded a commercial flight in Washington, D.C., bound for Jacksonville, Florida. Aboard was Tom Truxell, the SEAL OIC with whom he had shared office space at Binh Thuy. They enjoyed the flight together, sharing animated recollections of shared experiences in the delta. "Clayton," Truxell said at one point, "do you remember that missing swimming pool?" "Yeah," Spradley replied. "Y'all took it didn't you?" Truxell acknowledged that his SEALS had liberated the swimming pool, taking it to their forward base at Ca Mau. They thought they had a greater need for it than the rear echelon troops at Binh Thuy.

# 14

# DA NANG, 1970 TO 1971: MURDER, RAPE, AND THE BLACK MARKET

**When Edward J. Fitzpatrick arrived in early March** 1970 to take over NISRA Da Nang, he inherited from Don McCoy a smoothly running team of agents who were largely experienced and self-directed. Fitz stepped into an office beset with fraggings, narcotics, and the effects of racial tensions—and he had to run to catch up with the pace, but not for long. Well-liked from the outset, he enjoyed the loyalty of all who worked for him, without demanding it.

I remained in Da Nang for only a matter of weeks before flying south to take over the satellite unit at Cam Ranh Bay, under the command of NISRA Saigon. Later in the year, after several months at Cam Ranh and Saigon, I was asked to return to Da Nang to help with a caseload almost out of control.

There had been big changes by early 1970. Naval Support Activity, Da Nang, responding to Vietnamization cutbacks and redeployments, had moved to reduce its presence in the city. Both NISRA Da Nang's office and billet were axed and all were moved inside NSA's compound at Camp Tien Sa. The move was unsatisfactory, but it was necessary: the Navy was going, and eventually NIS would go too. The Naval Security Group detachment housed at Tien Sa left the country. We inherited their windowless Quonset hut with its high-gated fence and moved in. Agents found rooms in the BOQ.

Our office maids were transferred across to Tien Sa with us, and our interpreter Mr. Nam came along too. NSG had lived a cloistered existence, as their duties required them to, and they left us a small barbecue area and a place to have a few beers after work. The Quonset, despite being windowless, was spacious. Yeomen and clerks occupied the forward portion, Fitz occupied the office built for the NSG detachment commander, and a large room at the rear was set up with agent desks, filing cabinets, and other paraphernalia. In one corner, a very basic bunk had been set up alongside a battery of command radios and the telephone. This was where the rotating duty agent slept to answer after-hours emergency calls.

When I reported back to Da Nang, the move to Tien Sa was complete. Perhaps the first thing I noticed about the new space was its enforced insularity. We were no longer among Vietnamese; we had little contact with them and virtually no opportunity to get a feel for what was happening outside the Navy world. NISOV was by then so utterly focused on trying to cope with a huge load of serious criminal investigations that its other mission was going by the board. I had a gut feeling that NIS was just trying to ride out the wave without crashing. It made me uncomfortable.

The move back to the Da Nang agent team was effortless, and working for Fitz was a pleasure. Fitz had built a reputation as a man who led from the front. I admired him for it, but he worried me, too. He had a wife and large family back in the States, and he was a long way from being a trained infantryman. Simply, he would not send an agent out to do a job he would not do himself, and he often became personally involved in major investigations. I was always glad for his help, but still I was anxious.

Two incidents from this time illustrate Fitz's determination to provide best-quality investigative support, whatever the adversity: the first was the murder of a Vietnamese peasant woman by a Marine officer; the second was a multiple rape involving Marine Combined Action Group Team personnel.

The murder investigation began curiously with loose talk by reconnaissance Marine team members in a rear-area enlisted club. An NCO, back from operations in the hills south of An Hoa, talked about the mission over several hours and many beers. Recon marines were normally careful about talking shop outside their own circle of team members and were not known to share their experiences with other marines. What the NCO said was therefore noted, and when mention was made that the young officer commanding the unit had shot a Vietnamese peasant woman, others listened carefully. Word found its way to the First Marine Division staff judge advocate, who contacted Ed Fitzpatrick with a request for assistance.

Rear-area witnesses were located and interviewed. The information divulged implicated a young Marine first lieutenant as the killer of an unknown woman near an observation post manned by recon marines. In their role as forward eyes and ears for the division, these marines typically manned high ground, where they could observe the comings and goings of NVA and Viet Cong units in the fertile plain of the An Hoa Basin and similar hotly contested areas. The lieutenant had led a team to a ridgeline overlooking rice paddies and trails from the west used by enemy units marching in from Laotian sanctuaries and the Ho Chi Minh Trail. The team had a bolt-action sniper rifle, a highly accurate weapon equipped with telescopic site. Apparently the officer had used it to shoot a peasant woman working in the paddy field far below, possibly as a demonstration of his skill with the weapon.

There was understandable angst among senior Marine officers at these allegations. If the allegations were true, a member of their elite corps was a murderer. A thorough, professional investigation was imperative, and only one organization was equipped to do it: NIS.

A few major difficulties had to be overcome in this investigation. More than a week had passed since the alleged shooting had occurred. Even more problematic was the location of the crime scene in an area that had never been pacified and where major clashes with North Vietnamese troops had occurred regularly. Witnesses needed to be located and interviewed, the victim's body needed to be exhumed and examined, and a search needed to be carried out for physical evidence. And few of the NIS agents were trained infantrymen.

For NIS agents, the crime scene location revealed the longtime confused dichotomy between where we were supposed to go and where we were not. Guidance from headquarters policy makers had never been particularly specific: agents were simply told they should avoid travel to forward locations and uncontrolled areas. And if an agent were injured in a forward area, headquarters would require a good explanation for his trip to the off-limits area. On the other hand, NISOV command had sent a clear message to the commands it serviced: we should investigate major incidents. Imperiling successful prosecution of major cases by relying on military police investigators was unnecessary, they said. Ed Fitzpatrick and his agents never doubted that they should visit the crime scene out in Indian country. Let headquarters in Washington read about it in the report.

Division headquarters left security arrangements for the crime scene mission in the hands of the commanding officer of the reconnaissance battalion. The colonel was taking no chances either with the NIS team or with his marines. Marine CH46 helicopters would transport agents and the Marine security team to the area. Cobra gunships would escort them. Each agent would have a recon marine assigned to him in the event enemy forces were encountered.

The operation began as planned: agents boarded transport helicopters, joining heavily armed marines. A second CH46 joined them, escorted by Cobra gunships, which flew ahead to begin prepping the landing zone, where the victim was believed to be buried. Fusillades of rockets and mini-gun fire searched out potential enemy hiding places, and the landings began, a Marine security element pushing out to secure the landing zone.

Landings might prompt an enemy attack, and the agents had little time for a detailed crime scene search. Despite the nature of the unsecured area, Vietnamese witnesses were located and convinced to return to Da Nang for in-depth interviews. The victim's shallow grave was found. Agents had come armed with documentation issued by Vietnamese authorities in Da Nang authorizing disinterment for purposes of formal medical examination. The grave in sand was opened, and the victim's decomposing, shroud-wrapped remains removed and placed in a body bag.

Vietnamese witnesses told agents that the victim had been working in a nearby rice paddy when a shot was heard from the ridge above. She had dropped, mortally wounded. They could offer no explanation for the event. There had not, they said, been recent enemy incursions or actions between marines and VC or NVA. Interviews conducted later in the Da Nang rear area produced no new information beyond that originally reported at the scene.

The recon marine observation post (OP) was checked for evidence relating to the crime, but none was found. The medical examination confirmed only that a single high-velocity round had struck the victim, causing near-instantaneous death. The suspect exercised his right to decline interview by agents.

The investigation was classified secret, unusual for a criminal inquiry. Recon marines, their operations often classified in any event, kept the lid firmly on any potential leaks about what one of their officers had done. The matter was never referred for trial. NISRA Da Nang agents understood that the accused had been cashiered from the Marine Corps and some reparation had been made to the victim's family. There was a good deal of after-the-fact reflection about how difficult life could be for Vietnamese peasants living in actively contested areas, even without irresponsible young junior officers.

The first information received about the alleged rape was vague and unspecific and even failed to confirm the identity of the victim. She had apparently been prompted by family members to make a complaint at a refugee facility in the coastal community of Tam Ky, some distance from where the crime was said to have occurred. After further refining complaint information with interviews in the rear areas of Da Nang, Fitz decided to start the investigation with a visit to the Marine CAG units.

I had not been involved in the early stages of the investigation. By this time, I had worked with marines in the I Corps bush for nearly two years, and although I was not dismissive of the allegations, I was surprised CAG marines would commit a gang rape. CAG members were volunteers, many of whom extended their tours to participate in the program. CAG teams lived in Vietnamese communities, training and assisting the people in the defense of their lives and property. Combined teams were the product of a doctrine that Marine leaders began developing in the Central American Banana Wars, during which the value of marines living on the ground with local allies had repeatedly been proved. The concept was further expanded in Vietnam and it worked. Viet Cong influence diminished where CAG operated. NIS had little contact with CAG because it received very few complaints about team members.

In the latter stages of the war, the First Marine Division was heavily deployed in the Que Son Valley that formed the southern border of the AO. The Army's America 1 Division AO began at the valley and extended south to well below Chu Lai. The alleged rape apparently occurred in the Que Son Valley. CAG units were dispersed in small teams at strongpoints in various parts of the valley where security was problematic.

At the time, Que Son was definitely in Indian country. Large, bitter clashes between NVA and Marine battalions had occurred there since 1966. Viet Cong forces remained active, as we were soon to learn. For security reasons, we decided to take two vehicles, one of which was equipped with a variable-frequency military radio. With Fitz at the wheel of one jeep, me driving the other, and volunteers riding shotgun, we headed south down Route 1, past Dodge City, to LZ Baldy, the turn-off for Que Son. Special Agent John Dill IV, a former marine, rode shotgun for me.

Baldy, initially developed by the U.S. Army, had become an important Marine strongpoint and artillery support base. Located near Route 1—the national highway—and Route 535—the road to the Que Son Valley—its strategic value was obvious to all, including the enemy. Baldy had formidable defenses: aprons of concertina wire, trip flares, tanglefoot, claymore mines, and barrels of fu gas, a napalm-like substance stored in fifty-five-gallon drums that could be command-detonated by defenders. There was a Marine checkpoint on Route 535, some distance west of Baldy, on a muddy, rutted dirt road. We stopped there, spoke to sentries, verified radio frequencies, and listened while they radioed ahead to another security element farther inland to advise that we were using the road. As we were about to leave, a U.S. Army jeep pulled up with MACV advisory staff aboard. Marines noted their details, sent them through, and radioed the post ahead: "One doggy victor headed yours." We smiled; marines never missed a chance to address soldiers as doggies.

It was the rainy season, and the road had never been more than a cart track even when French administrators had carved it out decades before. We drove carefully but wasted little time on the way to the village of Que Son, headquarters of a rice-growing district. Mountains surrounded the paddy plain and ville. It was these mountains that harbored enemy forces. We saw evidence of enemy activity at the compound that was home to district advisers, where a cleanup was under way to repair damage from an overnight attack. Marines were repairing sandbagged bunkers, stringing fresh wire, and mending gate barriers. We continued westward several more miles to a tiny outpost just off the road. On nothing more than a small elevation in a flat plane of rice fields, the CAG team and their Vietnamese allies had built a small fortress to defend surrounding villages and the rice crop the enemy desired so much. There was some wire around the outer defenses, festooned with empty ration cans, which clattered in the wind; mortar aiming stakes had been driven into parapets and several fire points had been built of sandbags and empty wooden ammunition crates. A central bunker, noticeable for the array of antennae it supported, doubled as a CP and sleeping spot for the OIC. The CAG team did not receive many visitors from the outside.

A young, clean-cut marine dressed in cutoff utility trousers and boots strode down to us as we drove in. This was the lieutenant officer in charge. Fitz greeted him, identified himself, and explained why we were there. I looked around, taking in the verdant rice fields beyond and noticing sweating marines filling sandbags. They too had been hit the night before. "We kicked their ass," the lieutenant said when I asked what sort of a night they'd had. "Just a routine VC probe," he said.

Our suspects were not present. Knowing that time was against us—"the night belongs to Charles" being especially true in Que Son—we arranged for their return to Da Nang. But we did identify a potential witness.

We could do little else in Que Son Valley. Interpreter Mr. Nam believed our victim could still be in Tam Ky, farther south on Route 1. After a short joint conference, we decided to drive on. The return to Route 1 was uneventful, and an hour later we were in Tam Ky where Nam found the victim.

Though scarcely more than twenty-five, she was a typical peasant woman who had had several children and an obviously difficult life. She was hesitant to talk and did so only after Nam's repeated explanation that authorities genuinely wanted to find and punish those responsible for her attack. Finally she acquiesced, explaining how four marines had accosted then raped her in a bomb crater near her village. She did not think she could identify the perpetrators if she saw them again. "The large-noses all look the same to me," she told Nam. In his beautiful, flowing handwriting, Nam took a statement from her, and we started back up the road in the afternoon sun.

There was no useable physical evidence; it had been weeks since the rape, which had occurred in a contested area. The investigation outcome would depend almost entirely on witness interviews and interrogations. Fitz arranged that these be held in the NISRA office at Camp Tien Sa. Suspects and potential witnesses were carefully quarantined from each other, traveling in from the bush on different dates from different locations.

Carried out over several days, the interrogations corroborated and supported each other. The rape had occurred; it was not just a rumor created by a Vietnamese peasant with a grudge or desire for a compensation payment. The Judge Advocate General staff ultimately decided the case was not strong enough to expect a reasonable chance of success. It was not, however, for a lack of trying on the part of Edward J. Fitzpatrick.

In March 1971 the small cadre of Fitz's remaining agents congratulated him on the occasion of his transfer from Vietnam. He had defied the odds, had done his very best to make a difference, and had left a number of Vietnamese sore of heart at his departure.

Replacing Fitzpatrick as senior resident agent was Charles M. Bickley. Before NIS, Chuck, a quiet, thoroughly competent criminal investigator, had managed inquiries for a Southern California district attorney. He settled into the SRA office at Camp Tien Sa and quickly won the admiration and respect of the last of Da Nang's agent corps. Signs of the troop drawdown were everywhere; agents rotating at the end of their year tour in I Corps were not being replaced.

Although numerous violent crimes in the Da Nang region characterized duty at the NISRA, there was always an undercurrent of black-market and currency violations. NIS special agents worked these cases if resources were available at the time.

Special Agent Carl Skiff, between trips to remote firebases in the Que Son Mountains, quietly gathered evidence about a currency manipulation operation apparently under the control of a Marine staff sergeant at the R-and-R facility operated by the First Marine Division near Freedom Hill and adjacent the notorious Vietnamese ville Dogpatch. The suspect had access to U.S. currency—known to all simply as "green." Possession of green was illegal in Vietnam unless one was being processed to leave the country either on authorized leave or at end of tour. Personnel assigned to Vietnam were paid in MPCs, legal tender in military stores, post offices, and clubs in the country, but nowhere else.

The idea was to prevent personnel from either trading in currency with Vietnamese or engaging in barter and trade. Vietnam's national currency was fragile in the extreme and could not be exported from the country legally. The piaster had been overvalued on the official government exchange rate. Thus, Vietnamese had a strong incentive for wanting to move cash to external banks to purchase hard foreign currency, and service personnel had incentive to exchange MPC for piasters at favorable black market rates. The Vietnamese always preferred U.S. dollars, although there was a healthy market in MPC also.

An added element in the black-market equation was the Viet Cong initiative to acquire U.S. dollars to fund their fight against noncommunist forces. They needed hard currency to buy almost any item not readily available in the Vietnamese economy.

Skiff's suspect had access to green because marines processing to fly from Vietnam on five to seven days of external leave were allowed to exchange MPC for U.S. dollars. There were indications that the NCO was banking tidy sums from currency manipulation and perhaps also from sale of sought-after items offered at the nearby Freedom Hill PX. Dogpatch was always hungry for tape recorders, refrigerators, televisions, and other PX goods—and Vietnamese purchasers could pay in MPC, lavished illegally by

Americans on prostitutes and narcotics. The suspect's advantage was that he had the means to convert MPC to U.S. dollars, legal tender that could be exported virtually anywhere.

Skiff decided to infiltrate a trusted informant into the R-and-R facility in hopes that details about the suspect's *modus operendi* could be learned. A fellow Marine NCO was issued orders that placed him legitimately in areas frequented by the suspect, and the process of accumulating evidence began. Skiff soon realized that the suspect was a creature of habit; he moved around the R-and-R facility in predictable ways and was known to carry U.S. dollars on his person at certain times. Unauthorized possession of U.S. dollars was an offence in its own right. Skiff believed the suspect could be apprehended for possession of contraband and began preparing a surveillance and arrest plan.

Like most transit facilities, the R-and-R center at Freedom Hill was normally awash with new faces. Thus, special agents in normal Marine battle dress would go largely unnoticed. The agents took up positions inside the compound and waited for the suspect and Skiff's informant, who would give a prearranged signal if the offender was carrying contraband.

The operation went down like clockwork: The suspect walked from his comfortable barracks quarters across the adjoining parking area, and when the informant signaled, both men were quickly taken into custody, searched, and handcuffed. A wad of green was taken from the suspect's pocket. The suspect, a career marine, was transferred to the United States soon after for court-martial proceedings.

# 15
## THE MEN

**At its peak, NISOV had fewer than twenty-five** agents assigned. They were a diverse group: former military officers, police officers, grunts who'd gone back to school, and even a school teacher. All were volunteers. Without making gross generalizations, it is fair to say that most were conservative souls and few were shy about patriotism at the right time.

In the best of times, assignment to Vietnam might have merely offered exoticism and interesting work. In wartime, it offered danger and the unexpected. As they prepared to leave for Vietnam, newly assigned agents faced many unknowns.

This form letter to Special Agent Peter Hopkinson from NISRA Saigon Assistant Senior Resident Agent Don Webb indicated what the new volunteer might expect. In this case, Webb was kind enough to add a personal note to the standard message.

U.S. NAVAL INVESTIGATIVE SERVICE OFFICE
VIETNAM
APO San Francisco 96243

From: Commanding Officer, U.S. Naval Investigative Service Office, Vietnam
To: ———
Subj: Information for Special Agent reporting to Vietnam

1. *General.* As a Special Agent selected for assignment to Vietnam, you are entering a unique and valuable phase of your career. Your tour in Vietnam will expose you to more criminal and counterintelligence investigations and activities in one short year than your contemporaries will gain in many years of stateside duty. It will present you with more opportunities to exercise your judgement and make independent decisions than are available to any but supervisory personnel in the States. Thus,

with these opportunities to gain unique experience and exercise your initiative, this should be a rewarding tour.

2. *Assignment*. Presently, USNAVINVSERVO Vietnam [NISOV] maintains two NAVINVSERVRAs [NISRAs]: Saigon and Danang. USNAVINVSERVRA Saigon has satellite offices in Cam Ranh Bay and Binh Thuy, and USNAVINVSERVRA Danang has satellite offices at Chu Lai and Quang Tri. Every month one agent makes a trip to Bangkok to conduct investigations in Thailand. The preponderance of these cases are PSIs. The nature of combat operations encompassing sudden and dramatic shifts of personnel make it difficult to give you any assurance as to your initial duty assignment. Notwithstanding that factor, after arriving in Saigon and getting a short orientation, your initial assignment will be in either Saigon or Danang.

3. *Areas*. There is wide disparity in the living conditions between those in Saigon and those elsewhere in the country. Saigon is a big city which has grown larger and is overpopulated with both Vietnamese citizens and U.S. military and civilian personnel. Saigon has all the problems associated with overpopulation. Living conditions are crowded, garbage is piled high, traffic is unbelievably chaotic and prices are high. Danang is a small city which has been surrounded by the U.S. military. Danang has been declared Off Limits to U.S. military and civilian personnel. In other areas of the country, your life will be generally confined to living and working aboard a military base or cantonment.

4. *Saigon Billeting*. In Saigon you will be billeted in a BOQ occupied by U.S. and Free World Military Forces personnel. This BOQ was a former Vietnamese hotel which has had air conditioning, showers, and other "conveniences" added by the U.S. Military. These "conveniences" sometimes overtax the electrical and water systems and thus are not always operational, but they exist. Rooms are usually occupied by three permanent residents and the cost of the room is $5.00 per person per month. Laundry, room cleaning, water bottle filling (since tap water is not potable) and other miscellaneous services are provided by a Vietnamese maid costing you about $10.00 per month. Officers' open messes are available in several BOQs. Breakfast runs about 50–60 cents, lunch 65 cents–$1.00, and dinner $1.00 or more if you eat heartily. Beer is 20 cents, mixed drinks are 25 cents–50 cents. Entertainment is BOQ movies or floor shows or whatever you can find on the economy at exorbitant prices. If you like good French or Chinese food, floor shows and night clubs, you will find yourself spending plenty of cash. The curfew for Saigon, however, is currently 2200—0600.

5. *Danang Billeting*. All of the USNAVINVSERVRA Danang personnel moved into their new home on July 1967. It is a three story villa type structure which has all modern conveniences plus a few luxuries (from a Vietnamese standpoint). Maid service is available at low cost. There is an excellent Navy Officers' Club in Danang which boasts of the best facilities in-country. Breakfast is about 50 cents, lunch 65 cents, and dinner $1.00. Drinks are 25 cents–50 cents. Danang also has an older Army Club as well as an Air Force Club at the Air Base. A curfew of 2000–0600 is still in effect, and outside entertainment is minimal.

6. *Saigon Working Conditions*. The office space can only be described as adequate. It is air-conditioned and is conveniently located to the post exchange. Agents work six and a half days a week. You will find yourself fully occupied during these hours and on occasion will even put in some "overtime." There is a duty agent each day, currently a 1 in 5 rotation. Cases in Saigon are to a large extent criminal in nature and are in support of Saigon based commands or those units in the Mekong Delta or in coastal port areas. Counterintelligence collection is based largely on liaison with other government agencies, personal observation, and contact with Vietnamese sources or foreigners who are in some manner associated with the U.S. Navy/Marine Corps. There are four compact automobiles, two International Scouts, and one truck available for in-city travel while out of area travel is by any aircraft available. This will provide you with any thrills you might otherwise miss.

7. *Danang Working Conditions*. The office in Danang was formerly a combination office and billet. It has now has been renovated and equipped exclusively as an office. It is a large, well cared for structure and makes a comfortable office. It is partially air-conditioned, and rooms not so equipped have ceiling fans and open-air ventilation. The office hours are basically the same as in Saigon. The work is almost exclusively criminal in support of U.S. Naval Support Activity, Danang or U.S. Marine Corps commands. Any of the latter cases are in remote areas far from Danang and thus agents will occasionally find themselves uncomfortably close to combat area. There are eight vehicles available for local transportation and, as in Saigon, distant travel is by any available aircraft.

8. *Finances*. Most officers and agents find they can live on an average of $150.00 a month while in Vietnam if they do not partake of much outside entertainment or buy elaborate gifts. In addition to the regular salary, each agent while in Vietnam, receives a 25% differential which is subject to Federal income tax. Agents in Vietnam also get Separate Maintenance Allowance (SMA) which is tax exempt, in the following amounts:

$2,500 for wife; $2,900 for wife and one child; $3,300 for wife and two children; and $3,700 for a wife and more than three children. Additionally, agent personnel in Vietnam receive premium pay at the maximum rate which is 25% of the employee's rate of basic pay which does not exceed the minimum rate of basic pay for a GS-l0. Agents assigned to Vietnam are paid by the Naval Regional Finance Center (NRFC), Pearl Harbor, Hawaii. The NRFC will not mail an agent's pay check to Vietnam; therefore, it is recommended that each agent maintain a stateside bank account to which his check can be mailed by the NRFC,* Personal check cashing facilities are readily available in all locations to which you might be assigned. It is recommended that the agent arrive in-country with at least $100 available in cash or by check to tide him over until the first pay period. All "green" dollars and travelers checks are forbidden in Vietnam and must be turned in at the airport for Military Payment Certificates (MPC) used in Vietnam.

9. *Clothing.* Vietnam has two seasons—hot and wet and hot and dry. In the former, mildew is the great enemy; in the latter, dust. It is recommended that the agent not bring any good or expensive clothing White and solid colored short-sleeved shirts and slacks are the normal attire and sturdy washable varieties are recommended. Dry cleaning facilities are less than satisfactory. Only one summer suit should be brought for such use as out of country travel, leave, etc. Most agents prefer Hush Puppy type footwear because of the comfort and easy up-keep. Experience has shown that if you bring four or five pair of slacks, two-three pairs of shoes, half a dozen shirts, half a dozen sets of underwear, three or four towel and wash cloths, and an inexpensive vinyl raincoat, you will be adequately supplied. Presently, the only items that have been scarce are slacks and shirts. Electric razors will work on the Vietnamese current.

10. *Weapons.* Personal weapons are prohibited in Vietnam. You are to bring your ONI-issued weapon with you. This Office maintains a good variety of official weapons which may be drawn as needed.

11. *Mail:* Air mail to and from Saigon to the U.S. West Coast takes three days and five days to the East Coast, on the average. To and from Danang may take one or two days longer. The addresses:
Saigon: U.S. Naval Investigative Service Office, Vietnam APO San Francisco 96253
Danang: U.S. Naval Investigative Service Resident Agency, Danang FPO San Francisco 96695

---

* You must designate a commercial banking institution, as your paycheck cannot be mailed to your wife, mother, or anyone else.

We strongly suggest that you prepare for, and prepare your family for, initial and intermittent mail delays. By doing this you can preclude needless misunderstandings.

12. *Hazards:* It goes without saying that you will be operating in a combat area. There are no defined battle lines, and there is little question that the enemy controls more territory than do friendly forces, especially at night. The war can emerge almost any place, and you must face the fact that you are likely to observe it first hand during the course of your tour. This is not intended to magnify such hazards but merely to point out that they must not be minimized. Terrorism is almost an accepted occurrence in Saigon, and vigilance is mandatory. Mortar and rocket attacks are not uncommon, and it is essential that agent personnel know what to do when and if they are caught in them. Be aware of the fact that almost all Special Agents who have served in Vietnam have come under hostile fire at one time or another. If you are prepared for the possibility and exercise calm judgement, you are likely to emerge unscathed. Other hazards are of a health nature. Your required inoculations will protect you from the worst of these and weekly malaria pills will tend to offset that disease. There is little anyone can do to protect you from the "Ho Chi Minh Revenge," aka: diarrhea, and you are likely to suffer from it on a few occasions.

13. *PX.* Exchanges are available in all areas and carry a good supply of the necessities of life such as razor blades, shaving cream, tooth paste, books and magazines, film, etc. Luxury items such as cameras, radios, stereo equipment, etc., come and go, but may be special ordered at a considerable savings over stateside prices.

14. *Leave and R and R:* A five day trip to Japan, Hong Kong, Manila, Australia, Bangkok, Hawaii, Singapore, Taiwan, etc., is part of the benefits of a year tour. You are eligible for such a tour after being in-country a minimum of three months; however, due to the demand for R and R trips the time required in-country can vary from four to nine months, depending on the place you desire to visit. At present, Hawaii requires a minimum of six and one half months in-country. R and R trips are a package deal offering free round-trip transportation, low cost accommodations and does not count as leave. Workload permitting, other leave trips to the same areas may be taken on your own if you can arrange the required flights or can pay the fare in order to assure your return as scheduled.

15. *Passports.* Apply for an "Official U.S. Passport" well in advance of

departure date to avoid delay. Obtain a passport with multiple entrance and exit visas to Vietnam. Visas are not required to visit Thailand and Malaysia as long as one has a valid U.S. passport. Visas to Hong Kong, Australia, Taiwan and Japan may be obtained locally without delay.

16. *Miscellaneous.* Bring your U.S. Government drivers license and have it effective through your entire tour in Vietnam. Licensing procedures here vary and are bound to be a nuisance when getting established. It is also suggested that you bring a supply of any pills, vitamins, or other medication you may need until you can obtain a local source of supply. Again, the Exchange has a good supply of aspirin, cough drops, and the more popular patent medicines.

17. *Arrival.* All incoming personnel check-in at the USNAVINVSERVO Vietnam regardless of their ultimate duty assignment. For your benefit, it is suggested that you notify this Office, by letter or message, of the date, time and flight number of your arrival, in order that someone can be on hand to meet you and assist you in checking through customs, changing money, etc. Remember, you will be in a foreign country where the use of English is uncommon. In the event no one is at the Tan Son Nhut Air Base to meet you, call this office for transportation. From a Tan Son Nhut telephone, dial 98 and then our number which is 60845/60846 or 922-3967 during duty hours, and 922-3045 after duty hours.

18. If you have any further questions or need any further assistance to write this Office or the agent designated as your sponsor.

24 February 1970

Dear Pete,

I will address you thusly, having derived same from the name that was given me. You, as you most likely know, have been designated as my replacement in the wonderful world of Vietnam come sometime in July 1970. I will not be here to meet you since I will be going to my next duty station in May 1970; however, I thought I would drop you a line to let you know that your presence in Vietnam, or RVN as we refer to it, will be greatly appreciated.

I am enclosing a little blurb that is mostly propaganda but it will help you in some ways. I will also endeavor to add to it or explain certain parts of it so that you will know what to expect once your reverse freedom bird touches down at Tan Son Nhut Air Base (where you will enter RVN).

I have been here for 16 months having extended for six months, so it can't be all bad. Seriously, it is a very challenging but rewarding job. It requires unlimited enthusiasm, boundless energy, the hide of a water buffalo, and the eyes of an eagle. As an ONI agent, I'm sure you have these attributes and you will be in good stead over here.

Now down to the nitty gritty. Bring only wash and wear clothing. You will have a maid but her main job is to beat your clothes to rags on a wet rock. I brought six pairs of trousers and six shirts and I am still wearing them. I augmented my wardrobe with a few shirts and slacks from the PX at a very reasonable cost and I have stayed in pretty good shape. You will probably wear a suit over and you should have at least one suit and tie for out-country trips such as a Bangkok, Thailand, work trip, R&R, etc. Most of the guys wear Hush Puppies but I find Corfam leather holds up OK. That's all I wear. Either type will be fine. You will be given two field uniforms and a pair of boots after you get here for your in-country trips so no sweat there. Bring at least six sets of skivvies. This should last you through and you can always buy more at the PX if needed. Enough for clothing.

I don't know how you want to handle your finances but you should be made aware of the fact that your paycheck can only go to your bank of designation. A joint checking account with your wife at that bank might be the most satisfactory arrangement. You'll have to work that out. Green is no good here. We use Military Payment Script, affectionately known as funny money. You can cash checks on a stateside bank here for $100.00 at the Bank and $50.00 at the PX. This is how you get your funny money.

We live and eat at the Five Oceans BOQ located one block from the office. The rooms are adequate although nothing to write home about. The food is filling. You will have to pay your maid 1,000 piasters a month (local currency equal to about $8.20 US). You pay the BOQ 450 piasters a month (I have never figured out what that's for). The meals run about $2.00 a day depending on how much you eat or can stand.

## II

Case-wise we handle the full gamut. We have worked, are working, or will work every category in the book. You will also probably travel the entire country to get the work done but it is not too bad. You get used to it.

Upon arrival in country you may be assigned to either of the two NISRAs and subsequently may be assigned to one of four NISSUs. You will find that out upon arrival.

Everybody coming here has different questions so if I can be of further assistance or if you have any specific questions please let me know and I will attempt to answer them.

On that note I will close and wish you best of luck on your upcoming Vietnam tour. It will be a good one, I can assure you.

Sincerely,

DONALD L. WEBB

Most newly assigned agents received a letter similar to this, with or without a personal note. Armed with this information, they packed and headed off to a NIS assignment none would ever forget.

During my three years with NIS in Vietnam, I cannot recall ever hearing an in-depth political discussion between agents, but my colleagues were very aware of the changes—peaceful and otherwise—that were warping the American political scene throughout their tenure. Agents were privy to classified reports about organizations in the United States and elsewhere that openly advocated the violent overthrow of American government and institutions. The Weathermen were building bombs (and occasionally killing themselves with them) in Greenwich Village; the University of California was rife with insurrection; and militant racial groups on both ends of the color spectrum used bombs, guns, and intimidation to achieve their aims.

America's enemies were quick to exploit U.S. divisiveness, too—none more so than the North Vietnamese, who took succor from every newspaper article and television clip that added credence to the argument that a waiting game could win the war for them. The Vietnamese politburo preached that patient Confucian values and internal discipline would ultimately triumph over despotic Western values. Some viewed demonstrations at home as an affront to the many dedicated people in Vietnam who genuinely believed a possible communist takeover would be an unthinkable tragedy. When Jane Fonda traveled to North Vietnam, when NVA hospitals in South Vietnam were found to be operating with instruments and medication donated by zealots at home, and when captured American pilots were being tortured at the Hanoi Hilton, there was often little respect or appreciation for "rabble in the streets."

Far away in Vietnam, dependent on Armed Forces Radio and Television and *Stars and Stripes* newspaper for news from the home front, agents were frequently troubled by what they heard—particularly if they had not been home in nearly a year.

Mike Nagle on April 9, 1968, wrote to his mother, *"Received word of Dr. Martin Luther King's assassination and the subsequent wide-spread rioting. Was Los Angeles spared from this? Sometimes I'm kind of glad I'm not coming back to the States for a while."*

Later, in June, Nagle again wrote. *"Received word of Robert Kennedy being shot yesterday. I understand he is presently in critical condition in Los Angeles. It really makes me wonder, with the dissention, riots, and assassination what our country is coming to."*

The Soviets and their sympathizers exploited American divisiveness when they could. Service personnel on leave from Vietnam in Japan, Korea, and even Australia were contacted both by agents and by sympathizers. On the assumption they would speak out against the war and thus be of worth for propaganda, they were offered assistance to desert. Some were even courted for information about their duties in Vietnam, the initial contact in a potential espionage arrangement. In Australia, where there was strong antiwar sentiment and a well-delineated left wing, service personnel with access to sensitive information were the target of groups with established links to the extreme left. Because these events clearly fell within the NIS counterintelligence mandate, agents could be more than a little sensitive to the latest news from U.S. campuses. In boozier moments, if such things were discussed, a quick-fix solution designed to add levity to the conversation might be put forward. I recall a room 4 discussion in which it was suggested that World War II's B29 Superfortress fleet be reactivated and configured to drop huge quantities of fecal matter on street demonstrators, a slightly less bellicose purpose than the air raids on Japan for which they are famous. And when American astronauts walked on the moon in 1969, somebody said, "Tell those clever people at NASA to send us something to help us kill more [Vietnamese]—to hell with the moon."

Throughout it all, the Paris peace talks between North Vietnamese negotiators and U.S. diplomats ground ahead, punctuated by occasional cease-fires and bombing halts that seemed to change little for those on the ground in "the Nam." Mike Nagle's April 9, 1968, letter to his mother in California mirrored the thoughts of many: *"Sure hope these new peace proposals are productive. Many here feel the bombing pause was a grave mistake—as we can see the tangible results when the NVA supply lines are not bombed. Personally, I feel it's a good move if it in any way will help bring an end to this miserable war. Also very surprised Johnson declined to run for re-election. I think history will show that our involvement in Vietnam was a wise move—although I think the point has been made and we should do everything in our power to end it, save forfeiture of South Vietnam and/or surrendering what we have gained."*

Mike Nagle's youthful observations make interesting reading in hindsight, written a full seven years before South Vietnam finally collapsed under the communist onslaught.

Those who lived through the late '60s and '70s will recall it as the time of the Afro haircut, long hair, and ultimately, sideburns. Dedicated military men have long believed that part of pride in the uniform they wear is a carefully shorn, regulation haircut. Short hair, unfortunately, was definitely uncool for young servicemen on leave trying to impress the women of that day. Beyond the desire to be fashionably attractive to the opposite sex, "pushing the regulations" also became a means for some to express individualism and for true malcontents to go further, blatantly flaunting military regulation. Some blacks did their best to turn the debate into one of ethnicity. African American servicemen in less-disciplined outfits strode the streets with haircuts that would have done a Fijian policeman proud. There were sensitivities on both sides of the debate: I recall a senior Navy captain ordering an officer out of the officers' club because he had sideburns which extended unacceptably. The captain told the man his appearance was disgraceful.

The haircut debate never made it to the agent corps while I was in Vietnam, though I recall my good friend John Morgan being branded a subversive because he had hair long enough to touch his collar. John was an exception to the rule. In the Marine Corps field units during one of my last visits in 1971 to the Fifth Marines, I watched with quiet amusement as the battalion sergeant major approached a young first lieutenant, addressed him with great courtesy as Sir, and suggested he get a haircut before anything else. At chow, half an hour later, the lieutenant was shorn. The corps had its problems, but discipline in the officer ranks never seemed to be a part of it.

Through the twists and turns of the '60s and '70s and confusing, sometimes distressing events at home and in Vietnam, the agent corps served with integrity. Although not impervious to forces of the day, agents assigned to Vietnam maintained their commitment to the best traditions of the U.S. Naval Service.

# 16
# NEARING THE END

**Since they evolved from underwater demolition teams** (UDT)—the Frog Men of World War II fame—Navy SEAL teams have carried out important, often-secret missions using small, highly trained squads. SEALS are the functionaries of the Naval Special Warfare Group.

Important senior commanders have not always favored unconventional warfare, as the shady world of the Special Forces soldier is known. The elite image, special uniform accoutrements, and unusual equipment of the Special Forces have not necessarily won the approval of more conventional commanders. The U.S. Army's Special Forces program came under heavy attack after several officers in Vietnam were accused of complicity in the assassination of a double agent. It was well known that the commander of MACV, Gen. Creighton Abrams, USA, was no fan of the Special Forces. Pundits saw the assassination court-martials as a swan song for the Special Forces, and many would concede that it very nearly was.

When in 1971 NISOV agents briefed the CO of Naval Special Warfare at his Saigon office about serious criminal allegations against his SEAL team members, there was immediate and genuine concern that a couple of bad apples might spell the end of the entire program. Reductions and extreme budget austerity were the norm in the Navy at the time; nobody profited from the wrong type of publicity in that environment.

The U.S. Drug Enforcement Administration (DEA) had come to the San Diego NISRA with information gleaned from their local informant network: SEALS stationed at Coronado were alleged to have been instrumental in smuggling into the United States kilos of opium concealed in the scuba tanks that traveled with them on special Navy C130 flights used to rotate teams and their equipment in and out of Vietnam. These special flights moved SEALS outside the normal personnel logistic system, allowing them to keep classified special equipment under wraps—for instance, night-vision devices called Starlight Scopes carried a secret classification in 1971 and thus re-

223

quired special handling. Though Customs had cleared the aircraft and its occupants on arrival, none of the contraband had been discovered.

SEALS always seem to have favorite watering holes, whether abroad or at home. So it was in San Diego, where the bar of choice was also frequented by civilian accomplices in the opium-smuggling scheme. DEA agents quickly identified key players and probably set up an informant within the group. They learned that two SEAL team members, then assigned to Logistic Support Base Ben Luc, were planning to import more narcotics. But before the two suspects could make their next move, the U.S. attorney in San Diego decided the case DEA had built was adequate to support the immediate apprehension and return of the SEAL conspirators in Vietnam.

One of the accused SEALs was an officer, the son of a senior career naval officer then on active duty. His apparent involvement stung colleagues in Naval Special Warfare, even though his assignment was one of logistic support rather than command of SEAL operations. There seemed little doubt the man had taken part in the plan with greed and self-aggrandizement as his primary motives, none of which reflected well on his proud organization. The officer's co-conspirator was a petty officer second class with a history of many successful combat operations in Vietnam.

Navy JAG staff at NAVFORV were consulted and the decision was made to apprehend and incarcerate both men on the basis of documents furnished by the U.S. attorney in San Diego. Naval Special Warfare advised that the officer was at that moment on R and R leave in Sydney, Australia, but he was expected back on a night flight into Tan Son Nhut. The petty officer was at Ben Luc on stand-by status.

Special Agent Marshal Whidden and I, accompanied by a SEAL officer, drove from Saigon to Ben Luc to apprehend the petty officer. We used the hour or so of driving time to devise a plan for the arrest to minimize as much as possible the danger inherent in taking down a highly trained operative who we knew would be armed. The SEAL officer told us we could expect the man to be carrying, at least, a short-barreled revolver in the breast pocket of his camouflage utilities. We all agreed it would be best if the takedown occurred in an open area away from the SEAL hooches. This decided, we made a plan to have the Ben Luc communication station summon our man to receive an operationally urgent message. We reasoned he would drop whatever he was doing and walk the short distance from the SEAL area to the sandbagged bunker that contained the message center. That would provide us with our opportunity.

At Ben Luc, we briefed and requested the assistance of command staff. A junior sailor in the message center was detailed to deliver a note for our man that summoned him to the bunker for a message. This done, Marsh Whidden and I began slowly walking down the road we knew he would use. We were dressed in civvies and thought it likely we would be seen as visiting civilian engineers. The SEAL officer assisting us was in uniform; he hung well back from us. Within moments, our quarry approached us, walking hurriedly toward the communication bunker. Ignoring him, we continued an animated conversation about improving a drainage design until he was just past. Then we drew weapons, identified ourselves, and ordered him to remain stationary. The SEAL officer accompanying us had by then drawn his issue .45 pistol and covered the man from his right quarter. The accused was visibly rattled. I wasted no time removing a .38-caliber Colt Detective Special from his left breast pocket and handcuffing him.

Whidden remembers, "I recall my most vivid thought at the time of the arrest was whether or not our SEAL companion was going to shoot him on the spot. As I recall emotions were high and solutions to problems in Vietnam were a little different than they would have been Stateside. I certainly didn't want to be in his line of fire, that's for sure."

We marched him directly back to his nearby quarters, where he had a small private cubicle in the main sleeping hooch. There I began a careful search of his personal effects, looking especially for correspondence and other evidence that would illustrate the dynamics of the conspiracy. Whidden moved into an adjoining area to search gear belonging to the coaccused.

The man's cubicle contained a formidable arsenal: captured Chinese AK47 assault rifles, an SKS, even an Australian self-loading rifle whose barrel had been shortened—a favorite weapon of the Australian Special Air Service, with whom the SEALS operated. There were concussion and fragmentation grenades, flares, and other pyrotechnics that would have rendered the hooch a very unpleasant environment in the event of fire, rocket attack, or accident. In a wooden ammunition box, I found a number of letters. These contained information that would support charges against both accused. Marshal Whidden's search produced evidence, but of a much more circumstantial nature. The search complete, we loaded up and drove back to Saigon, where the accused was incarcerated. One down, one to go.

Given the nature of the SEAL team camaraderie and the communication equipment at their disposal, we considered it lucky that the accused officer was out of Vietnam. We reasoned that, even if they wanted to, finding and alerting the man in Sydney would be very difficult. So when the chartered Boeing 707 landed at Saigon's Tan Son Nhut Airport that night, a team led by Senior Resident Agent Fred Givens was waiting for it. Givens, renowned in the organization as a man who could look after himself, had been a Texas Ranger. Quiet, always calm, Givens never seemed to have problems with ne'er-do-wells once his blue eyes fastened on them. With Givens in charge, we had a strong measure of confidence that our man wouldn't be tempted to do anything silly. And so it was. The NIS agent team was first aboard the plane when the door was opened. Givens asked cabin crew to page the accused and we watched him make his way forward past rows of bleary-eyed service personnel just back from a week in the fleshpots of Sydney's Kings Cross. Identified, he was handcuffed, ushered off the aircraft, and taken into security spaces, where a full search was conducted of his person and luggage. We did not elect to interrogate him.

As an officer, he was entitled to incarceration in facilities for officers only. The Army maintained a stockade with a section reserved for officers at the massive Long Binh facility that accommodated the U.S. Army Vietnam headquarters elements. Known in Vietnam as the Long Binh Jail (LBJ), it was in those spartan confines that our accused spent his first night awaiting transport to the United States to stand trial. We reflected that a hard bunk at the LBJ must have been a harsh change from the soft living and gentle company of Sydney.

Both men were returned to the United States and tried in federal court. We later heard that convictions had been obtained for both.

Marshall Whidden remembers especially the camaraderie between NIS agents and SEALs. "The one thing that stood out most in the SEAL drug smuggling case was the camaraderie that developed between the SEAL team guys and us. We always had good relationships, probably because our organizations were both kind of bastard outfits and they did do some jobs for us through the years. That was a terribly embarrassing event for those guys, especially the teams in Vietnam, and it would have been convenient for them to turn against the messenger. But to their credit they didn't and in fact it made the relationship stronger. I remember some mock knife fighting in room 4, them against our man and the usual winner, Uncle Fred Givens."

National presidential elections were scheduled in August 1971. President Nguyen Van Thieu, running for a second four-year term was opposed by both former President Nguyen Cao Ky and Gen. Duong Van "Big" Minh until both men suddenly withdrew, claiming the incumbent had rigged the election. Students at Saigon University demonstrated, as did Buddhist activists who also contended that the election process was faulty. Students spilled into streets not far from NISOV headquarters. Because of concerns about anti-American feelings, all hands were ordered to limit their travel and exposure in cities.

Thieu won the election by a larger majority than the previous one and was sworn into office on October 3. Communist gunners expressed their displeasure by firing Russian rockets into Saigon, killing several Vietnamese civilians. Viet Cong and NVA regulars mounted similar attacks elsewhere around South Vietnam.

By the last quarter of 1971, U.S. force withdrawal and Vietnamization were apparent in every quarter. The Cholon PX closed, marking an end to the compound area that first housed the Navy headquarters in the early '60s,

Headquarters, Support Activity Saigon. The building that first housed the Provost Marshal and then NISOV was no longer available to Naval Intelligence. Further, the Five Oceans BOQ, home to agents and officers since 1962, was also closed. The U.S. Army was getting out of Saigon in a hurry.

As it had at the outset, the Navy again found a home in Cholon with U.S. Army MPs. Only a short distance from the office being vacated was a multistoried former Vietnamese hotel, which then housed an Army CID unit. The Army unit was also downsizing, leaving two floors available for NISOV billeting and office space.

No office move is ever easy after an organization has been in place continuously for nearly a decade. For a unit with security responsibilities, and thus the paraphernalia required for safe custody of classified material, moves are further complicated. Naval Investigative Service Office, Vietnam, had numerous four-drawer document security containers, not unlike armored filing cabinets. The containers were protected against forced entry with combination locks and steel plating. There were desks, typewriters, personal effects, unclassified reference documents, the entire contents of the NISRA evidence locker, photographic equipment—a seemingly endless list.

The entire office staff, from the CO to our one assigned seaman, turned out to help. Drawers were removed from security containers and transported in trucks, closely guarded by armed agents. Moved items were carried individually from the trucks past the armed sentries at the MP building, the heavier items stockpiled in the breezeway between the two wings of the building. Teams raised the heavy items upward with block and tackle. This was not the work federal agents normally did, but it was unavoidable. Our various "customers" had to wait until we were reestablished, with radios and telephones operating again. All but the commanding officer, Cdr. Gene Moore, and Supervising Agent Dick McKenna moved their gear into rooms in the building adjacent the offices; the CO and McKenna remained billeted at the 98 Phan Dinh Phung villa under the watchful eye of the housekeeper, Hai.

Whidden said of the move, "The only time I can remember security being tighter is when we were transporting a truckload of liquor to the NIS company bar from Tan Son Nhut."

In retrospect, I think the move probably exacerbated the already prevalent feeling, even in our command, that we were all on borrowed time: the United States was going to leave Vietnam in any event—that the reassuring rhetoric that was being proffered to our South Vietnamese allies was hollow. I had been in country at this point for more than two years; I found it disquieting when Vietnamese asked me if things would be all right after we all left, but I had neither the foresight nor the cynicism to realize what was happening. I could not believe, after the monumental sacrifices that had been made, that the United States would walk away—and I said so. I reassured Vietnamese friends and associates about their future. Mea culpa.

By the latter part of 1971 the U.S. presence in Cholon had dwindled. We and our MP hosts were largely on our own. We no longer had messing facilities, as the Five Oceans was closed. I found myself purchasing food from street vendors, who came out in the evenings to sell bread, warm beer, and a few specialty items such as boiled mussels. Bunkie John Morgan had an electric frying pan (which frequently blew electrical circuits) and occasionally created meals for us with frozen food purchased by the CO on his shopping runs to the commissary. None of us had authority to shop at the commissary. More often, I could be found at dinnertime on the sidewalk in front of the old hotel sitting on a stool with a bowl of cooked muscles, French bread, and a quart of warm Tiger beer.

Marshal Whidden: "The food was certainly one of the up points for the tour. Probably one the greatest treats was simply eating a butter-smeared loaf of French bread freshly purchased off a local street corner and washed down with a bottle of beer. There were some great restaurants and soup kitchens. Those that stand out most were the great Cholon Chinese restaurants. Many times it got exciting as we had to sit with a handgun in our lap, under the dinner napkin, to have ready to discourage disabled veterans, cowboys, and just common Asian criminal folks."

None of this was genuine hardship, merely a reflection of the state of things at the time. Our caseload remained largely unchanged; agents drove to Nha Be and downtown to COMNAVFORV every day to cover the latest incidents. Few high-profile investigations were under way at the time, but we dealt with an increasing number of incidents involving Vietnamese Navy personnel. Most U.S. Navy facilities were being handed over to the VNN in one form or another, meaning that the Vietnamese command area now encompassed areas from which non-U.S. personnel had previously been excluded. The incidence of burglary and theft rose appreciably.

Providing needed services to the scattered U.S. Navy commands, which in many instances were becoming isolated in much the way we were, became more of a challenge for NISOV. Cutbacks and Vietnamization affected transport and communication too.

In Da Nang at this time, Special Agent Ed Giblin, later to become SRA in Saigon, operated a one-man office in the vastly reduced area of Camp Tien Sa, then in use by U.S. naval advisers. This was the third office space NIS in Da Nang had used since the original office in the city had been given up the year previous. Giblin, with a petty officer yeoman to manage the phone and clerical duties, was doing his best to stage an orderly withdrawal from I Corps. He operated in a climate of pandemonium until the decision was made to pull him permanently back to Saigon.

The area south of Saigon that encompasses the Mekong Delta remained important in the allied naval effort, but increasingly, Vietnamese Navy units were taking over combat operations and patrolling. The U.S. Navy role was steadily moving back toward advisory status as the Americans turned over equipment and withdrew men. For Naval Investigative Service special agents, this had several important ramifications: getting to commands and people was more difficult; it was no longer possible to rely on U.S. military aircraft and vessels for a ride; and advisory staff was more difficult to locate.

I had established useful ties with the CIA proprietary airline Air America. As the once-dependable Navy and Army medevac chopper service no longer was so, I would occasionally rely on the Air America pilots to get me where I needed to go, often in fixed-wing Pilatus Porter turboprop aircraft. Catching these rides was a matter of getting out to the Tan Son Nhut Terminal and waiting to see what developed on the flight manifest. Porter flights were not always rostered, but pilots always seemed willing to help if they could. One memorable mission was my first ride in a Porter, during the 1971 monsoon. I needed to get to Moc Hoa, on the Plain of Reeds near the Cambodian border. We didn't leave Saigon until late morning; a heavy, dark cloud cover had already built up. I was seated next to the pilot, a former Marine aviator who seemed to have an air of adventure about him, and was learning about this unique aircraft, designed by the Swiss to land in inhospitable places like glaciers. The pilot guided the aircraft with a stick, in the manner of fighter pilots, and he adjusted flap setting by reaching overhead to a handle and sprocket, which looked as though it had come off a bicycle. Rotating the sprocket drove a chain that operated the flap gear. It was basic, but it worked very well.

We leveled out at perhaps three thousand feet and adjusted to a north-westerly course. As was typical at this time of year, water stood everywhere below: in the paddies, rivers, and canals. There was more water-covered terrain than dry land, and closer to Cambodia, there was even more flooding. I began to wonder what the airstrip at Moc Hoa would look like. My anxiety increased as we began our descent after the short flight. I could see a strip ahead, and the pilot nodded above the roar of the big turboprop to signal that was our destination. More of the strip was covered in water than not. The pilot turned and yelled in my ear, "Do you need to get in there?" I nodded affirmatively, still wondering how he planned a landing.

I soon found out: the pilot made the sort of approach one would expect for landing on an aircraft carrier. With flaps down, emulating perhaps a landing pelican, we swooped over the end markers of the tarmac and the pilot reversed propeller pitch. We simply stopped in the air and dropped a foot or two to the ground. I was amazed—and sat there with a silly grin on my face. My ex-Marine jet jockey grinned back and helped me open the door. I grabbed my rifle and gear, closed the door, and walked quickly to the edge of the strip. Moments later, the pilot had revved his engine with brakes full on, then released them to roll a few yards and stagger into the air. A minute later he was out of sight, and I was alone except for a couple of Vietnamese in uniform, who were sleeping under thatched shade some distance away. I sat on some sandbags, cradling my rifle, waiting for another aircraft.

An aircraft eventually stopped, an Army Dustoff Huey assigned to the medevac squadron in Binh Thuy. Alighting next to a fuel hose connected to nearby storage bladders, the crew chief disembarked and began fueling while the pilots remained at their controls. Crouching, I ran up to him, waving to the pilots, and asked if they could drop me at a forward base not far away. The crew had a short discussion via the intercom, then the chief gave me a thumbs-up and I crawled aboard and strapped in. The Dustoff was empty then, but the state of the floor suggested it had not been until quite recently, streaks of congealing blood revealing where a body had been pulled out the door.

Moments later, we were in the air gathering altitude over the inundated plain, afternoon sun reflecting off the glistening stalks of inundated fields of reeds. I was comforted in the knowledge that my briefcase and I would be in a reasonably secure position for the night. In the countryside, I noticed the dearth of familiar American faces much more.

There were good reasons for that. Troop levels at the beginning of 1971 were pegged at 280,000. By the end of the year, they had declined to 159,000. The South Vietnamese were assuming more responsibility for actual prosecution of the ground war, and their casualty rates reflected this.

In theory, Vietnamization seemed to be working on the ground—although the United States was committed to an aggressive air campaign to support them. Large B52 strikes continued to hammer NVA troop concentrations in Cambodia, Laos, and Vietnam. One had to wonder how long they would last if that airpower were not on call to support the ARVN. We heard news almost daily about seemingly unending peace talks in Paris, which optimists hoped might provide a tolerable political solution and get American prisoners of war released. The only thing certain was that we all seemed to be leaving Vietnam.

Being the most ground-experienced agent in the office had its disadvantages: I could be sent anywhere. More than two years of in-country experience had taught me where units we serviced were and how best to locate people assigned there. Agents always had the option of asking the command to send a person of interest rearward to Saigon, but inevitably the person concerned would want to know why he was traveling. The often-valuable commodity of surprise, along with access to an individual's personal effects and compatriots, might be forfeited if agents took the easy option. An agent finding his way out to a field unit and doing his job on the spot usually achieved best results. So we went to our customers.

In late 1971 South Vietnam was a long way from being at peace, but it became possible—with careful planning—to drive places where previously helicopter flights had been the only option. I drove from Saigon to Can Tho twice. The second time I was halted at a new bridge just completed with American foreign aid; VC sappers using ammonium-nitrate fertilizer mixed with diesel fuel had demolished some of the support structure. The irony of seeing empty fertilizer bags bearing the familiar hand-clasp U.S. Agency for International Development logo was not lost to me that day. They lay on the banks of a small picturesque river, the bridge approaches shaded by palm trees and bamboo. Cars, jeeps, and trucks were backed up for miles, Vietnamese drivers and passengers becoming uneasy as the sun reached its zenith and began to fall. ARVN military police (QC) were having problems keeping jeeps off the damaged bridge. They resorted to halting traffic by firing M16s overhead.

The only other U.S. vehicle I could see was a grey Navy International Scout, which I soon learned had Navy SEALs on board who were growing uncomfortable with events, as I was. After a brief conference we decided to bluff our way past the QC using my Military Security Service identification. Taking the initiative, the SEALs pulled off on the steeply sloping road shoulder and drove toward the increasingly agitated QCs. Following closely behind, I held the MSS card out for inspection and was approached. The SEALs, after briefly stopping, pulled away immediately; I quickly said "MSS" to the Vietnamese and followed the speeding Scout, as a burst of fire erupted from the ARVN. We drove fast, made the ferry crossings across the Mekong and Ba Sac Rivers, and were safely at Binh Thuy that evening. As I nursed a beer that night, it occurred to me this had been an unnecessarily risky trip, the sort that had killed complacent travelers in Vietnam for years. I would, I resolved, be more alert to potential dangers in the months remaining in my tour.

I continued to run leads in the delta, working with the Binh Thuy agent. Special Agent Rudy Dees had an unenviable caseload, with which I assisted from time to time. Being billeted with and therefore close to Army and Navy aviation units at Binh Thuy made helicopter transport fairly dependable and hassle-free. We ranged over Cape Ca Mau to the Navy Sea Float outpost at Nam Can, where industrious sailors had constructed the first base aboard flat barges anchored in the river. Never far from a fight, Sea Float sailors drew fire just by venturing upstream around the river bend. They were surrounded by hundreds of square miles of mangrove swamp and, to the northwest, by the infamous U Minh Forest that had been home to NVA battalions for many years. SEAL teams operated with great success in the region, taking the guerrilla war to the enemy. The area had a well-earned reputation as Indian country. In the opposite direction, the riverside border towns of Chau Doc and Tan Chau had advisory outposts, some the legacy of Special Forces units venturing across into Cambodia. If a case lead or a complaint came our way, we responded.

Naval Air Facility, Cam Ranh Bay, operated helicopters that flew regular milk runs from the depot in Saigon. When I first arrived, these were old, green US34Ds, which had obviously come from the Marine Corps inventory. The 34 looked like a flying tadpole because of the monstrous radial aircraft engine housed in the nose under the pilots. It was an aircraft with character, and I usually enjoyed my 34 flights high over the rivers and canals of the delta, looking past the door gunner as we overflew the remote, triangular forts the French left behind.

The 34s were scheduled for replacement with the much larger twin-rotor CH46 helicopters. Summoned to an LST anchored in the Gulf of Cambodia, I joined one of the last flights in the venerable bird. It was a long flight, by helicopter standards, and on this occasion there were no views. Clouds and fog covered the coast as we winged over the final vestiges of terra firma somewhere down the coast from Ha Tien. The flight over water seemed to last a very long time. I was not wearing a headset, so could not hear pilot conversations, but we had reduced our elevation considerably and I sensed we were no longer flying in a straight line. I eventually caught the eye of the crew chief/door gunner and said slowly so he could read my lips, "Lost?" He nodded his head in the affirmative, then slid across and said, "The fucking ship won't give us directions to their position." I nodded my understanding. Ships' positions were classified, especially when they were anchored in hostile territory. More minutes passed before the long, grey shape of an LST loomed out of the fog and we gratefully set down across her open tank deck. There was not a great deal of fuel left in the old bird. I jumped off with the mail and was replaced by men due for rotation home. The crew chief busied himself getting enough fuel into the tanks to get them to the next airfield that had high-octane aviation fuel available. Soon, they were flight-ready. The pilot cranked over the big motor, which caught immediately, belching smoke out of cavernous exhaust stacks. Moments later they were circling the ship and climbing above the fog.

It had been a long time since I had been aboard a ship at anchor in open waters. The atmosphere was eerily quiet without the thump of screws and the sound of all the machinery that goes to drive a ship through the water. With the helicopter gone and weather worsening, sailors came out on the tank deck, stripped their clothes off and began lathering up with soap in the freshwater falling from the skies. Freshwater shortages are endemic to LSTs; this was a not-to-be missed opportunity for men who had endured water rationing for a long time.

My business aboard the ship did not take long. By mid-afternoon I was beginning to consider my next move. Being marooned aboard a stationary

LST in the Gulf of Cambodia until the next resupply mission flew in was not an attractive option, so I asked the CO if another underway vessel might be in the area. He agreed to check for me. This was not as simple a matter as it had once been; Vietnamization was at this point well advanced, meaning friendly small vessels then in the area were most likely those of the Vietnamese Navy.

The weather was not improving, and as I watched waves sweep across the open water, I began to wonder which would be the better option: the pitch and roll of the notorious flat-bottomed LST or a smaller vessel under way in foul weather. A young sailor approached me and said, "Sir, a swift boat will be coming alongside for you," breaking my reverie. He beckoned to the railing where a Jacobs ladder was being readied, and I heard the swift's engines as it throttled back to approach us from astern. I looked down as crewmembers dropped fenders over the side to prevent a damaging collision, a real possibility in existing conditions.

As crewmembers threw lines to the boat, I had a close look at her. Fifty feet long, the patrol craft, fast, was a sleek, shallow-draft vessel designed to work coastal waters and rivers. With its alloy hull, it cut a rakish appearance except for the pilothouse perched only a few feet back from the bow peak. It was a practical design, but perhaps lacked the romantic silhouette of a patrol torpedo (PT) boat. On top of the wheelhouse was a gun tub, mounting a pair of .50-caliber machine guns. Looking down into the gun mount, I could see it would command an excellent field of vision above the waves. On the aft deck behind the wheelhouse, crew scurried around the centrally positioned 81mm mortar–machine gun combination mount. Unlike conventional mortars, this one could actually be aimed in the manner of a typical deck gun.

Only one Westerner, a young U.S. Navy petty officer who towered over his shipmates, was on board. As soon as the vessel had been made secure alongside and the engines had been shut down, he had covers off the two massive Detroit diesels and began to check them.

My gear was secured to a line and lowered over the side of the LST to waiting hands below. A good deal of slop splashed up between the two hulls, and my pack swung in an arc with the vessel movement. I gritted my teeth and swung over the side, grimly clutching the Jacobs ladder, which by then was swinging in much the way my gear had. At the end of the ladder there was nothing to do but jump to the rapidly rising deck of the Swift. My landing was neither soft nor gentle, and it caused some good-natured grinning from the Vietnamese. How, they must have wondered, was this tall Yankee going to fare in the seas ahead?

I was offered a comfortable spot below but prudently elected to find a standing position in the wheelhouse where, I reasoned, there was likely to be more fresh air. It was a wise decision. We were soon under way, this apparently also a signal for crewmembers to begin preparing a meal in the space below. They slaughtered a chicken, heated water, and broke out the *nuoc mam* fish condiment. Nuoc mam has wonderful flavors but also an overpoweringly pungent fish odor, which some have compared to unwashed athletic socks. The aromas wafting around the vessel as we plunged into waves that threw water clear over the pilothouse were not conducive to comfortable travel. It took a great deal of concentration to convince my churning stomach that I was not, nor would I become, seasick. A grizzled older Vietnamese coxswain hung onto the wheel skillfully, occasionally checking my color with a cheerful grin. Shirtless, he had a collection of tattoos and illustrations on his chest, the most prominent of which was the statement, "Sat Cong," meaning "kill Viet Cong."

The swift made landfall at An Thoi on the island of Phu Quoc without my disgracing myself. I thanked my hosts for the ride and made my way to the Navy outpost, established in the early '60s to support the Vietnamese Navy's junk force. Successive groups of American advisers had transformed the outpost into a reasonably comfortable spot, replete with spectacular ocean views. With a clean beach and fresh breezes, it certainly offered conditions vastly superior to those the inland Brown Water Navy had to endure. The only drawback I detected was its proximity to several thousand hardcore enemy prisoners of war interned on the island.

At the Navy base, I soon learned the next aircraft back to mainland South Vietnam would not be departing until the following morning, when a USAF C123 Provider was due in to the airstrip. Asking about space availability, I was told, "Don't worry about it; just show up, you'll be okay." Just to be sure, the next morning I was at the airstrip an hour before flight time. With more than two years of experience dealing with U.S. Air Force air movement personnel, this seemed a wise precaution.

I need not have worried. The morning was beautiful, with a gentle breeze blowing in off the Gulf of Cambodia and seemingly unlimited visibility. No U.S. Air Force personnel were present, only Army aviation maintenance men and armorers servicing Cobra gunships and loading rockets into pods for the next mission. I watched the sweating armorer at work until my reverie was broken by the arrival of an aging military fire truck festooned with fully outfitted firefighters. They were Vietnamese civilian employees. Their helmets, jackets, and boots were of U.S. manufacture, all correctly buttoned and buckled, but many times larger than the small-framed wearers. I was quietly amused. I reasoned that the fire truck's arrival was a good indicator my aircraft was inbound and was soon rewarded for my patience as the twin-engine cargo plane touched down, reversed props, and taxied quickly off to the seaward parking area.

By this time, a crowd of Vietnamese Navy personnel and dependents had clustered on the verge of the hardstand area. I did not see live pigs included in the woven baskets and cloth bundles each had, but they were clearly moving house—everything else seemed to be with them. In the meantime, the aircraft was refueled and pilots carried out the preflight check of their charge. I caught the eye of the crew chief, who beckoned me over with a casual turn of his head just as the Vietnamese dependents broke ranks from the grass verge and headed en masse for the aircraft loading ramp. I was lucky in the ensuing skirmish, winning for myself a sling seat far forward, next to an open window. The aircraft quickly filled with chattering Vietnamese, their gear piled unceremoniously onto the cargo ramp. I heard the sound of breaking glass amid the chaos. With the ramp soon up, a harried crew chief pushed forward to the cabin area, shaking his head as he reached me, saying "nouc mam." He was soon followed by the odor of the renowned Phu Quoc fish sauce, then leaking on the cargo deck. The pilots made haste to get us under way, and minutes later I was watching An Thoi's beach fade away behind us as we climbed into the cooling atmosphere. I wondered if this would be my last trip to Phu Quoc; as luck would have it, it was.

In this same time frame, NISRA Saigon received a request for assistance from one of the Navy barrack ships (APLs) anchored in the Mekong near the Cambodian border. Irregularities in the ship post office had been discovered, and it was feared that the postal clerk was stealing from the mail. I inherited the case, which from the outset seemed fairly straightforward, as did locating and getting to the ship. The APL was a floating barracks configured to function as an assault support vessel. She was home not only to a resident helicopter gunship from the Navy Sea Wolf squadron but also to a variety of river patrol craft.

By this time, the old CH34s had been stood down: the Naval Air Facility Cam Ranh Bay Detachment Tan Son Nhut now had a CH46 Sea Knight, which had already been christened *Ha Tien Hattie*. The seaport of Ha Tien, adjacent the Cambodian border, was the farthest point the aircraft flew to; somebody thought the name a good one and stenciled it in black over the Marine green fuselage. The big Boeing Vertol twin-rotor helicopter could carry much bigger loads, faster than previously. The aircraft were new to the Navy detachment, but they were not new by any means. "Checking the bulkheads and seats in the old CH46s to make sure you didn't get lined up with a known active hydraulic leak—that was normal," Whidden recalls.

On this occasion, an agent who had a case to work near Tan Son Nhut Air Base dropped me off at the Navy depot. Seated around a Navy grey SEA hut were perhaps twelve sailors dressed in green utilities. Each, in his own way, was trying to kill time until the flight was called. Some read tattered pocket books or copies of *Stars and Stripes* newspaper; others who had found a post or wall to lean against were trying to doze. One or two smoked, staring into the distance. I reported in, signed the manifest in the office, stood on the scale, and then wandered out to check on progress with our bird. *Ha Tien Hattie's* crew chief was closing the inspection ports on the rear rotor. As he did so, the pilots walked out past me and began their preflight check.

Perhaps ten minutes later, we were called over to the helicopter. Passengers perched in sling seats anchored along the fuselage, most men cradling their issue rifles between their knees. Turbines whined, big overhead rotors picked up speed, and we began taxiing, finally lifting off and rapidly gaining altitude over the perimeter fence of the air base, with scores of Vietnamese cyclists and pedestrians who looked the size of ants below us on the highway. Saigon fell away, and we soared over rice paddies on a southbound course.

The APL, my destination, was our first stop. Our pilots approached the small landing pad on the vessel with caution, though they were accustomed to landing on underway ships. Standing behind the man guiding us in on the tiny ship platform was a fireman dressed in a reflective fire suit that covered him completely. As we hovered and then landed, I could see our image reflected in his face protection panel. We exited from the rear ramp and moved quickly off the landing zone and down the ladderway. As I surveyed the barges, boats, and men who were all a part of this combat platform, the helo pulled pitch and clattered off over the broad muddy expanse of the Mekong to its next destination.

Permanently moored alongside were large flat barges. These served both as mooring points for PBR vessels and as a venue for the recreation area, a plywood SEA hut christened the Last Chance Saloon. Air-conditioned, it dispensed cold beer to the men who walked "ashore" down the ship gangway. The Navy had found the means to allow men a few beers in off-duty time without violating its longtime policy of dry ships. As I watched, two sailors walked out the door to the barge edge and began relieving themselves. The ship's master at arms had by then joined me at the elevated railing. "Biggest urinal in the entire United States Navy," he commented. Who could argue with him?

The investigation was routine: after briefing the executive officer and obtaining a command-authorized search, I examined the suspect postal clerk's locker and personal effects. Material including jewelry and watches was recovered together with documentation that indicated the items were the property of others. The clerk elected not to speak with me about the allegations. I took photographs, bundled up evidence, and completed preliminary paperwork, then went topside. It was late afternoon, the sun beginning to dip low over the flat delta countryside. From upriver, two Cambodian patrol boats approached us. I had not seen the Chinese-built boats this close before, so watched with curiosity as they throttled back and approached berthing positions alongside. From my vantage point, I could see the Cambodian flag with its distinctive stencil of the temples of Angkor fluttering from the mast. How quickly things had changed, I mused. Not long ago, this same boat might well have fired on Americans; all had changed since the allies crossed into Cambodia to clean out the North Vietnamese.

A nearby pair of gunners mates test firing .50-caliber machine guns into the river below shattered my reverie. Satisfied their repairs had rendered the weapons combat-ready, each then shouldered one of the fifty-pound guns and walked toward the armory. Soon they would once again be fastened into mounts on PBRs.

At the evening meal in the wardroom, I noticed with interest the conduct of Vietnamese and visiting Cambodian naval officers. They obviously did not like each other, though each group was quite capable of communicating with the other if it wished to do so. I was aware of the animosity, which had origins that stretched back to ancient times, but had never been this close to it. How long, I wondered, could an alliance of convenience with this sort of history be expected to last? Of course, it did prove to be temporary.

The following day I faced the challenge of how best to get back to Saigon. The ship was not expecting aircraft visits. With Vietnamization, air traffic movements were far fewer than in previous times. I elected to take my chances at an airstrip likely to be busier, Chau Doc. A Vietnamese PBR took me south down the canal that crossed the tributaries of the Mekong. Chau Doc, a longtime border post, was situated at the confluence of the canal and the southern main Mekong tributary, the Ba Sac.

We cast off after breakfast, joined another PBR, and made our way down the canal. The VNN crew was friendly, but language barriers made real communication difficult. They were not in a hurry, and I relished the opportunity to watch river-dwellers whose stilted structures and picturesque boats lined the banks and tributaries. There were friendly calls and waves for the young sailors. Had the crew not been manning machine guns, I might easily have imagined myself in an idyllic setting. I tried to imagine how it must have seemed to the French who had plied the waters at the turn of the century.

Chau Doc, with its aging, crumbling French architecture and towering banyan trees, seemed to have avoided the war. I admired the minarets of the mosque. There were no Americans to be seen. This too was a step back in time, the spell broken only when I heard the distinctive thump of a Huey landing in the distance. Bidding the boatmen good-bye, I found my way to the helo pad and was in Binh Thuy that afternoon, in time to bum a ride back to Saigon. It would be hard to describe the life of a traveling field agent as boring.

Marshal Whidden's recollections of agent air travel in Vietnam are memorable. "I flew to Da Nang on an Air America C46 to pick up a frozen turkey, parlayed from the Army, for Hai to prepare for Christmas dinner at the CO's villa. I then manifested the bird on the return flight as T. Turkey so as to have a seat on which to stow the old bird coming home."

Whidden recalls that Vietnam special agents were often challenged to improvise their travel arrangements. "Being dropped off in a clearing in the jungle to hopefully to be retrieved later by another helo—or having a T39 stop on a darkened runway in NKP [Thailand] at 0400 because you could not get manifested on a flight the normal way [and after all having good friends in OSI does pay dividends]—that was normal. Of course explaining the situation to the Air Force general who happened to be aboard his aircraft was even more challenging. I don't know why the pilot ever stopped for me."

When the Vietnam agents marked the 1972 New Year, all were housed together in the Army CID building in Cholon. The Army had drawn down its staff numbers too, and there was talk that another move was not that far away. In the meantime, Special Agent Ken Seal came aboard as supervising agent; he would remain so until Ed Giblin finished his tour and NISOV was downgraded in March to a resident agency under control of NISO Philippines—exactly as it had begun seven years previously.

In January 1972 I inherited an informant at the Newport Dock facility, a young SeaBee who reported increasing signs of large-scale theft of goods from waterside by Vietnamese Navy personnel, apparently with the complicity of U.S. Navy men assigned there. I monitored the informant regularly, awaiting an opportunity to catch the offenders with the goods, in what I hoped would be a sting operation.

In mid-March I quietly finished both my third year in the Republic of Vietnam and my NIS career, flying out of Saigon on a commercial flight to the Philippines to pursue a business career in Australia, away from Vietnam and the war. Marshal Whidden took over the informant at Newport Docks.

I left behind me a lot of memories and people I felt certain I was betraying simply with my departure. I had, in effect, turned my back on it all. Certainly I was relieved when the Pan Am flight cleared the coast—I had survived—but a part of me remained in Vietnam. So too did some very close friends and colleagues.

By the end of March 1972 Whidden's informant was confident that a large-scale theft of material was being planned at Newport by Vietnamese naval officers. A Vietnamese officer had approached the informant and had asked him to prepare fictitious documentation to facilitate the removal of a vast quantity of building material from U.S. control. These supplies were readily salable on Saigon's black market. The informant was told he would be well paid once the material had successfully cleared the heavily guarded gates of Newport.

Whidden told the SeaBee to play along with the would-be thieves: establish a day for the operation with them in advance to allow preparation for the sting. With a firm date set, Whidden approached our counterparts at VNNSB to participate in the operation by arresting Vietnamese suspects. In his seventh year of working for NIS, Lo Han Thang assisted with day-to-day planning as the operation matured.

Whidden recalls, "On the day of the arrest we set the trap at Newport. Even though we went to a great deal of trouble to disguise our presence we must have been obvious—but I guess the bad guys were pretty slow and had no inside people because they never picked up on it."

Two armored cars were positioned in semiconcealed positions outside the entrance to Newport to block the convoy of trucks loaded with stolen material should the offenders decide to attempt to run the gate. NIS special agents dressed as guards and workers and positioned themselves at various vantage points to monitor progress as trucks were loaded. "The hardest part was hiding the Security Bloc troopers who were there in mass, mainly in jeeps—some with vehicle-mounted machine guns."

It was a long day. The sting had been set up in the morning, but for some unknown reason, the suspects remained inactive until well into the afternoon. Whidden had no contact with the informant and so grew increasingly concerned at his inability to control events. He bought VNNSB troopers drinks and candy to discourage them from wandering around and potentially compromising secrecy.

When the key players, all Vietnamese Navy officers, finally arrived, things moved quickly. Ten two-and-a-half-ton trucks were loaded with everything from cement to toilets. They then formed up and drove to the gate as a convoy, expecting to be waved through as one. As they arrived at the gate, Whidden gave the signal. The gate was blocked and the trucks surrounded by the edgy, heavily armed Vietnamese. Whidden: "Thank God no one fired a shot because had they opened up they would have killed all the drivers and loaders who most likely were innocent of knowingly doing wrong."

A large wad of notes was seized as evidence from the suspects, and several hundred thousand dollars worth of U.S. property was returned. The U.S. naval command was pleased, not only because a theft was thwarted and a strong message sent to would-be opportunists, but also because NISOV had run another successful operation with their Vietnamese Navy counterparts.

Whidden recalls the aftermath: "We put the source up in a hotel in Saigon for the next couple of nights, for his own safety, paid for meals and entertainment as a reward, and then he was shipped out to preclude any retribution."

Commander, U.S. Naval Forces, Vietnam, R.Adm. Robert S. Salzer, USN, later commended the informant in a letter for his official personnel file.

John Morgan left soon after the incident to take a post in the Philippines. Marshal Whidden and Ted Hicks stayed longer, enduring yet another office move to spaces in the central Saigon compound of the commander of U.S. Naval Forces, Vietnam. Their workload shrank as more naval personnel departed; those remaining were likely to be career sailors disinclined to stray from the established rules. Counterintelligence matters remained a low priority. Two new agents, Bob Bagshaw and Ham Maedor, were later assigned to work the Saigon office but were short-toured after a matter of months; Bagshaw moved on to Nam Phong, Thailand.

Ultimately, both Whidden and Hicks were transferred to Subic Bay, Philippines. Certainly one of the busiest offices in the NIS network, its area of responsibility included nearly dormant Vietnam—where only the offices of the Military Sealift Command continued to operate—as well as Thailand, where Marine aviation units had deployed from Vietnam. There they worked for Special Agent Don Webb (of Saigon fame). Periodically, they returned to Saigon to run investigative leads.

Marshal Whidden: "After we totally withdrew from Vietnam, we probably made trips back in country, from the Philippines, every two months or so. I don't think anyone other than Ted Hicks, John Odom, and I made those trips, except the final one. Sometimes the agent would stay two weeks in Vietnam, sometimes a month or longer. No one else wanted to go. In conjunction, we would normally make a swing through Bangkok and run to ground those leads that had built up in the interim. It usually required a good bit of travel throughout the country. We also started covering, on a monthly basis, the Marine Base at 'the Rose Garden,' Nam Phong, Thailand. For about a year we would fly in by C130 and one, sometimes two, agents would stay for a thirty-day period. That was another experience unto itself. Live in a SEA hut, shit in a ditch, and roam the countryside. What an idyllic life. That's when John Odom and I started somewhat seriously considering the option of leaving government service to become chicken ranchers in the Northern High Country of Thailand."

In February 1973 the U.S. Army assumed responsibility for military message communication from Vietnam. This created some challenges for agents used to the naval communication station, from which even sensitive reports could be quickly dispatched with no questions. The Army wanted to know what was in the reports, and this could lead to awkward questions about where some reported information had originated.

This same month Marshal Whidden was dispatched from NISRA Subic Bay as agent afloat aboard the USS *Oriskany*. "I was aboard in the gulf when Peace with Honor [President Nixon's much vaunted peace plan with North Vietnam] was announced. Two battle groups steamed all night to form up

together to parade in celebration. It may have been a sad—even dishonorable—time in American history, but it was a glorious spectacle on that morning. I don't recall how many ships were present but there were four carriers.
Much to my wife's chagrin I left her pregnant and alone living on the banks
of the shit river in Olongapo City—her first excursion out of the US of A—
to accomplish this mission. Many more would follow."

Of course, North Vietnam never intended to honor the peace agree-
ment and aggressively continued its prosecution of the war against the
South—which no longer had direct U.S. military assistance—until the final
capitulation of Saigon in 1975.

In March 1973 Special Agent John Odom, a counterintelligence special-
ist assigned to Subic Bay, made his first trip into Vietnam accompanied by
Marshal Whidden. Odom was ordered to determine what potential threats
of terrorism existed in the Saigon and Mekong Delta areas, particularly anything that might be directed against the ongoing Supply Cambodia out of
Thailand program, the supply initiative designed to prop up the fragile pro-
Western government of Lon Nol, who was then engaged in a bitter fight for
Cambodia against the communist Khmer Rouge. The plan was relatively
simple: supplies were shipped from the United States to Thailand, restaged
onto barges, then taken by tugboat across the Gulf of Thailand to the port
of Vung Tau, where a tributary of the Mekong could be accessed.

Odom reactivated Lo Han Thang, then working for the Army in Saigon,
to help source information about threats to shipping. True to form, Thang
unearthed reports that the enemy had advanced a plan to attack the large fuel
depot on the Saigon River at Nha Be. A longtime target of the communists,
the port was then lightly defended after the U.S. Navy withdrawal and was
apparently quite vulnerable. The plan unearthed suggested the Viet Cong
would attack the depot and attempt to scuttle or sink a ship across the water-
way, thus isolating the Port of Saigon. Though the attack did not come as
and when predicted, it did occur later, causing considerable disruption to
South Vietnam's military fuel supply.

Odom also continued the long-standing relationship with our Vietnamese counterparts, the Vietnamese Navy Security Service (VNNSS), still under the command of Captain Thanh.

Often working alone, Odom sensed that the security situation in Saigon
had changed. Initially he used the Embassy Hotel as a base, but nighttime
activity in the hallways and on the street soon convinced him that little stood
between him and any determined attacker in the street, and he moved to the
Grey House, an Air America establishment near Tan Son Nhut Airport.
The house was located within a secure compound guarded by Nung merce-
naries, and it had a fine bar and restaurant and a place to safely park a
vehicle. The Navy's Military Sealift Command (MSC) offices in central Saigon
provided him an office.

A sense of uncertainty about the future of South Vietnam was becoming more pervasive. During this time an unattended warehouse opposite the MSC offices in Saigon was found to contain boxes of unsecured classified messages; an investigation into the origins of the boxes was launched immediately. It seemed quite possible that, at best, unauthorized persons had access to sensitive classified material; at worst, the enemy might have been reading the Navy's mail for a considerable period of time. Odom made inquiries and determined that a U.S. civilian office employee had neglected to properly destroy classified documents accumulated in the safes over time. The excess documents had been put into boxes and stored across the street in rented warehouse space, where they remained for many months. Fortunately, when the boxes were finally opened, they were found to contain almost nothing but ship movement reports classified as confidential and really of no value at all once the vessel had moved on.

The threat that first brought John Odom to Vietnam later became a reality when one of the tugs used to push transport barges to Cambodia was sunk, reportedly by Viet Cong swimmer-sappers, at Vung Tau. On the scene, Odom soon learned that the ARVN colonel in charge of port security regarded the sinking with some suspicion. He decided to look into the matter further, and his investigations seemed to indicate a conspiracy by the Korean tug owners to collect compensation from the U.S. government. Perhaps realizing the lucrative barge transport program would not last much longer, the Koreans seemed to have sunk their vessel at its moorings. As the investigation proceeded, the owner of the vessel, Madam Wu, contacted Odom unexpectedly at the Embassy Hotel. The agent had previously seen her at the Vung Tau Wharf without knowing who she was. Madam Wu wasted no time telling the agent that she needed his cooperation and asked what kind of compensation would be required for him to leave the case alone; Odom declined the bribe.

Later, the Koreans turned up the heat by calling a meeting with officials at the Korean embassy. Odom attended the meeting after first advising U.S. embassy staff and was subjected to a range of questions aimed at undermining his investigative conclusions. In the end, the agent returned to Vung Tau, borrowed diving equipment, and inspected the sunken hull personally. His inspection clearly indicated that the blast that damaged the tug had been from within, not from the outside as had been suggested. Odom wrote his report. The Korean claim for compensation was dismissed.

Of rather more interest in Odom's counterintelligence assignment was a chance contact in Vung Tau with a Vietnamese woman who was consorting with a colonel in the Czech Army. In the 1970s Czechoslovakia was firmly cemented into the Soviet-dominated Eastern Bloc, so any opportunity to gain information about a military officer was keenly sought after. Odom learned the man had been assigned to the International Control Commission, the body originally charged with overseeing provisions of the 1954 treaty between North and South Vietnam. The colonel had traveled extensively, presumably also into the North. His Vietnamese lover was more than happy to share her secrets about his family, career, and personal habits. Her conversations with the colonel inevitably returned to the theme of the love they had for each other and the colonel's unhappiness in his Czechoslovakian home. The CIA was grateful for Odom's reports.

# 17
## THE FALL

**When in April 1975 the fall of Saigon looked imminent**, a final decision had to be made about the last remaining NIS office in Vietnam. Subic Bay Senior Resident Agent Don Webb decided to close the small office maintained for visiting agents at the Defence Attaché Office (DAO) compound at Tan Son Nhut Air Base. Electing not to send either of the relatively uncontrollable former Vietnam agents, he dispatched instead Special Agent Gary West, a young man who he knew would carry out instructions without question. West was told to make his own judgment call as to what he brought out and what was left for destruction.

West decided to leave everything: counterintelligence manuals, crime scene kits—the detritus of years of agent activity in Saigon. He came out with virtually only what he was wearing, leaving the final destiny of the office in the hands of Army demolition experts, who began wiring charges and preparing safes and their documents for destruction by thermal grenades and white phosphorous.

Whidden and Hicks, back in Subic, were increasingly restive as events began to overtake some vaguely laid plans to travel to Saigon to rescue former NISOV employees, in particular Lo Han Thang. Whidden broached the subject with SRA Webb, who refused permission on the grounds that the situation in Saigon was too unstable and dangerous. The evacuation plan had been left too long. Groups of disgruntled ARVN soldiers were reported to be interfering with evacuation plans. Whidden got through to U.S. Army personnel in Saigon and asked them to look after Thang and his family; it was the best he could do. Two trusted allies, Maj. Andy Gambara, U.S. Army Military Intelligence, and SAC Josh Billings, U.S. Army CID, agreed to help.

Thang was at the time working in the DAO compound at Tan Son Nhut. In the days before Whidden's call for help, some Vietnamese had been evacuated from nearby Bien Hoa Air Base, but with NVA armor drawing nearer, Bien Hoa was no longer a safe option. The enemy was in Saigon within days.

Back in the Philippines, with communication to Saigon uncertain, Whidden began to worry about whether Lo Han Thang and his family had been evacuated. He drove to the massive U.S. Air Force facility at Clark Air Base and enlisted the assistance of OSI agents to try to locate the family among the many refugees then being sheltered after often harrowing flights from South Vietnam. Thang's name did not appear on flight manifests; neither could he be found among the evacuees. Whidden noted with considerable disgust that many of the early evacuees were not direct-hire Vietnamese employees of the U.S. government. Many seemed to be politicians and even streetwise "cowboys" off the boulevards of Saigon. Distressed, the agent returned to Subic Bay and passed the word to other concerned agents: Lo Han Thang, his wife, and his daughter might be casualties.

Several days passed before Whidden returned to Clark, enlisted the help of OSI agents, and was again disappointed to find no trace of the Lo family. SRA Don Webb expressed concern about the amount of time Whidden was devoting to the search.

On the third trip to Clark, Whidden again strode into OSI intending to request help. Sitting in the waiting area was Thang. "Where the hell have you been?!" were Thang's first words to the vastly relieved Whidden. Always the professional, Thang and his family had traveled under an assumed alias, never knowing for certain whether his shadowy past might be known to the Viet Cong, which might have had sympathizers close to the evacuation machine.

Everyone realized that the Subic Bay naval facilities would bear the initial brunt of seaborne evacuations after the fall of the South. Thang's first job upon arrival was to assist in the screening of hundreds of Vietnamese evacuees, many of whom would not have even basic identification. The agents thought it over, researched the Vietnamese repatriation process, and then decided it would not be in the best interests of their Vietnamese friend to remove him and his family from the bureaucratic pipeline that would ultimately give them a new life in the United States. A cash collection was taken up for them in anticipation of their next stopping point on the way to America: Guam. In the meantime, Ted Hicks's sister and her husband agreed to sponsor the Lo family in Southern California.

Whidden: "We, individually and as an organization, owe a great deal of gratitude to Maj. Andy Gambara , U.S. Army MI, and to SAC Josh Billings, U.S. Army CID. These two men were both American patriots in the truest sense. We would have been unable to do as well as we did in-country, after the pull out, without their assistance. After it was all said and done, a lot of folks owed them a debt of gratitude."

Harrowing stories surfaced from the final hours of Saigon. Defenders of the Defense Attaché Office compound spoke of having to shoot their way through the streets of Saigon, defending busloads of evacuees on the way to their aircraft. So too came a witness to the final moments of the NIS office at the compound, who said the building had literally melted under the weight of thermal grenades aimed so as to destroy classified material and property.

When it came, the fall of Saigon precipitated a massive evacuation of Vietnamese aboard virtually any vessel that would float. The U.S. fleet, stationed off the coast, rescued many of these brave souls; others elected to strike out directly for the Philippines and the U.S. Navy base, Subic Bay. Significantly, the CIA had evacuated its important Can Tho facility by vessel, dispatching their personnel down a tributary of the Mekong and into open waters, bound for Subic.

As the deluge of refugees began to reach Philippine waters, their vessels were boarded by junior officers of the U.S. Navy, who raised the Stars and Stripes to facilitate entry into the U.S. base, under Philippine law. All weapons were ordered surrendered; these were either cast over the side or impounded for later destruction.

NIS agents were charged with systematically screening all evacuees to ensure their status as genuine refugees. A facility on Grande Island, normally a recreation area for the naval base, was quickly erected with a Marine security force present. NIS agents used PBRs to reach the vessels on their way into port. What they saw was frequently distressing: people without food or water in leaky, overloaded, and decidedly unseaworthy boats. Many of the evacuees were themselves in physical distress after many days at sea.

Said Marshal Whidden, "The welcome we got when we boarded those boats was just unbelievable. The bravery and dignity the Vietnamese people presented was incredible. They were scared—they were terrified—but they weren't rabble."

One of Whidden's keenest recollections of the flotilla arrival at Subic was passing a heavily laden South Vietnamese Navy water carrier in a PBR. Hearing a plaintive cry—"Marsho!"—he turned to see the waving figure of VNN Commander Khoa, a longtime NIS ally of the VNNSS. But their happy reunion was marred by the news that Khoa's commanding officer, Captain Nguyen Van Tan, had stayed behind, apparently to gather his family, and had not made it out. Tan was thought to have been heard on the evening Saigon fell on the captured South Vietnamese Navy radio, calling for Navy men to return to port with their vessels. The broadcast had obviously been made under duress.

Included in the seaborne mass of humanity were general officers of the South Vietnamese military forces, the mayor of Saigon, and even well-known movie stars. Many carried their remaining wealth in the form of small gold bars or gold leaf. All was receipted for and locked in a CONEX shipping box under the control of armed Marine sentries.

With the CIA contingent came scores of large bags, packed with U.S. currency—the agency's black money for operations in the Mekong Delta.

This too was seized and put under guard. The agency itself sent teams of case officers in to assist with screening. Agents proficient in Vietnamese and Khmer arrived from stations around the globe. CIA interrogator-translator teams came from Okinawa and set about identifying their people and those of the Vietnamese Military Security Service. Agents carefully scrutinized all the internees. Clothing, manner of dress, and reactions to fellow evacuees were all carefully observed and noted. All were interrogated at least once; a few were polygraphed also.

Throughout it all, a frustrated press corps tried unsuccessfully to access Grande Island and its temporary inhabitants. The Navy and Marine Corps successfully kept all at bay, never hesitating to seize and destroy film taken in the restricted area. Many in the military felt strongly that the press had done neither the armed forces nor the country a great service in Vietnam, so the regulations on the media were prosecuted with a good deal of vigor.

The screening lasted for weeks. It should have been the swan song for the former Vietnam agents, but for John Odom, there was one final episode: Khmer Rouge soldiers seized USS *Mayaguez* and took it to an island near the Cambodian mainland. After refusing to return the vessel, the communist forces were attacked by U.S. Marine infantry and airpower. Marine counterintelligence teams on the island later seized everything of possible intelligence value they could find, scouring Khmer Rouge casualties, their camp, and facilities. They found diaries, photographs, official papers, and even French brandy. Odom and a team of specialists carefully scrutinized it all before forwarding parcels onward for formal evaluation.

With that, the war was truly over.

From the perspective of personal experience, perhaps Supervising Agent Dick McKenna's letter to his agents at the end of his tour says what most of us felt in some way. "Good-byes are sometimes hard to express—and my attempts on my final parting proved to be a complete failure as far as you so and so's are concerned. But I must say to you all what is in my heart. Working with you for the past year was an honor—a finer group of men exists nowhere. You are individually and collectively that factor that adds up to a unique, once in a lifetime experience. It is rare that one has the opportunity in life to share the frustrations, the tensions, the joys, the laughter of a group so molded by common goals and interests—and I feel privileged to have been part of that group. You made my tour, and I shall remember each one of you."

Through the entire story of Naval Intelligence involvement in Vietnam—from 1965 to 1975—only one personality played a continuous role throughout: Lo Han Thang. Officers, agents, and enlisted rotated through Vietnam every twelve months. Thang remained, always representing continuity, a man who consistently could be counted on—a man tried, trusted, and true.

Thang was a man tempered in the crucible of contemporary Vietnamese politics. Born in the North, he had begun his education when France was defeated at Dien Bien Phu. When the Geneva Treaty of 1954 was signed, effectively dividing the country into communist North and pro-Western South, the Lo family knew there would be no future for them under Ho Chi Minh's pro-Moscow regime. They made ready to take what few belongings they could carry with them and found their way to the port of Haiphong, whence the U.S. Navy was ferrying those who wished to leave down the coast to Saigon, Republic of Vietnam. How curious that then-Lt. Bob Kain, already introduced as Naval Intelligence's first agent in Vietnam, was then an officer aboard one of the LSTs so assigned. Perhaps Kain's ship removed the Lo family to their new home in the South; we'll never know for certain. More than four decades have passed since a young Vietnamese boy passed through the cavernous jaws of the ship that carried his family to a new home; the ship's name has faded with time. Not all of the Lo family settled in Saigon. Two sisters migrated to France, where they settled and remained.

A bright student, Thang mastered English and found employment with the interpreter pool of the American embassy in Saigon. From that job, the Office of Naval Intelligence recruited him to become a full-time interpreter and functionary. He was bright, diplomatic, and well connected with various Vietnamese government agencies. Agents liked and trusted him. Soon Thang was actively involved in counterintelligence operations with ONI special agents.

As the office grew with the mission and a NISO was established, Thang was assisted by other Vietnamese with language skills. But his primacy was never in doubt, nor was his loyalty to the agency and its personnel. A skilled interviewer, Thang had the ability to talk with Vietnamese and learn facts without suggesting a particular outcome. This was a strength few other interpreters had.

His Navy employment ended in 1973 when NIS ceased a full-time presence in Vietnam. The Army was glad to have his services, but he continued to assist Naval Intelligence agents until the very end, in 1975.

That Thang was successfully evacuated with his wife and young daughter only hours before Saigon fell reflects little credit on the people who employed him all those years; his escape was much more a function of his own toughness, determination, and professionalism. I think, as I know most agents do who shared the dangers of the Vietnam War with Lo Han Thang, that we could have done a far better job of looking after our trusted ally. And his story certainly is not unique.

# 18
# EPILOGUE

**The last of the NIS special agents with Vietnam** experience had reached mandatory retirement age by the new millennium. Several rose to senior rank in the organization, leaving lasting marks of a leadership style that was forged in the crucible of war. Most, now in their sixties, enjoy retirement, though several have gone on to excel in private enterprise.

Lo Han Thang is settled in Southern California. The infant daughter he and wife Phuong carried out of Saigon in the final hours of freedom is an honors graduate of the University of Southern California. The family has not returned to Saigon, even for a short vacation. They are another truly American success story, as are many Vietnamese who were forced to flee their country.

Of the Vietnamese officers and families of VNNSS who successfully escaped Saigon when it fell in April 1975, several families were sponsored and accommodated by the U.S. Navy officers with whom they had previously served. The Brooks and Schneider families—among others—assimilated and patiently restarted the lives of their traumatized former allies. In the three decades since the end of the war, the sponsors have witnessed a remarkable litany of educational and professional successes among the children of those families, now all proud Americans.

In 1999 retired YNC Jon Springer, still believing his Vietnamese wife, Cang, and two children had been lost in the Vietnam War, was stunned to learn that they had made good their escape from Saigon immediately before the fall in 1975. Cang's sister had married an American civilian who arranged for the trio to leave Vietnam as a part of his family. After stints in various refugee facilities, they settled temporarily in California before establishing themselves in Las Vegas, Nevada. One of the daughters, who had never believed her mother's story that her father had been killed during the Tet Offensive, had determinedly used the Internet to find her natural father. Not only was Jon Springer reunited with his daughters and their mother, but he also found that he was a grandfather four times over. This may be the only happy ending to come out of the Tet Offensive of 1968.

In his effort to gather together his large family of eight children, VNNSS commanding officer Capt. Nguyen Van Tan had run out of time; he was captured soon after North Vietnamese troops overran Saigon and rushed off to North Vietnam for interrogation. Incarcerated in a series of brutally primitive jungle camps in the mountainous provinces of Vinh Phu, Thanh Phong, and Nam Ninh, he was subjected to isolation, torture, and years of interrogation while he worked as a hard-labor prisoner. A small man, Tan, aged forty-three when captured, lost sixty pounds while in captivity. For more than sixteen years, the North Vietnamese worked to extract secrets from their captive. They also incarcerated Tan's brother, a former civilian counter-intelligence officer. The two brothers saw each other only once while in captivity, at a camp near Phan Thiet in former South Vietnam. Both were subjected to further brutality by their captors after the chance meeting.

Throughout his captivity, Tan's ailing wife waited for his eventual release, which was assisted by concerned former U.S. Navy colleagues. V.Adm. Rex Rectanus and others rallied to assist Tan, and in June 1991 he was finally released and repatriated to the United States with his wife and four of their children. His wife died a month later.

Now remarried, Tan has settled in southern California. So has his brother, who survived fourteen years in the North Vietnamese gulag. The four children who were repatriated with Tan are now grown and settled, three others remain in Saigon, and one is a resident of Sydney, Australia. A grandson is a serving U.S. Navy officer, now stationed in Japan.

My return trip to Vietnam in the late 1990s was in some ways a step back in time. Some changes are noticeable: zealous revolutionaries have renamed streets, and new high-rise buildings line the horizons in both Saigon and Hanoi. In many respects though, a trip to Saigon was an experience in *deja vú*. French colonial architecture has survived, though in many cases it is now showing its age.

However, the modern Vietnam is a very young country. More than half of the population of 65 million is less than twenty-five years old. They do not remember the war. They are here today, looking determinedly at the future, and I have no doubt they will continue to accelerate moves toward a true market economy and away from the state control that has been a feature of government for more than three decades. As war-era revolutionaries retire and die, more change can be expected. The Vietnamese remain as resourceful and courageous as ever. They are committed to catching up with Asian neighbors and doubtless will do so.

In Cholon, the NISOV office has been demolished to make way for a service station. The HSAS compound that once housed the PX is sealed shut and appears to have been that way for several decades. On the corner opposite, Fuji's Restaurant has been totally razed; no traces remain even of the bamboo grove and gardens, which once were a pleasant escape from the bustling streets outside the walls. Much of the city center remains as it was in the sixties. The Continental Palace, Caravelle, Rex, and Majestic hotels have had facelifts, the town hall has been restored, and the park statuary has been changed. Hordes of motorcycles remain, and in the evening hundreds of young people and children turn out to walk among parks and fountains.

Thieu's monument of ostentation, the Presidential Palace, has been preserved as a national museum, as has the tank that symbolically breached its gates on the evening Saigon fell in 1975. Young female guides suitably indoctrinated into Vietnam's modern socialist ideal escort visitors. The grand halls, lovely art works, and rooftop helicopter pad with a parked Huey have been carefully maintained as examples of capitalist excess. A basement war room, resplendent with wall maps marked to show the progress of the war, is also a popular attraction.

The American embassy, once the hub of Saigon, simply looks old and tired, its concrete starkness now streaked with dark mold and decay. The new government does not encourage visits.

Da Nang, reflecting its perennial status as a commercial seaport, has been rebuilt in many areas. The White Elephant is gone, as is the 20 Duy Tan Street residence where Naval Intelligence was first established. The billet at 23 Doc Lap, curiously, has survived change, its rooms converted into tiny apartments. I found a widow and her young daughter living in the first-floor room Carl Sundstrom and I shared in 1969. Despite conspicuously displayed NLF awards, she received me graciously into her tiny home, which has had little or no maintenance over the years. Nearby, General Lam's villa now houses a bank. Its well-manicured neocolonial facade has seldom looked better. Opposite 23 Doc Lap, the old French villa that took the fatal rocket strike that night in 1969, now serves as the offices of an oil company.

With assistance from sympathetic communist nations, the national highway over Hai Van Pass north of Da Nang was widened and improved. Were it not for the collection of French, pre-French Vietnamese, and former South Vietnamese bunkers clustered around the crest of the pass, visualizing just what a hostile environment these mountains had been would not be easy. Whether the victim of allied defoliants (as the communists claim) or desperate, starving peasant woodcutters, the forests that graced the mountains are largely gone. What remains are magnificent, unforgettable views: to the south, the village of Nam O, Red Beach, and Da Nang's grand harbor; to the north, the idyllic lagoon and sand isthmus upon which is built one of the Orient's most picturesque villages, Lang Co. During the war southbound convoys assembled and joined the gun trucks and armor at Lang Co for the perilous trip over the pass. The assembly point today is a roadside market, among which the occasional European backpacker can be seen bargaining for marble trinkets or cold drinks.

Hue is less than an hour farther north. The airport at Phu Bai and the French military buildings, which once sheltered the most important Marine enclave north of Da Nang, are now largely abandoned. The airport itself receives daily flights from the domestic airline; otherwise, it is as quiet as the sand dunes around it. Another ten minutes north through the rice paddies, the outskirts of Hue appear. Little seems to have changed; perhaps the only big differences were the absence of concertina wire, sandbags, and sentries in modern Hue. The Catholic cathedral, a glorious monument to the best of Gothic-French Oriental architecture, arises in the west—its spires reaching up above groves of palms and bamboo. And soon, I was on the banks of the Perfume River—precisely where I had stood in awe on my first visit to the Imperial City in mid-1969. On the river were sampans—Vietnam's own unique brand of bustling pedicabs—cyclos, and pedestrians—and beyond, the towering flagstaff, this time resplendent in the colors of the Democratic Republic of Vietnam. There could be no surer reminder of the war's outcome.

The south bank of the Perfume River, where I stood musing, was the epicenter of some of the most savage house-to-house combat of the war. To my delight, few indicators remained of those desperate times when U.S. Marines blasted their way through the university buildings, provincial headquarters and a prison, and even the hospital—removing some very determined VC and North Vietnamese regulars. The tamarind trees had fully recovered, spreading a leafy canopy over the waterfront boulevard. Villas constructed in the art deco style of French Indochina were worn and perhaps moldy, but lacking nothing for character. I felt a little like I'd come home, after three decades away.

An old French hotel near the railway station served as home for more than a week of exploration. This time it was possible to visit the outlying legacy of the Nguyen dynasty—the imperial tombs. During the war, a visit to the rural surrounds of Hue was a very dangerous enterprise, and I had left Vietnam disappointed that I'd never seen any of them. Now, the Perfume River's many sampans provide a peaceful, placid journey upstream to the burial sites, each carefully chosen for position by its intended occupant. All are an expression in symmetry, beautifully considered landscaping, and artistic expression. More than two decades of war and turmoil have left their mark—on some more than others—but the pockmarks of small-arms fire hardly detract from the simple beauty and aura of peace to be found at the imperial tombs. This was a side of Vietnam I'd never seen, and I often found myself reflecting with envy on the life of a Hue-based prewar French colonial.

Venturing into the cloud-shrouded mountain ranges that stand a short distance to the west of the Imperial City is a journey into a different world. The narrow track built by the French and later improved by Americans to supply the important firebases protecting the city is today not in good repair. But it is passable, and the striking mountain country that the road winds through quickly overcomes any discomfort. Firebase Bastogne, home to the 101st Airborne is now a grass-covered hill, still surrounded by the ville that unquestionably developed during the war as a venue for trade with American service personnel.

As the plains and paddy fields fade, Bru villages begin to appear, built on steep hillsides. The Montagnard people, the aboriginals of Indochina who performed sterling service as irregular soldiers under the leadership of the U.S. Special Forces, are paying the price for their reputation as killers of Vietnamese. They have been forcibly moved by the government and survive today as subsistence farmers practicing slash-and-burn agriculture. A benefit, albeit an extremely hazardous one, is scrap metal and unexploded ordnance from the war. Bru households feature cluster bombshells, unexploded mortar rounds, and piles or artillery shrapnel.

The Ashau Valley, a name that struck a quiet chord of terror in those who operated against this traditional harboring spot of the NVA, nestles in the Annamite Cordelera adjacent to the Laotian border—whence the Northerners came via tributaries of the Ho Chi Minh Trail. Until 1966 a U.S. Special Forces camp supported on-going reconnaissance of the trail. Then the NVA decided on a strategy of attrition against vulnerable and difficult-to-supply border camps. Operating during the monsoon, when clouds cover the ranges and limit air observation and attacks, they moved antiaircraft batteries onto the low hills and mountains that circle the camp and its airstrip and systematically began heavy artillery attacks followed by infantry. U.S. soldiers and their Montagnard irregulars were substantially outnumbered; they were eventually driven out, withdrawing overland until plucked from the jungle by Marine aviators based at Phu Bai. Ashau today is a small school and a collection of grass huts for the Bru students, all lying within throwing distance of shattered bunkers and unexploded bombs. Visitors are not encouraged to visit Ashau, but determined ones get through. The Cubans generously helped their communist allies extend and pave a former branch of the Ho Chi Minh Trail northward from Ashau clear through to Route 9, which connects the coast with Khe Sanh. The new road snakes its way under mountaintops, which once bore names like "Firebase Bradley" and "Tun Tavern."

Khe Sanh is given over to coffee and pepper plantations; they cover much of the former Marine base that the media was so fond of equating to the 1954 French defeat at Dien Bien Phu. Today, the once-scarred hills are once again verdant. But Khe Sanh base still retains its aura. Piles of unexploded ordnance are recovered weekly, at considerable physical cost to the collectors, and a thriving trade in excavated military memorabilia goes on: buttons, badges of rank, boot soles, scraps of webbing.

In the midst of the DMZ stands a low hill named Con Thien, or "Hill of the Angels" to the Vietnamese. Marines heavily fortified this geographic reference point after early battles with the NVA, to block enemy attack routes into the zone and points beyond. As a firebase, its small perimeter took hundreds of rounds of heavy artillery fire from North Vietnamese guns concealed to the north. Its muddy trenches, interlocking water-filled shell holes, rats, and stench compared in many respects to the conditions of trench warfare in World War I. Driving through pine plantations, I found with some difficulty the bloody hill where so many lost their lives; it was surrounded and covered by banana plantations.

A visitor to Vietnam who knew the country during the war will probably at some point ponder about what difference America's brave attempt to rescue South Vietnam made. As I stared out over verdant rice paddies in the former demilitarized zone during my first visit since the war, I was prompted to think that, despite a preponderance of altruism, we had mattered very little in the context of Vietnam's troubled two millennia of history. My American compatriots are now dying at an alarming rate, joining their Vietnamese enemies upon whom age is also taking its toll. Their leaders and educators have reared the youth of Vietnam on a diet of one-sided war stories; but with time, this too will fade into the realm of ancient history. Time marches on, and in this instance, it's no bad thing.

Returning to Hue, the city that had once again drawn me back, afternoon rains provided a context that connected my memories and the contemporary images of this visit. During the war, rain often granted me a visual and aural escape from the cacophony. Low clouds would sweep in, the atmosphere heavy in anticipation of the following deluge, as large raindrops began falling on palm leaves and trees—a patter that became a steady drumming that blocked out all. At those times—when the air became damp and fresh, leaves and flowers took on a fresh sheen and were reborn, and time stood still—I was very much at peace with myself and Vietnam. I felt almost as if it was somehow intended that I should have the experience of the storm in that troubled place as a reminder of the greater scene. So it was, all those years later, that the rains brought me back to the temporary tranquility of that earlier time, accenting how very little had changed with the Perfume River and her peoples in thirty years. Vietnam's entire past, after all, was based on stoic endurance, and I was but a grain of sand in that history.

# GLOSSARY

| Term | Explanation |
|------|-------------|
| AO | Area of operations. |
| *ao dai* | Traditional Vietnamese lady's dress. |
| APL | A floating barracks ship. |
| ARVN | Army of the Republic of Vietnam, the South Vietnamese Army. |
| ASA | Army Security Agency, a highly classified command charged with signal security and electronic intelligence acquisition. |
| BEQ | Bachelor enlisted quarters. |
| BIs | Background investigations. |
| boonies | From *boondocks*; out in the wilds; the bush. |
| BOQ | Bachelor officers quarters. |
| C47 | Douglas DC3, a twin-engine transport. Most were built during World War II. |
| C117 | Super DC3, an upgraded version of the C47. It had larger engines and a different tail assembly. |
| C130 | Lockheed Hercules, a four-engine turbo-prop transport aircraft in service with all service branches except the Army. |
| CACO | Casualty assistance coordination officer. |
| CAG | U.S. Marine Corps Combined Action Group. Part of the Marine Corps strategy in Vietnam to assist friendly villagers to protect their crops and assets from the Viet Cong. |
| CBMU | Construction battalion maintenance unit, a unit designator for naval engineers (SeaBees) often assigned to maintenance duties, as opposed to construction. |
| CH46 | Twin-rotor Boeing Vertol medium helicopter widely used by U.S. Marines and, to a lesser extent, by the U.S. Navy. |
| chow | Food. |

257

| | |
|---|---|
| CHP | California Highway Patrol. |
| CIA | U.S. Central Intelligence Agency. |
| CIB | Combat infantry badge, a U.S. Army decoration. Also, Combat Information Bureau. |
| CIC | Army Counterintelligence Corps. |
| CID | Criminal Investigation Division. Criminal investigation component of the U.S. Marine Corps and U.S. Army Military Police commands. |
| CINCPACFLT | Commander in chief, Pacific Fleet. |
| CO | Commanding officer. |
| Cobra | AH1 Bell Huey Cobra, a purpose-built helicopter gunship. |
| COMNAVFORV | Commander, Naval Forces, Vietnam |
| COMUSMACV | Commander, U.S. Military Assistance Command, Vietnam. Originally Gen. W. C. Westmoreland, succeeded in 1968 by his assistant, Gen. Creighton Abrams, U.S. Army. |
| CP | Command post. |
| CS | A refined form of tear gas. |
| DAO | Defense Attaché Office. |
| DEA | Drug Enforcement Administration. |
| *dinky-dau* | Corrupted Vietnamese term for crazy. |
| DMZ | Demilitarized zone. The area along the eighteenth parallel that separated North and South Vietnam. |
| DNI | Director of Naval Intelligence. |
| DRV | Democratic Republic of Vietnam (communist North Vietnam). |
| EOD | Explosive ordnance disposal. |
| flak jacket | Body armor. |
| FLC | Force Logistic Command. |
| frag | A fragmentation hand grenade. |
| fragging | The act of murder by use of a fragmentation hand grenade. |
| grunt | A field marine. |
| gunny | Gunnery sergeant, a Marine Corp senior NCO, E-7. |
| HAL-4 | Helicopter Attack Squadron 4, the Sea Wolves; Navy helicopter squadron assigned to the Mekong Delta region. |
| Ho Chi Minh Trail | A network of improvised roads and trails extending from North Vietnam to the south, most of it in neutral Laos and Cambodia and thus out of reach of U.S. ground troops. |
| hooch | A hut, often of the SEA design, used as rear-area |

accommodation in Vietnam. Also describes an improvised field shelter.

| | |
|---|---|
| HSAS | Headquarters Support Activity, Saigon. |
| Huey | Utility helicopter. The Bell UH1 series of utility helicopters were the workhorses of the Vietnam War. |
| I Corps | Pronounced "Eye" Corps, the first of four corps areas adopted by Vietnamese and consequently, U.S. forces. I Corps was the northernmost corps, IV Corps being the Mekong Delta Region. |
| ICC | International Control Commission. |
| IIR | Intelligence information report. |
| investigative lead | A logical next step or task in the investigative process, often an interview or a simple inquiry. Leads were sent to NISOV for action by other NIS offices, and similarly, it was often necessary to request another office or agency to complete leads. |
| JAG | Judge Advocate General, the legal arm of the U.S. military organization. |
| JPRC | Joint Personnel Recovery Center. |
| LAAM | Light antiaircraft missile. |
| ladderway | Stairs, in naval jargon. |
| LCM | Landing craft, medium. Ramped landing craft capable of carrying vehicles and personnel. |
| LCU | Landing craft, utility. |
| lifer | Derisive term for a career military man. |
| LSB | Logistic support base. |
| LST | Landing ship, tank. |
| Lt. Cdr. | Lieutenant commander. Naval officer rank 0-4, equivalent to a major. |
| Lt. j.g. | Lieutenant, junior grade. Naval officer grade 0-2, equivalent to a first lieutenant in other services. |
| LZ | Landing zone. |
| M1 Garand | Semiautomatic, .30-caliber rifle first issued to U.S. troops in early World War II. |
| M16 | Issue U.S. rifle which began service in Vietnam during 1966. |
| MACV | Military Assistance Command, Vietnam. |
| MAF | Marine amphibious force. |
| magazine | An ammunition storage facility, especially on a warship; on a modern military firearm a magazine carries ammunition, ready to fire. |
| MI5 | British national counterintelligence agency. |
| MIA | Missing in action. |

| | |
|---|---|
| MP | Military Police. Applies to both Army and U.S. Marine Corps. |
| MPC | Military payment certificates. |
| MSC | Military Sealift Command. |
| MSD | Vietnamese Military Security Directorate. |
| MSS | Vietnamese Military Security Service. |
| MSTS | Military Sea Transportation Service. |
| N-22 | Counterintelligence officer of COMNAVFORV. |
| NAD | Naval advisory detachment. |
| NAF | Naval air facility. |
| NAS | Naval air station. |
| NAVFORV | Naval Forces, Vietnam. |
| NCO | Noncommissioned officer. The enlisted ranks E-4 to E-9. |
| newbie | A recent arrival to Vietnam; a new guy. |
| NILO | Naval Intelligence liaison officer. |
| NIS | Naval Investigative Service. |
| NISOV | Naval Investigative Service Office, Vietnam. The command headquarters for NIS, located in Cholon, Saigon. |
| NISRA | Naval Investigative Service Resident Agency, a NIS field office. There were two in Vietnam: Saigon and Da Nang. |
| NISSU | Naval Investigative Service Satellite Unit, typically one-man outposts assigned to area requiring the full-time presence of a NIS special agent. There were NISSUs at Binh Thuy, Vung Tau, Cam Ranh Bay, Chu Lai, and Quang Tri. |
| NLF | National Liberation Front. |
| NSA | Naval Support Activity. |
| NSG | Naval Security Group, a highly classified command charged with electronic intelligence missions. |
| NVA | North Vietnamese Army, the regular standing army of the DRV. |
| OIC | Officer in charge. |
| OICC | Officer in charge of construction. |
| OP | Observation post. |
| OSI | U.S. Air Force Office of Special Investigations, the Air Force counterpart to NIS. |
| padre | A military chaplain. |
| PBR | Riverine patrol boat. |
| PCF | Patrol craft, fast; swift boat. |
| PCS | Permanent change of station; a permanent transfer. |

| | |
|---|---|
| PF | Vietnamese popular forces, South Vietnamese militia. |
| PFC | Private first class. |
| POW | Prisoner of war. |
| PX | Post exchange, a retail outlet designed to provide military personnel with quality goods at the best prices. |
| refueling pod | Device fitted on aircraft to allow fuel to be taken from aerial tankers while in flight. |
| revetment | Typically, blast walls erected to protect equipment from damage by rocket and mortar attack. |
| RFPF | Vietnamese regional forces militia; ruff-puffs. |
| RVN | Republic of Vietnam; South Vietnam. |
| SEA hut | Southeast Asia hut. A temporary building design utilizing basic timber framing, plywood decking, fly screen, and roofing iron. |
| SeaBees | Naval mobile construction battalions. |
| SEAL | Elite Navy commandos. |
| skivvies | Underclothing, in particular, underpants. |
| skivvy honcho | A man possessed of winning ways with the opposite sex. |
| skivvy house | A brothel. |
| SRA | Senior resident agent. Senior agents at Saigon and Da Nang NISRAs. |
| SU | Satellite unit. |
| TDY | Temporary duty (as opposed to permanent station change) orders. |
| UCMJ | Universal Code of Military Justice. |
| UDT | Underwater demolition team. |
| VAL-4 | Navy fixed-wing squadron assigned to the Mekong Delta region. |
| VC | Viet Cong. |
| VCI | Viet Cong infrastructure. |
| Viet Cong | Enemy guerrillas, often local people. The main fighting force of the communist National Liberation Front. |
| ville | Any Vietnamese settlement or village. |
| VNAF | South Vietnamese Air Force. |
| VNN | Vietnamese Navy. Naval forces of the Republic of Vietnam. |
| VNNSB | Vietnamese Navy Security Bloc. In 1970 became VNNSS. |
| VNNSS | Vietnamese Navy Security Service. |
| YNC | Yeoman chief petty officer (E-7). Senior naval NCO |

with clerical specialties.

XO     Exective officer. Second in command, under a commanding officer.

# INDEX

# ABOUT THE AUTHOR

**Douglass H. Hubbard Jr.** is a consultant who has lived and worked extensively in Asia, Australia, and Africa. He served in Vietnam longer than any other member of the U.S. Naval Investigative Service. He has contributed to Australian and American magazines.